Canada in the Frame

MODERN AMERICAS

Modern Americas is a series for books discussing the culture, politics and history of the Americas from the nineteenth century to the present day. It aims to foster national, international, transnational and comparative approaches to topics in the region, including those that bridge geographical and/or disciplinary divides, such as between the disparate parts of the hemisphere covered by the series (the US, Latin America, Canada and the Caribbean) or between the humanities and social/natural sciences.

Series Editors

Claire Lindsay is Reader in Latin American Literature and Culture, UCL.

Tony McCulloch is Senior Fellow in North American Studies at the Institute of the Americas, UCL.

Maxine Molyneux is Professor of Sociology at the Institute of the Americas, UCL.

Kate Quinn is Senior Lecturer in Caribbean History at the Institute of the Americas, UCL.

Canada in the Frame

Copyright, Collections and the Image of Canada, 1895–1924

Philip J. Hatfield

UCLPRESS

First published in 2018 by
UCL Press
University College London
Gower Street
London WC1E 6BT

Available to download free: www.ucl.ac.uk/ucl-press

ISBN: 978–1–78735–301–5 (Hbk.)
ISBN: 978–1–78735–300–8 (Pbk.)
ISBN: 978–1–78735–299–5 (PDF)
ISBN: 978–1–78735–302–2 (epub)
ISBN: 978–1–78735–303–9 (mobi)
ISBN: 978–1–78735–304–6 (html)
DOI: https://doi.org/10.14324/111.9781787352995

‘How charming it would be if it were possible to cause these natural images to imprint themselves durably, and remain fixed upon the paper!’

W. H. F. Talbot, *The Pencil of Nature Part 1: Introduction*

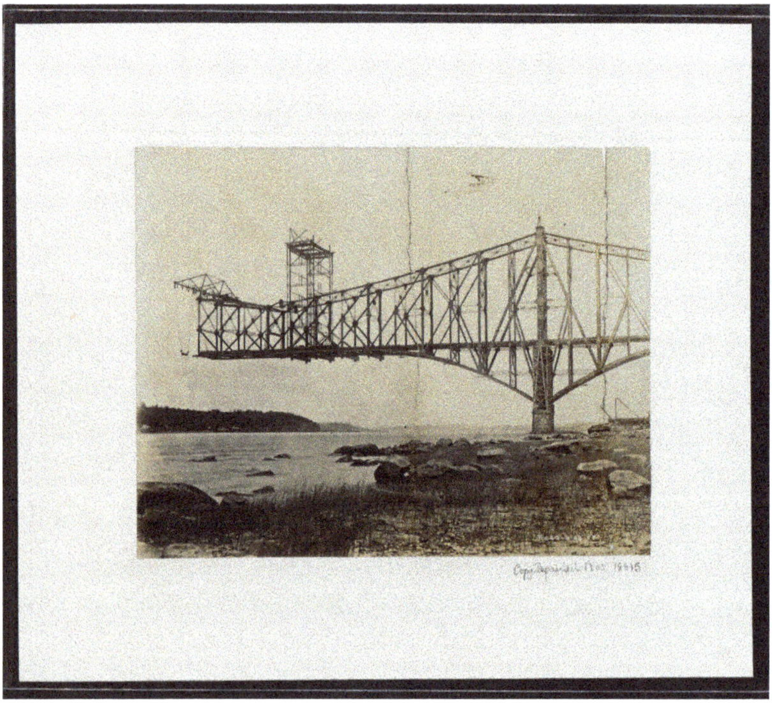

Fig. 0.1 The construction of the Quebec Bridge. Since day one of working with the Colonial Copyright Collection this photograph has stood out, portraying Canada's process of modernisation as well as the unique and incomplete view of it conveyed in this collection. Photograph: 'Quebec Bridge'. Copyright F. E. Cudworth, 1907 (copyright number 18815).

Acknowledgements

'Canada in the Frame', as a project of various stages, has been evolving now for over 12 years, covering tentative MA research, the all-consuming investment of a PhD, the continuing work of a curatorial career and various supporting projects at the British Library. As a result, there is a wide-ranging group of people to thank and acknowledge here.

First to mention are Felix Driver and Carole Holden, without whom the original research behind this work would not have come about. More importantly, without their guidance I would no doubt not be writing these acknowledgements. Phil Davies and the Eccles Centre for American Studies have also been continual supporters of work on the collection discussed in the following pages. Elsewhere in the British Library many people contributed information and expertise to this work. John Falconer, P. R. Harris, Barry Taylor and Stephen Bury are just a few of the people from whom I have learned about the collections and the Library's heritage. Further afield, this project would have been the poorer without the input of scholars from Queen's University, Kingston. Most specifically, Joan Schwartz has been a constant source of excellent information and enthusiastic evangelism for this work and the collection that underpins it. Without the efforts she and a number of others put in it could still be sitting in boxes, known only to a few and used by none. Our understanding of Canada and photographic history is the richer for those who take such collections under their wing.

I would also like to thank Richard Dennis, James Ryan, Tony McCulloch and the many members of the British Association for Canadian Studies; they have all contributed to and supported this project in some way and made the work the richer for it. Finally, thanks are due to two departments and institutions: the Americas Team at the British Library and the Department of Geography at Royal Holloway, University of London. Both have nurtured this project and had a profound effect on my life. Continuing to work at the British Library is a pleasure each and every day, while being an RHUL alum is a source of great pride and fond, photogenic memories.

Projects like this also evolve in unexpected ways. 2012 saw a collaboration between the British Library, the Eccles Centre and Wikimedia UK to bring the collection discussed here online and into the public domain. Working with Wikimedia UK (specifically Andrew Gray, our Wikimedian in Residence at the time) allowed the British Library to reconnect the Colonial Copyright Collection with audiences across Canada and the rest of the world. The digitisation work also instigated a significant shift in attitude: if we can put the images into the hands of the wider public for free, why not also the research? And so the publication of this monograph with UCL Press is a fitting culmination of the broader project. I cannot thank Lara Speicher and the editors of the 'Modern Americas' series enough for their faith in the work and their enthusiasm for publishing this research. I must also thank the two reviewers who gave such constructive and helpful feedback on the monograph. Truly, all involved with UCL Press have made this a better, more engaging piece of scholarship.

Finally, family has been a huge part of this work. Thanks are due to my parents for the support that got me on the road to here and to my wife Madeleine, who has read the innumerable drafts, jottings and ramblings that comprise this work. That the peer reviewers and readers of this book find it enjoyable and useful owes a lot to her keen eye, insightful questioning and, most importantly, patience.

Contents

List of figures

Introduction: photographs, people, place

Galleries, libraries, archives and museums, largely public spaces with a range of foci and organisational structures, have one structural thing in common: they all tend to hold large amounts of material that is 'hidden'. Whether it is seldom displayed in public, loosely catalogued, unwieldy for use or out of sight for various other reasons, this material is rarely used by researchers and even less frequently seen by the public. To be clear, such material is not 'lost'; it rather inhabits a twilight zone of use, known of by curators and some researchers, but requiring work to bring it out of the shaded fringe of the institution.

HS85/10 (and a variety of storage locations loosely linked to this reference) is the shelfmark of one such collection currently held at the British Library. Collected between 1895 and 1924, the photographs held here offer a unique view of late nineteenth-century and early twentieth-century Canada. Gathered from across a growing, federated nation using copyright deposit as a mechanism of accumulation, this collection provides a grass-roots, open and somewhat untidy view of Canada, its people and the practice of photography between these years. Names familiar to Canadians with a vague sense of photographic history, such as Notman, are found here. So are the names which those readers with a deeper knowledge might recognise: the Byron Harmons and Charles Ayletts of Canada's early twentieth-century photographic history. The value of the collection, however, lies in its wide spectrum of Canadian photography.

Canada in the Frame looks at this collection, infrequently used and far from its place of origin, and asks two questions: What does it show us of Canada and its photographic history? What peculiar view do these photographs, viewed from the old 'Heart of Empire', give of a former part of the British Empire in a post-colonial age?

An uncommon collection

The British Museum Library's collection of Canadian copyright photographs, deposited between 1895 and 1924[1] and now housed at the

British Library, covers a dynamic period in Canada's national history and provides a variety of different views of its landscapes and peoples.[2] As a copyright collection, its contents were actually generated by a curious productive mechanism: namely the calculation, or sometimes the whim, of the individual Canadian photographer. In practice this is a collection composed of materials *sent* rather than gathered, a fact that has particular consequences for its interpretation today. In short, the key factor in the collection's assembly was a notion in the mind of individual depositors that the value attached to the images submitted would justify the cost of copyright deposit. The result, therefore, is a photographic collection whose composition is skewed by factors rarely considered within the confines of scholarship of the museum, archive or library.

The Colonial Copyright Collection of Canadian photographs held at the British Library is not widely known and certainly has no plausible claim to be one of the great photographic archives. It is not in the same circle as collections at the Musée d'Orsay or the Victoria and Albert Museum, for example, which bear witness to the birth and development of photography as a technical and artistic practice. Nor does it represent sufficiently the oeuvre of a single photographer in a way comparable to the archives of celebrated photographers such as Fox Talbot or Canada's own William Notman.[3] Instead it consists of an assortment of images of various subjects in different formats and styles, made by a variety of photographers across Canada and submitted to the British Museum Library under relatively short-lived copyright legislation.

While the existence of the collection depends on the status of the photograph as (potential) commercial property, its development into the form in which it exists today combined two further impulses: firstly the desire to collect and archive as much raw intellectual property as possible from across the empire and secondly the aspirations of the photographers submitting work for copyright. The result is a diverse and eclectic collection which, viewed as a whole, offers a kaleidoscopic vision of Canada's landscapes and peoples in the closing decade of the nineteenth century and the opening decades of the twentieth.

The origins of the law under which the collection came into being reflect, in part, the archival and imperial imperatives that shaped the development of the British Museum Library during the nineteenth century – especially under the influence of individuals such as Keeper of Books Antonio Panizzi, whose stewardship saw a significant strengthening of its status as a legal deposit library. Through Panizzi's parliamentary lobbying, the British Library's collections attained a global reach. This included the acquisition of material from all over the world, encompassing, without being limited to, the territories of the British

Empire.[4] The globalisation of the collecting impulse, articulated through an imperial vision, was not unique to the British Library, of course, nor is this collection the only one of its kind to be produced in this way. From the mid-Victorian period numerous scholarly and scientific institutions, as well as innumerable British government departments, museums and universities, sought to establish subject collections and archives of worldwide scope. Meanwhile wealthy individual collectors, such as Sir Henry Wellcome, used their global networks to reinvent an earlier tradition of scholarly collecting associated above all with Sir Hans Sloane, a key figure in the history of the British Museum and of many other London collections.[5]

The advent of photography – and growing interest in its potential uses within the realms of science, art, government and commerce – led to the formation of various kinds of photographic collection emerging from the middle of the nineteenth century. These were generated and arranged in a variety of ways, depending on the context. In recent years a number of scholars have considered the development of these collections. Their discussions illuminate the myriad forms in which photographic materials were produced, circulated, collected and used, and reveal the importance of understanding the specific social and institutional contexts in which collections took shape.

While the Colonial Copyright Collection has received relatively limited attention from scholars, it has not altogether languished in obscurity. Since the late twentieth century, for instance, concerted efforts have been made by curators and librarians to catalogue the collection.[6] However, it has nonetheless remained within something of an archival twilight zone, partly due to persistent uncertainties over how to categorise and define the use of photographs originally deposited in an apparently haphazard manner as an appendix to a wider and seemingly more systematic archival endeavour. The interpretation of such a collection, in which the agency of individual donor photographers is uneasily yoked to the institutional dictates of archival acquisition by an imperial copyright library, presents specific challenges as well as opportunities. However, rather than portray the collection as a poor cousin of other archives, supposedly less arbitrary and heterogeneous, the aim in this book is to shed light on the Colonial Copyright Collection's wider significance.

Geography as a concept and as a discipline has provided a number of ways into the analysis of this collection. In this and subsequent chapters, the ideas of historical and cultural geographers are deployed as tools to generate new perspectives on the collection, with particular regard to relationships between colonial settlement and image-making, the visual economies of colonial expansion and the historical geography of Canada. It is fortunate too that there is a wide body of scholarship on the history of photography in Canada (some of this also being published by geographers). This book connects to the writings developed by authors from across the academic, library and archival sectors, contributing to a discourse well established since the late twentieth century.[7] On top of this, the key to understanding such a collection is to engage effectively with its complexity; as a result, a wide range of other literatures will be drawn upon, including work in Canadian history, imperial history, the history of photography, history of science, anthropology and museum and library studies.

The purpose of this introductory chapter is twofold. Firstly, it provides an historical perspective on the development of colonial copyright legislation, in order to illuminate the legal and institutional context in which the collection was established. Secondly, it seeks to outline in greater depth the key concepts which have informed the research – especially arguments concerning the 'imperial archive', as developed by Thomas Richards and others; the notion of 'visual economy', drawn from the work of Deborah Poole on the Andean image world and adapted here for use in a very different context; and recent work which has emphasised the value of a spatial perspective on the historical geography of colony, Dominion and empire.[8]

Colonial Copyright Law in historical perspective

Colonial copyright legislation was the driver by which these Canadian photographs were collected. It played a fundamental part in the process whereby published materials drawn from around the British Empire were acquired by institutional depositories in the metropole and in the colonies, comprising what might be called a 'paper empire'. This term is often linked with its use by Thomas Richards in *The Imperial Archive*, but the notion of a paper empire – an imperial system founded upon the flow and collation of information through the medium of paper – is also employed by academic geographers such as Miles Ogborn.[9] In *Indian Ink* Ogborn describes the East India Company's world as 'one made on paper, as well as on land and sea', illustrating the central role of printed knowledge, especially in the functioning of imperial projects.[10]

Central to the idea of an empire run on paper is the significance of flows and accumulations of knowledge for the effective implementation of imperial and colonial projects. However, in Richards's writing the idea of a paper empire, represented by the figure of the imperial archive, is somewhat monolithic; it is housed in gigantic repositories and sifted through by legions of civil servants. Yet the paper empire was in fact much more fragmented and disjointed than this. It was also managed by a diaspora of invested imperial and colonial parties, as illustrated by Ogborn's discussion of the centrality of paper to the operations of the East India Company.

Institutions such as the British Museum, including its library, were instrumental in the development of an institutional knowledge framework involving the flow of large amounts of printed materials around the empire. The development of copyright to protect intellectual property and, in this context, the implementation of the Colonial Copyright Law were central to this process of accumulation. The latter established the terms and mechanisms by which the British government could require the submission of material from colonial authors, publishers and institutions to British libraries. In principle, the idea of colonial copyright was intended to extend the protection of British copyright law to all intellectual property producers who resided and published within 'all of Her Majesty's Dominions, Protectorates and Dependencies across the Seas'.[11] While this law provided considerable benefit and protection to the authors and publishers of literature and artistic work in other countries, the British government and various affiliated institutions were significant beneficiaries too.[12] The resulting stores of material and knowledge were held in high esteem as ways of educating about and understanding the empire, as evidenced by organisations such as the Royal Colonial Institute.[13]

However, as with many colonial mechanisms defined by the metropole, Colonial Copyright Law failed to assert fully the degree of control, or reap exactly the type of information, sought by the imperial administration. In reality it was very difficult to enforce the submission of material from Dominions and governed territories. The terms of submission were unrealistic, penalisation for non-compliance was rare and, in the exceptions where they were enforced, the charges levied as penalty for non-compliance were hardly greater than the cost of printing and posting an extra copy of the copyrighted work to the submissions office in London.[14] As a result, representatives of various British government departments[15] were drawn into continuous correspondence with the governments and printers of colonially governed nations, all of whom saw their chance to negotiate better deals for their authors and themselves in terms of copyright laws. In the run-up to the passing of Canada's

1895 revision of its copyright law (in which stipulation for submission to the British Museum Library was inserted), there was a flurry of correspondence between government offices in Canada and Britain. The British government eventually redrafted its Colonial Copyright Law with some minor amendments favourable to the government of Canada.[16]

Imperial rule could therefore significantly affect how much and what kind of material producers needed to offer up for copyright to be granted. In the particular case of Canada, the copyright legislation resulted in the submission of an expanded body of materials, including photography, from 1895 onwards.[17] In this context the British government and the British Museum Library exerted pressure by consistently reminding the Canadian government of its 'duty' to submit material to the British Museum Library.[18] It was agreed that compliance would produce benefits for the Dominion government of Canada, in the form of reduced tariff duties on published imports and submission of British documents to Canadian institutions,[19] but these benefits manifested themselves as a relaxation of colonially imposed restrictions.[20]

A paper by P. B. O'Neill, 'Canadiana Deposited in the British Museum Library Between 1895 and 1923', provides a useful account of the key points of the Colonial Copyright Law, highlighting the interaction between the various governments and institutional bodies who benefited from it.[21] He points out that the British Museum Library actively pursued submissions from Canada under the Colonial Copyright Law and reveals how much government lobbying went into drafting, redrafting and implementation. However, some details in this account are erroneous, for example the statement that the library had a 'purely local' interest in Canadian copyright deposits and relied solely upon actors local to London to elicit the material.[22] This implies that the copyright deposits were desired simply for metropolitan users and were acquired solely through London's political and legislative mechanisms, masking the fact that Antonio Panizzi and his successors as Keeper of Books actively pursued Canadian material (and Commonwealth submissions in general) through myriad channels (Parliament, the courts, Commonwealth Office, etc.) and sought to maintain as complete a record of Canadian intellectual property as possible.[23] As such, O'Neill's account hints at but underplays both the globalised nature of this exchange network and the British Museum Library's role as an actor within it.

The development of a legal and institutional framework that both facilitated and managed the flow of intellectual property and knowledge from around the empire to the metropole has left a significant legacy in Britain's institutions. Indeed it has developed the collections of some, such as the British Museum Library, so significantly that the geography of the archive itself has also been fundamentally changed by the deposition of these materials. Further, the complexity of Colonial Copyright Law and the discussion outlined above suggests the care that must be taken in dealing with the Colonial Copyright Collection's photographs as a result of their complex history.

Carole Payne's work *The Official Picture* has navigated similar waters when analysing the still photography division of the National Film Board of Canada.[24] Payne argues that this collection displays the 'banal nationalism' that underpinned the brief of the National Film Board at this time. The Colonial Copyright Collection – heavily mediated by the aims of the metropole, its associated paper empire and the photographic market within which Canadian photographers operated – should be analysed within its own context, one defined by distant imperialism and a developing Dominion nationalism. All of which is to say material born of such a system inevitably has a complex genesis, which must be carefully considered when analysing the photographs today. The material biographies, collection heritage and diverse meanings embedded within these images are precisely the factors which make the Colonial Copyright Collection significant today, and it is these which form the focus of the substantive chapters of this book.

Making a photographic collection

In spite of the difficulties set out above, the legacy of the development and enforcement of Colonial Copyright Law is a substantial collection of books, pamphlets, papers, music and photographs that currently resides in the stores of the modern British Library. This material was not always in the form or of the quality desired by those with vested interests in it acquired through the law. The result was an uneven absorption of this material into the collection and the creation of material satellites, arrayed uneasily around the rest of the British Museum Library's collections. Such was the initial fate of the Colonial Copyright Collection of Canadian photographs, their unmediated submission and material form proving problematic to the institution's prevailing collections logic. That the material was retained at all is due largely to the significance of Canada to the empire; thus information about the country was important to developing a geography of knowledge from this paper empire. Although a similar process was undertaken to gain the same materials from other British colonial territories, materials from these territories were treated in different ways, dependent upon the significance of the material and influenced by the importance of the territory of origin. In other cases they were simply not received at all.

As a result, although photographs and photographically illustrated materials were submitted from other territories, they either lacked the volume to create a collection or were consumed by larger ones (such as those of the India Office). Consequently, only the Canadian photographs have coalesced into a freestanding collection, known within the British Library and in this book as the Colonial Copyright Collection.[25] While all the material in this collection is photographic in form, it is worth noting that photographs of paintings and statues also form part of this collection. In terms of their action as copyright deposits, these photographs themselves are rarely being copyrighted; rather they act as mechanisms through which another piece of unique art can be registered for copyright.[26] Such images have subsequently become part of the Colonial Copyright Collection as the British Library today understands it due to their material form, and this nuance of content and copyright law is easily overlooked. While only a few such images are mentioned in this book, they do present an opportunity for further work on the collection and an avenue through which the changing collection's definition of material can be perceived.

It is important then to consider not just the regulatory processes that led to their collation, but also how the materials were created and how they were received by the institution – both important factors influencing what any collection becomes. This involves consideration of the images' material form. Photographic images have always come in myriad forms, and these have significant impact upon the way in which the image itself may be used, stored and read.[27] Further, the materiality of the image can also present starting points or significant factors in considering what these images tell us of Canada between 1895 and 1924.

Many major institutional photographic collections are acquired and developed through some sort of direct mechanism of material accumulation. In the case of the Victoria and Albert Museum's photographic collection, for example, the material has been acquired through the careful and considered selection of items by curators according to specific institutional criteria. By contrast, a collection such as that of the Royal Geographical Society has been accumulated largely through the production and deposition of images from individuals participating in expeditions of many different kinds, of which only a few were directed by the Society itself. While the exact mechanism of selection may vary from collection to collection, the process of acquiring photographic material is in principle driven by some sort of curatorial mandate – explicit or implicit – that ultimately is under the control of the institution.

The contents of the Colonial Copyright Collection, however, are dictated not by curatorial choice but rather by the eye of the photographers who created the images – and in particular by their perception of the potential of these images for financial gain. The images were acquired by the library essentially because they fell within the remit of copyright, not because a curator or librarian wished to acquire those specific items on the basis of their relevance to the institution. Each of the images had to be copyrighted in Canada by application to the Department for Agriculture in Ottawa, which was given responsibility for processing the copyright applications from across the nation and transferring them to their relevant recipients in Britain. The process was administrated without reference to the quality or content of the images: the only significant factors in obtaining copyright were that the form should be filled out appropriately, the copyright deposit fee be paid in full and the relevant images attached. It was also important that the appropriate number of images be attached, as the Canadian government required that a copy of the image also be provided for the collections of the Library of Parliament in Ottawa. These copies thus form a sister collection which still exists in Canada as part of Library and Archives Canada.[28] On its journey through the system, the copyrighted item would be received and processed by various intermediary civil servants. Provided that the image passed the above checks, it would be filtered along an administrative chain leading across the Atlantic Ocean and eventually to the British Museum Library acquisitions department, where it would be stamped (Fig.0.2) and added to the collection.[29]

As a result, the contents of this collection cannot simply be reduced to the collecting impulse of the library. Moreover, the photographs deposited were rarely mediated by the critical criteria of intermediary producers, such as those involved in the production of printed, illustrated and cartographic work at the time. Here then we see the ephemerality, mechanisation and individualisation of the photographic and image-making process combining to usurp the role of the curator in creating this collection. The legacy for the British Museum Library was a certain curatorial ambivalence concerning the collection and what it actually represents. Alongside notions of the paper empire, which shed light on the development of systems of colonial copyright, we therefore need to deploy other concepts which acknowledge the role of photographs and photographers in systems and networks of exchange. In this regard, the idea of a visual economy, originally developed in a very different context,

Fig. 0.2 Illustration of stamp.

represents a useful way of understanding the process by which images in a photographic collection such as the one under consideration may accrue value across space and time.[30]

The notion of a paper empire, as highlighted earlier, is important to understanding the collection's relationship to the wider imperial endeavour. As Thomas Richards asserts, the British Museum had an administrative role in the archiving of empire through the collation of, and provision of access to, knowledge about Britain's colonial territories.[31] On this basis we could interpret Colonial Copyright Law as an attempt to enforce greater control on the empire through the accumulation of a panoptical body of knowledge governed by an overarching legal system. However, as Richards notes, the practical reality of attempting to control or understand empire through the accumulation of a panoptical imperial archive meant that the project was ultimately doomed. This is due not only to the impossibility of collecting all the required information, but also to the difficulty of collating it into useful bodies of knowledge.[32] The Colonial Copyright Collection is one such body of material that could not be codified within the logic of the imperial archive.[33] Instead it is better situated as part of an unruly paper empire, diverse in form, content, type and the perceived quality of the information circulating within it.

As Richards argues, the notion of the imperial archive was essentially a powerful fantasy which nonetheless had real, material and far-reaching effects. It came to shape both the form of colonial government and the development of metropolitan institutions such as the British Museum. However, the case of the Colonial Copyright Collection suggests that this was only one of the impulses behind the development of imperial – and colonial – collections. In order to characterise the distinct mechanisms that generated the form and content of this collection, we need to deploy concepts which allow more room for commercial processes, institutional politics and colonial agency. We also need to engage with the collection through a framework that embraces the plurality and heterogeneity of the embedded materials and affords space to consider how their significance and meaning shifts as they move across spaces and are engaged with at different times. In this context, Poole's notion of a 'visual economy' is suggestive. As used by Poole in the very different context of the Andean image world, the concept refers to the complex networks of exchange within which photographs operate, and to their status as objects with an economic value. For all the evident differences, her core concerns with the geography of image-making, the circulation of images across spatially extended networks and, above all, the commercial contexts in which photographs are made and exchanged have distinct echoes in this study of the Colonial Copyright Collection.

Poole's emphasis on the ways in which photographic images accrue value through circulation depends on a spatial perspective of what she calls the visual economy. In short, the passage of images over space is key to modifying the way in which they are used and exchanged. In parallel, recent work on the historical geography of empire has emphasised the significance of the networks and sites through which imperial knowledge circulated. For example, Butlin's recent work *Geographies of Empire*[34] illustrates the multiple and complex colonialisms at work internationally during the nineteenth and twentieth centuries. In detailing the different national colonialisms he also illustrates the various institutional, legal, commercial, scientific and other colonial networks that existed within these empires.

Butlin's work draws from extensive scholarship by historical geographers that has analysed the complex networks which drew colonial metropole and colonial territory into a spatially extensive and fragmented common framework.[35] In the case of the British Empire, this body of work has suggested that the flow of information, legislation and action in the colonial system was neither homogenous nor bound by a single logic; instead it was a system composed of multiple sites and actors, each of which affected the various colonial processes in which they were involved.[36] It is through this understanding that we should view Colonial Copyright Law and the geography of knowledge that formed around it.

Throughout the colonial period the library, the archive, the museum and the exhibition space were significant sites in the making of meaning.[37] Major exhibitions such as the Great Exhibition in Crystal Palace or the various incarnations of the world's fair and the Toronto Industrial Exhibition[38] were important in the establishment of frameworks of understanding through which the modern, rapidly changing colonial world could be articulated. Through these events the geography and aesthetic of the fair and the exhibition demonstrated to the public a way of seeing the world. This was of crucial importance in a world where the pace of change was so great, and the sites facilitating the development of Europe and the Americas were often so far beyond the everyday perspective of the ordinary citizen.[39] Significantly such sites represented a geography *within* a geography, a fixed site that articulated and displayed to the public a way of seeing an expanding world. However, the exhibition was not the only medium within the urban centres of colonialism that was responsible for the making of meaning or the creation of authorised knowledge.

The British Museum Library effectively authorised a certain geography of knowledge through curatorial, administrative and pragmatic decisions concerning its collections. The role of the institution in the generation of this geography is illustrated initially through the lobbying of the government by the British Museum over the Colonial Copyright Law. The result of this lobbying was the flow of material from Canada and other colonies to London and the British Museum Library's repositories. Within this context the library can be understood as a colonial hub in the network, with the bulk of material moving in the system flowing to the library and a significantly smaller proportion flowing from London and back out to the colonies.[40] The dynamics of information exchange between colonial territories is indicative of the type of colonial relationship between them: the larger the degree of reciprocity, the more significant the colony was to the coloniser. Consequently, as colonies increased in importance they negotiated relationships increasingly similar to those direct exchange mechanisms that existed between colonial powers at the time.

A similar dynamic was present within the institution, for example in the fact that the British Museum Library de-accessioned a significantly higher proportion of material from minor colonies than it did from those deemed to be of greater significance.[41] Within this context material from the Dominions was regarded as second only to material from India in terms of its retention value, hence the survival of the Canadian photographs from the copyright deposits. Nonetheless, the photography within the Colonial Copyright Collection was not acquired as a result of an institutional commitment to its inherent value, and it came to be regarded as peripheral material within the library. As O'Neill has illustrated, the images were treated as deposit records rather than as significant cultural and intellectual artefacts that needed to be accessible to the public and researchers.[42] This was because the images were copyright records and submitted by numerous, mostly unknown photographers across Canada,[43] while the status of photography as a 'lesser' art reinforced this approach.[44]

The photographs within the Colonial Copyright Collection contained a myriad of photographic subjects and material forms submitted from across Canada. That so many images were submitted during the period covered by the collection reflected the significance of a rapidly developing consumer market for photography.[45] There was a growing market for photographically illustrated books, portrait photographs, commemorative images, *cartes de visite*, photographic advertisements and newspaper illustrations.[46] Further, photographers found themselves able to cater to these markets with increasing ease as the photographic and print technologies underpinning their trade became more efficient, cheaper and smaller.[47] The images deposited in the Colonial Copyright Collection were produced to cater to these niches. The sheer diversity of different photographic subjects and formats that comprise the collection contributes to the perception, on an initial view, that the material is merely ephemeral in nature. That these images were submitted by individuals seeking to protect their work from the opportunism of others certainly limited their status as items of lasting value, worth entering formally into the collections.

Notwithstanding some curatorial concerns over the suitability of these images for the collections of the British Museum Library, their origins ensured they had a certain status. As one of the great British Dominions, Canada was increasingly viewed, within the paternalistic vernacular of the British Empire, as something less like a dependent child and more like a developing sibling.[48] Given the selective disposal of – and even resistance to the submission of – similar materials from less significant colonies, it is clear that the Canadian Colonial Copyright materials survived due to the perceived importance of the territory from which they hailed – even if they did survive by being separated from the main collections and placed in the Woolwich Arsenal Depository.[49]

This fact illustrates that Colonial Copyright Law and its utilisation by the British Museum Library facilitated the articulation of a geography of knowledge. It also perpetuated colonial perceptions of value based fundamentally on the geographical origin of the material. This geography is one of inclusion and exclusion, illustrating not just the limits of knowledge of the colonial world but also defining how much of the colonial world is worth knowing. In this world, some places are more visible than others. The purpose of this book is in a sense to chart the geographies rendered visible through the collection. In this respect, the prominence of certain sites and scenes reflected both the geography of commercial photographic practice and the imaginative geography of an emergent Canadian modernity.

Interpreting a photographic collection

While noting the significance of technology, copyright and the institutional context to the creation of the Canadian Copyright Collection, it is also important to consider the effect that the material properties of the copyrighted images have had on its subsequent history. Photographic collections come in many shapes and sizes, as well as being accessible to wider publics in a variety of ways. In storage terms the Colonial Copyright Collection is still somewhat fragmented in its organisation, in part as a result of its material properties. While the majority of the collection is situated within the main body of the library, having been bound into black albums or collated into storage boxes during a recent conservation programme,[50] a substantial body of material is held in other parts of the library as a result of how it has been catalogued. Most notably, a substantial cache of images has ended up as part of the Maps collections of the library on account of their utility as topographic views.

The blurring of lines with regard to where the material has ended up in the collection is further evidence of the difficulty in situating this body of copyright-acquired material within the prevailing printed and bound order of the institution. It is also indicative of the effect that the materiality of the image has had on the subsequent absorption of elements of the Colonial Copyright Collection into the wider collections of the British Library. These pragmatic decisions based upon size, durability, storability, etc., as well as on the views of various curators through the life of the collection, affect the way each item is positioned within the institution, causing it to accrue value and shift in meaning over time.

This situation is similar to that of 'Box 54', discussed by Edwards and Hart in *Photographs, Objects, Histories*,[51] where the aggregation of materials creates new meanings and juxtapositions. In the case of the Colonial Copyright Collection, the processes of production, copyright, deposition and subsequent processing within the library have created a set of complex object biographies.

The difficulty in placing the images of the Colonial Copyright Collection within the library's collections illustrates another major difference between this and more classical photography collections. While no collection of material can be perfectly codified, there are those which manage (or are made) to perform a coherent narrative, especially through the use of public display.[52] The role of publications aimed at a general public readership can also be significant in reinforcing dominant ideas about the nature of such collections, as can be seen through the coffee-table books of the Royal Geographical Society.[53] The Colonial Copyright Collection has been treated to one such work in the past, entitled *Canada: The Missing Years*;[54] this book creates a bounded, limited notion of the collection. The title attempts to frame the view provided through the collection as a whimsical gaze into a forgotten past, while the book makes no attempt to engage with the individual photographers whose work makes up the collection, nor its myriad material forms. The idea of gazing back onto a single vision of a 'lost' Canada is also at odds with the dynamic, plural and contested Canada on view in contemporary historiography.

It is also important to consider the role of the photograph as a material object with a specific kind of agency. As noted above, what has been produced in Canada, moved across the globe and stored in the British Museum Library is not just a collection of images: it is rather an assortment of objects with their own material histories. The object of the photograph comes in various shapes and forms (as well as sizes), with Colonial Copyright Collection images deposited in formats ranging from postcards to individual photographic prints and photographically illustrated publications.[55] The multiplicity of these formats was continually growing and changing during the period in which the collection developed, and this is significant to how we perceive the collection as a whole. Further, the material also wears and degrades, with consequences for the future preservation of the photographs and form of the collection (as illustrated by the contemporary storage forms of the collection shown in Fig.0.3). The image as an object with particular material properties is significant, as our first engagement with photographs is often negotiated through their material condition or feel, as opposed to what they actually

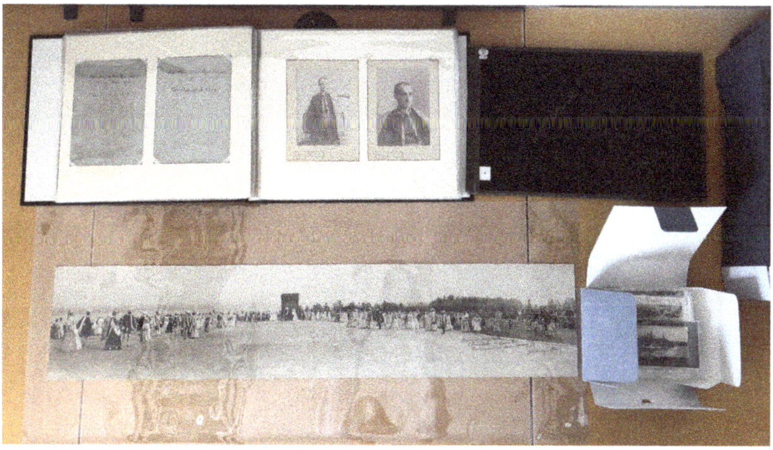

Fig. 0.3 The Colonial Copyright Collection in its various forms.

show. This is the central point made by Edwards and Hart in their edited work *Photographs, Objects, Histories*.[56]

As will become clear in the substantive chapters of this book, the materiality of the image and the conditions of its photographic reproduction have an important effect upon the view perceived today. These chapters will also illustrate that the materiality of the photograph's reproduction had an effect upon the circulation of the image, the patterns of its consumption and the perspective it provided to audiences at the time the image was produced. For the researcher, materiality continues to have consequences as items become damaged, degrade unevenly, wear in specific ways and become accessible under different archival conditions as a result of their material properties.

Extending from this, consideration must also be given as to how the materiality of these images will continue to affect engagement with these photographs in a period where our contact with photographic objects is increasingly digital. As has been widely noted, this does not remove questions of materiality; rather it creates new modes of engagement and encourages thinking about different types of materiality.[57] This is especially pertinent as the Colonial Copyright Collection – along with other photographic collections, both personal and institutional – increasingly moves into a digital domain, a process highlighted in the conclusion of this book. Whether it be through the changing technologies around at the time of production, the effect of time or the shifting technological landscape of today, it is clear that the Colonial Copyright Collection carries with it significant materialities. Engagement with these characteristics not only heightens the sense of the complexity of the collection, but also presents 'ways in' to considering the material, as will be discussed in subsequent chapters.[58]

When seen in the raw, the heterogeneous materiality and dynamics of the Colonial Copyright Collection forces us to some extent to engage with the inherent plurality of its contents. That the collection can be viewed as an agglomeration of individual images and corpuses of work distinguishes it from collections based around single albums, ostensibly more coherent bodies of work (which have often been highly mediated by the producer and the curator) or tightly regulated institutional collections. Indeed, when viewed as a whole the collection might be said to have some affinities with domestic photographic collections.

This is a big theoretical leap and I should clarify that by this I do not mean domestic *albums*. Instead I mean something more like those collections of photographs that have fallen into shoe boxes and been stored in attics, often taken out, sifted and sorted into new forms, but never falling into a stable cohesion. I also situate the Colonial Copyright Collection in this frame because of the work of Roland Barthes. In *Camera Lucida* Barthes discusses at length how photographs, their subtle details and their unknown connections with our own knowledges and other histories develop *punctums* in their structure.[59] There is overlap here too with the work of Martha Langford, whose work *Suspended Conversations* is driven by the open statement of the photographic album.[60] These unknown connections are very much the sparks that have created the substantive chapters of this book, as well as the engines that have driven their investigation.

While Barthes uses the term on an emotional level to describe 'that which punctures', *punctum* is also used to highlight the occasion when an image makes unexpected and challenging connections beyond the basic *studium*.[61] As with various types of domestic photography collections,[62] the Colonial Copyright Collection is full of hidden and unexpected significances. To express it another way, both the Colonial Copyright Collection and family photograph collections can be understood as palimpsests; indeed this notion of a layering of information over time is appropriate to working with individual images within the collection.

The key, therefore, is to interact with the collection in such a way that draws out these significances and allows them to be considered in depth. That way, the method to this book can be more systematic than Barthes's serendipitous rummaging in his mother's attic. Indeed, this connects to the points made earlier about the development of rich object biographies through the processes of collecting and preserving the Colonial Copyright Collection. Not only have these biographies been mediated and developed via the collection, but also the collections of the British Library as a whole present further opportunities to investigate and develop these biographies through engagement with a wider range of materials. In each of the following substantive discussions a variety of materials – from newspapers, maps and philately to official publications and institutional conference papers – have been consulted in order to contextualise the interpretation of these photographs through the materials arranged around them.

Undertaking research into a collection such as this requires engagement with a broad body of significant academic theory that has grown up around photography in general, and colonial photography in particular, over the last few decades. Such work has influenced recent writing on vision, empire and geography by historical geographers. It is clear from this literature that colonialism provided an important impetus and opportunity for the realisation of the desire to see and perceive the world in imperial terms.[63] Authors such as Sontag,[64] Ryan,[65] Schwartz and Ryan[66] and MacQuire[67] illustrate how the expanding role of technology in textual, visual and audio communication was bound up with the intensification of the colonial process during the latter half of the nineteenth century and the first decades of the twentieth; they demonstrate, moreover, that photography was integral to developing colonial understandings of place. This is the broadest visual context within which the Colonial Copyright Collection of photographs may be situated. It is a collection born of the desire of multiple actors to visualise the territories of British colonialism in a form that could be readily circulated throughout the empire for economic benefit. Running in parallel to this economic imperative is an imperial one. Here the collection of images at the British Museum Library can be seen as part of a multifaceted project of knowledge accumulation centred on the imperial metropolis, as discussed above.

For much of its history, there has been considerable debate over the photograph's capacity to illustrate to the viewer that which was factually true about the subject of the image.[68] Within the nineteenth and early twentieth centuries there was also a strong belief that the deployment of photography would help to illustrate the utility and reality of colonial territories and peoples, allowing their essential natures to be made visible.[69] As a result, the camera was often perceived as a tool for data collection, with the photograph itself often being positioned as an authoritative document rather than an artistic product.[70] This attitude was reflected particularly in the literature of scientific disciplines such as anthropology and geography, where photography was represented as offering the possibility of entirely objective witnessing. However, in other spheres, notably those of artistic practice or popular tourism, the story was somewhat different: in this sense, the subjectivity of the camera was celebrated, or at least not quite so hidden.[71] In this context the inclusion of photographs within the remit of copyright legislation, originally designed to cater for literary and artistic works, suggests that within certain realms value was placed precisely on the skill and imagination of the photographer. The camera, like the pen, was a tool for creating value and, as the record of copyright deposits shows, the photographer's claims to authorship predominantly remained anything but invisible.[72]

The notion of visual economy, as we have seen above, has provided one useful tool for rethinking the agency of the photographer in the making of a collection such as the one examined in this book. Another tool for interpreting the collection which has proved useful in this context is more metaphorical in nature. It involves viewing the collection as a series of deposits, one layered upon the other. Subsequent to their deposition in the British Museum Library new layers of information and interpretation were built up over time, shifting and changing perceptions of the spaces, places and peoples contained in the images themselves. Researching the images is thus more like tracing a geological transect than mapping an individual moment frozen in time, while the landscape of the collection is more palimpsest than map.

As emphasised in this section, the Colonial Copyright Collection of photographs is composed of images produced during a period in time of tremendous change in Canada and across the world. However, the archive itself has changed significantly since the moment of creation and deposition, and the way in which we view and engage with images has also changed markedly.[73] The once dreamed-of paper empire has thus continued to evolve. Far from being the static repository of knowledge some had hoped for, the collection is an organic cache of knowledge that develops, shifts and changes as it interacts with institution, researcher and society. The undertaking of research for this book, and its application in a variety of other forms, may provide a new chapter in the life of the collection. In this phase of the collection's biography further interconnections and arrangements will be uncovered and articulated, developing the rich material and imaginative properties of the photographs themselves.

Picturing Canada

The remaining chapters of this book deal substantively with the contents of the Colonial Copyright Collection by considering some of its most notable subjects, genres and forms. Each chapter is stimulated by the content of the collection itself, with the flow of deposits over time, the body of work by individual photographers and the discourse between individual images informing the development of the case studies found below.

The selection of case studies is driven by a desire to show a representative form of the collection while also analysing the patterns and foci that develop from the disparate visual economy of Canadian photography between 1895 and 1924. 'Disparate' is used here to suggest the distances and relative personal separation of the photographers who submitted work to this collection, rather than as a reference to the overall subjects that seemed to grab Canadian photographers and the markets to which they provided images. Indeed, the subjects and themes that prevail in the collection, and the dynamic connections that can be perceived between photographers and their photographic subjects over time and space, are striking. The case studies also aim to illustrate the complexity of this visual economy, its role in the paper empire and, in the case of Lord Beaverbrook and the Canadian War Records Office in Chapter 6, how Canadians became increasingly involved in reshaping the dynamics of the visual economy not just of the Dominion, but of the British Empire itself.

That there are so many common themes photographed by the individuals whose work comprises this collection is underscored by the aggregating of the six substantive chapters of this book into two thematic parts. Part 1, 'Disseminating Modernity', focuses on how images of a rapidly modernising Canada were produced and shared between 1895 and 1924. This allows the argument to illustrate how important the postal service – and, specifically, the picture postcard – were to underpinning the visual economy of late nineteenth- and early twentieth-century Canada. In turn, the postcard as a mechanism of circulation opens up a discussion of how these material objects themselves moved around the country – namely on transport networks such as the railway, also discussed in this Part of the book. The section also lingers on the imaginations of modernisation which were circulated through these networks: what subjects were circulated and what messages, sometimes contradictory, were articulated. Part 2, 'Photographing Canada's Peoples in a Changing World', looks at the other predominant theme of the collections: the peoples of Canada, their diversity and their agency in a changing nation increasingly visible on the world stage. Photographers from across Canada turned their lenses on individuals from Canada's First Peoples, migrants from throughout Europe, Canadians going to war and various other subjects. This section considers how these images formed understandings and imaginations for viewers within Canada and also began to shape how Canadians were perceived by the wider world.

Each of these Parts is divided up into chapters, the contents of which require some elaboration here. Chapter 1 focuses on how these images circulated from producer to consumer, looking at how they came into contact with viewers and how their meanings were received. The collection covers a period in time often understood to be the 'golden age' of the postcard as a novel and popular means of communication.[74] As will be shown, these postcards, and the dissemination of images in the post, were a key way in which these images circulated in Canada and reached their audience. At the same time Canada was coming to know itself in new ways, both in terms of its situation within the British Empire and the development of new technologies that allowed different and more comprehensive views of its varied landscapes. The chapter focuses on how the picture postcard acted as a means by which these ideas and developments were communicated, both within Canada and globally, most notably through the promise of aerial photography.

Chapter 2 examines the photographic record of Canada's rapidly expanding cities, using images in the collection to discuss views of civic and entrepreneurial projects that were occurring in different parts of Canada. Two case studies frame the discussion: the photography of the opening of the parliament buildings in Victoria, B. C., by J. W. Jones and the photographic work commissioned by the T. Eaton Co. of Toronto. The chapter explores what these two contrasting sets of images show us about visions of urban development across Canada. In so doing Chapter 2 illustrates the various social, financial and political processes that were shaping Canadian cities in the late nineteenth and early twentieth centuries. This chapter also exemplifies the varied operation of visual economies of photography through the two different ways in which the sets of photographs came into being and circulated.

Chapter 3 focuses on Canada's railways and the views of them provided through the collection. Photographic imagery represented both the potential bounties and the dangers of the railway – particularly significant as between 1895 and 1924 the railways threatened both to underpin and undermine the country simultaneously. Using views from a variety of official and unofficial sources, this chapter uses the collection to illustrate the ubiquity of the camera and discuss how it affirmed, questioned and undermined the populist view of the railways propagated at the time and throughout the twentieth century.

Chapter 4 considers the depictions of various First Peoples groups from across Canada. While there are many notable photographic collections dedicated to First Peoples and other indigenous groups across the world, the Colonial Copyright Collection provides a unique perspective by virtue of its composition. Given that the collection is comprised of images submitted by myriad photographers from across Canada, of various levels of professionalism and photographic renown, it provides an opportunity to consider an unusually wide range of photographic depictions of First Peoples groups. The chapter explores some of the different ways in which photographic depictions of indigenous groups can be affected, both by colonial stereotypes and more localised concerns.

Chapter 5 turns to the range of people migrating to the new Canadian nation. This unpicks some of the grand narratives of the settlement of 'The Last Best West', with everyday life and multicultural influxes of people juxtaposed to show a fuller picture of migration to Canada. The eclectic nature of the collection allows the coming together of photographs illustrating both differences and similarities within the many different groups arriving in Canada at the time of the Colonial Copyright Collection.

Finally, Chapter 6 reveals the wider, nation-building narratives communicated domestically and worldwide through war photography. Canada's growing international military involvement as a result of the South African and First World Wars is often held up as an example of Canada's emergence as an independent nation. The breadth of material submitted for copyright illustrates the mobilisation of Canadians on the home front and front lines, and offers some reflections on the value of visual imagery in understanding both the horror and propaganda of war. As noted above, the chapter also considers the role of photography and copyright in changing Canada's role with the empire and its metropole.

Each of these chapters is shaped by the form as well as the content of the Colonial Copyright Collection, as the structure of the archive continues to affect the agency of these images even in the contemporary period. Partly for this reason, the conclusion gives explicit consideration to the present condition and potential future uses of the collection. This chapter considers the role of the archive and the images it contains in the digital age, within the context of new approaches to the production, consumption and preservation of photographic images. In so doing it elaborates on parallels and differences between the past and present agency of the archive, suggesting how lessons from the past are still relevant in an age where paper empires have in the main given way to digital domains.

Part 1
Disseminating Modernity

1
Circulations: the photograph and the postcard

The chapters in Part 1 will consider, in turn, how the camera captured the impact of the aeroplane, modernising city and expanding rail network in Canada. Before that, however, it is important to focus on the most notable way in which these images circulated: as postcards. The postcard was both born of and represented nineteenth-century technological modernity. For some, including the historian Asa Briggs, the picture postcard is an *objet par excellence* of the late Victorian era, illustrative of an increasingly intense, visually stimulating, networked and globalised world.[1] Literature on the history of the postcard, such as Frank Staff's *The Picture Postcard and its Origins*, often refers to the first two decades of the twentieth century as its 'golden age'.[2] Yet while this golden age represented a high point in the international consumption of the postcard, it was not a new invention even in the late nineteenth century. Rather, the postcard evolved through centuries of writing habits, paper printing developments and various postal reforms.

Transport and communication developments – including the railways of Chapter 3 – hastened the movement of people and things across the world, creating both the distributive mechanisms and the market for the postcard. At this time the postcard came in a huge variety of forms, ranging from the kinds of cards still familiar today to intricate, embroidered structures that could be shaped to stand on a dresser. Postcard imagery also contained a plethora of photographic, cartographic and hand-illustrated subjects, serving an international and voracious consumer market. In places such as Germany, where postal and printing developments advanced more quickly, postcards were established as fashionable and exciting by the late 1880s. This trend was enlivened by the publication in 1895 of the first German 'Gruss Aus. . .' ('Greetings From. . .') card. These proved unexpectedly popular, hugely influencing the future form of the postcard industry and the legacy of what the postcard is today. Canada was not immune from this craze in communication; by the beginning of the twentieth century the postcard had become an established consumer taste across the nation.

The parallel development of ever more efficient printing and photographic technologies paved the way for the postcard to become an inexpensive and popular way of communicating over distance. The No.3 Folding Pocket Kodak, a small, portable camera on sale from 1900 to 1914, could print the developed image directly onto a specially designed card that had a back laid out for posting as a postcard.[3] These sorts of technological developments, along with the public's increasing enthusiasm for postcards that could be used as greetings cards, tourist mementoes or illustrations of places visited to friends and family back home, allowed the field of postcard production to be entered by the local, jobbing photographer – able to produce interesting and unique images to meet the public desire quickly, easily and in limited print runs.

This massive increase in the volume of postcards was accompanied by a shift in the circulation of photographic images. The photograph moved from being a relatively expensive material object, enjoying limited circulation among the higher social classes, to a mass media object which most members of society could afford to own and send. The images that circulated in this way were often more significant than framings of postcards as ephemeral might suggest. Researchers of visual imagery have shown how the postcard represented and reduced complex, multi-layered messages into stereotypical visual forms. For example, Geary and Webb (a curator and an archivist respectively) edited a collection on *Delivering Views: Distant Cultures in Early Postcards*, which uses examples from elsewhere in the empire to illustrate how essentialist ideas of 'distant' places were sent home by postcard.[4] Canada was no different; here the postcard was a catalyst to the creation and circulation of new views and ideas, as well as expressing and communicating the modernity of Canada in the twentieth century.

Canada in the post: the golden age of postcards

Before 1902 most photographers in Canada sold their images to national or even international printers, publishers or commissioning companies ('sponsors') who provided a market to photographers able to produce unique and interesting local views or particularly good images of national and provincial civic events (as in the case of J. W. Jones in Chapter 2).

After 1902 the Colonial Copyright Collection experienced a significant increase in photographic deposits – evidence in part of the popularity and profitability of this market for photographers in Canada. With the improvements to printing technology and photographic equipment that had occurred by the beginning of the twentieth century, it soon became possible for localised amateur and semi-professional photographers to print their own images cheaply and efficiently and to sell them in limited runs. This consequently was much more profitable than selling the copyright of the image to a large national or international printer.

The coming of the postcard allied to these developments also provided photographers with a distinct reason for copyrighting their work and made it financially sensible to do so. The technological, economic and circulatory changes that were the very drivers of the postcard industry also necessitated protection of images that were well received. Further, reduced photographic production and printing costs mediated the overhead expense of submitting for copyright. Photographers were thus encouraged to submit their work for copyright as it became both less expensive and more beneficial.

Local photographers were able to produce high quality postcards annotated with the card's title and photographer's name. This was achieved by scoring the details onto the original negative, resulting in etched white writing on the final reproduction of the card – a detail seen in many of the images of the Colonial Copyright Collection and indicative of their use as postcards. At the same time the lack of this evidence does not necessarily mean a copyrighted image was never reproduced as a postcard. Many postcards from this period survive only in private collections, and the photographers who deposited images in the Colonial Copyright Collection would have printed their own cards in small volumes for sale leaving little or no formal record. However, the material clues on the deposited images (their size, subject, layout, negative markings, etc.) often suggest that an image might have been reproduced as a postcard or view-card.

The view-card would have been produced in a similar shape and style to the postcard, but printed in higher quality; it was usually sold as a personal keepsake to tourists and other visitors. The distinction, therefore, is that while in many ways the view-card was similar to the postcard in form, style and content, it was not designed for posting. As noted in the Introduction with reference to Elizabeth Edwards's work in particular, photographic objects carry considerable biographical traces in their material form.[5] In the context of the Colonial Copyright Collection, the markings on images discussed earlier provide a clear insight into the potential use, economic and exchange values of many of the images.

The deposits known to be postcards (either registered as postcards or in a more raw photographic state) are an unusual blank canvas. Deposited by the copyrighter, they have not themselves been used for correspondence, so they provide none of the pithy or mundane insights into the sender and receiver common to many postcard collections. This allows the imagination to fill in some of the blanks, while the images and material form of the postcards still communicate messages about their place of origin. They also show the importance of the postcard in transforming the visual economy of the nation, as the prevalence of mass produced, affordable images was still a relatively new phenomenon.

Other sources also help reveal the use of images as postcards. *Greetings From Canada*, an enthusiast's publication detailing the variety of postcards posted in Canada between 1900 and 1916, contains several postcards decorated by images deposited in the Colonial Copyright Collection.[6] The Azilda train crash (Fig.1.1, see also Chapter 3), the ruins of the 1904 fire in Toronto (Fig.1.2) and the social views of the arrival of the Moose Jaw homesteaders in 1909 (see Fig.1.3 and a discussion

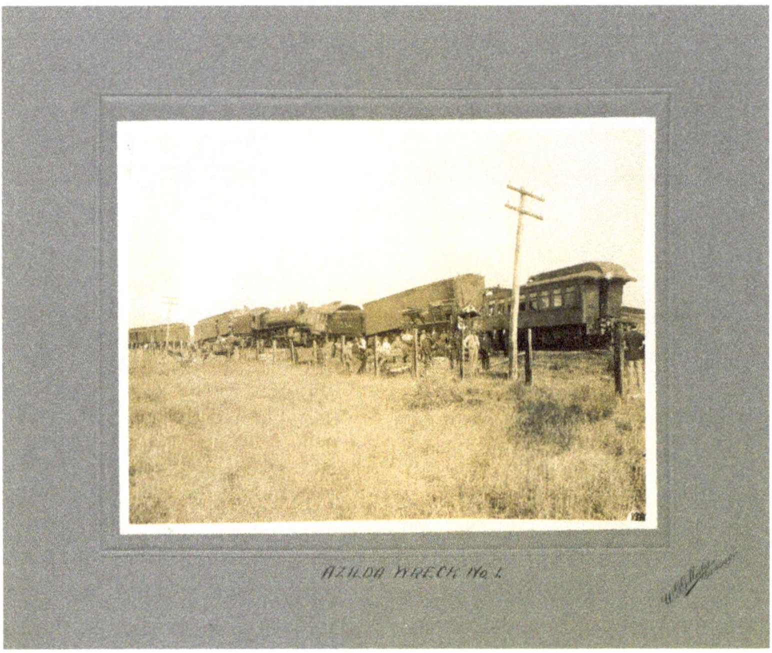

Fig. 1.1 'Azilda Train Wreck, No.10'. Copyright William G. Gillespie (copyright number 17688).

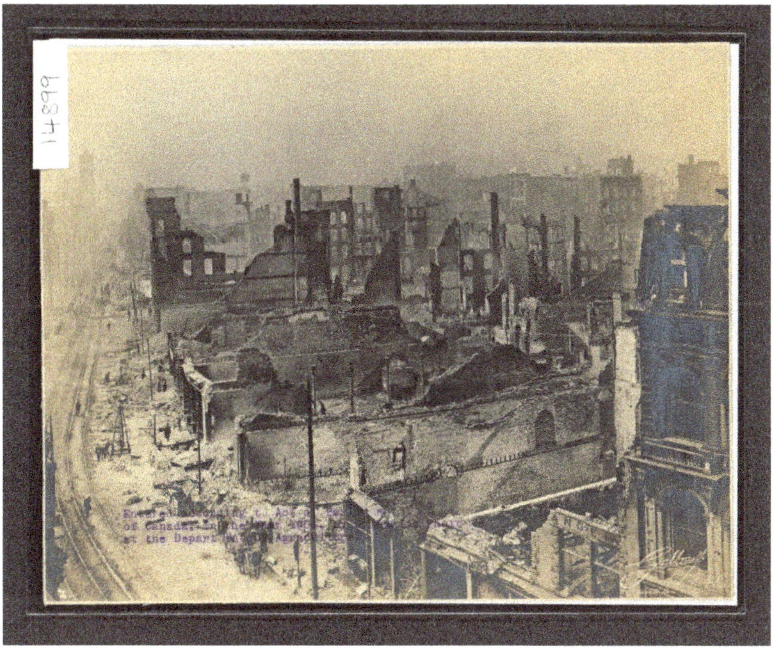

Fig. 1.2 'Ruins of Toronto Fire, 1904'. Copyright Galbraith Photo. Co. (copyright number 15423).

in Chapter 5) are all displayed in this book as examples of some of Canada's more unique postcards. Similarly, the contents of the postcard collectors' website delcampe.net suggests that the postcards of copyright depositors such as Byron Harmon (Fig.1.4) and Albert Rafton-Canning are still popular among enthusiasts for their beautiful views of the Rocky Mountains.

The absence of supplementary archival evidence for many of these photographs does not diminish the significance of the Colonial Copyright Collection as one of the most substantial and complete archives of potential, if not actual, postcard production across Canada during the late nineteenth and early twentieth centuries. This is particularly important as many Canadian historians and postcard scholars regard the sphere of the local producer as the most dynamic part of the postcard production market. It has often been suggested that the work of local photographers gives a more authentic picture of the visual diversity of the place and the nation than the larger, less visually dynamic publishers, who often struggled to source material from more marginal locations due to problems in their supply chain.

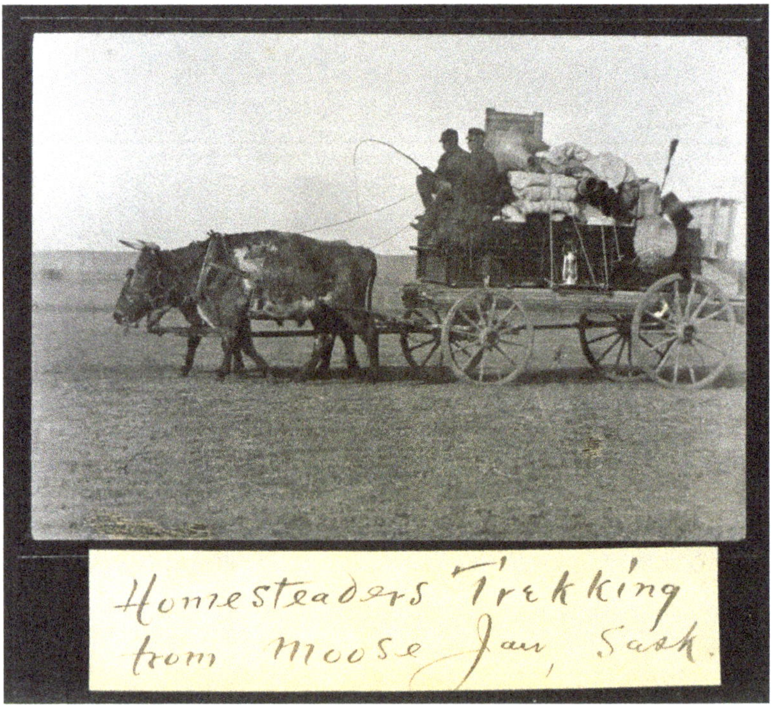

Fig. 1.3 'Homesteaders Trekking From Moosejaw, Saskatchewan'. Copyright Lewis Rice, 1909 (copyright number 20797).

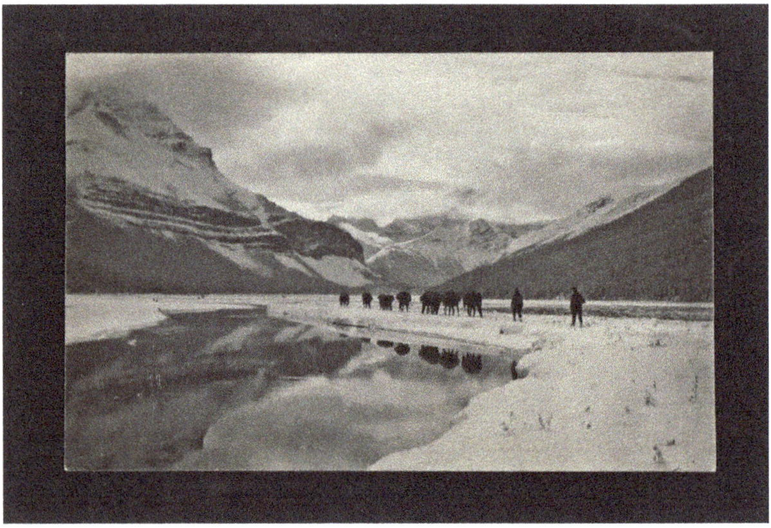

Fig. 1.4 'Approaching Wilcox Pass'. Copyright Byron Harmon (copyright number 24781).

Alongside new production capabilities, the desire of local enthusiasts, tourists and collectors provided an incentive for postcard producers constantly to produce new images. This resulted in a further explosion of views and subjects depicted through the lens of local photographers and on sale to the public. As a result, by the end of the 1920s few public gatherings, natural beauty spots or striking views of human settlements were left un-photographed; wherever there was a view to be captured, a photographer had journeyed to the spot and portrayed it through the camera's lens. One example is the work of photographer Byron Harmon (also featured in Chapter 3), who depicted large parts of the national parks and the edge of the Rocky Mountains around Banff, Alberta, from exquisite viewpoints scouted on his walks around the area. Harmon printed the images himself for sale as postcards made available to locals, tourists and travellers – the most substantial market being those individuals passing through on the transcontinental railway. Harmon also experimented with novel photographic and reproduction techniques, depositing a number of stereoscopic photographs (with postcard backings) for copyright in the early twentieth century. Two of these can be seen in Figs 1.5 and 1.6.

The advent of the photographic postcard therefore represents a significant change in the means and meaning of communication at a distance in Canada. It also corresponds with the development of the Canadian postal service, one of a number of modes of communication established with a mandate to encourage national integration and identity formation.[7] The Canadian postal service was therefore the main mechanism

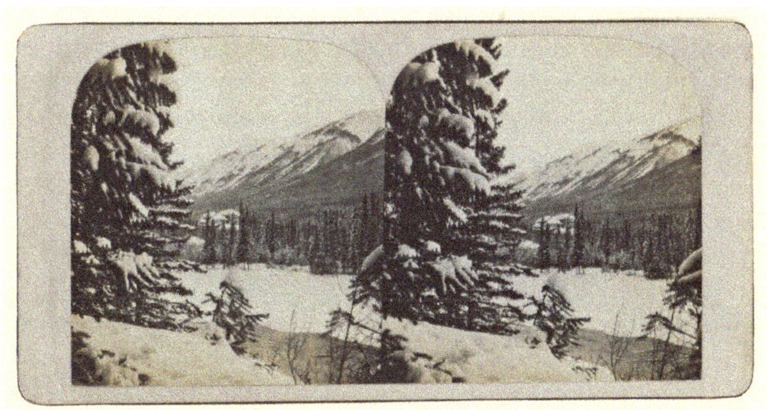

Fig. 1.5 'CPR Hotel, Banff', 1908. Copyright Byron Harmon (copyright number hs85 10 19332).

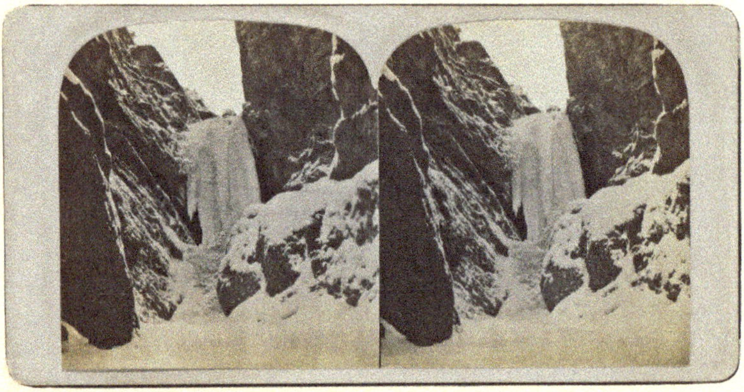

Fig. 1.6 'Frozen Waterfall on Mt Stephen', 1908. Copyright Byron Harmon (copyright number hs85 10 19331).

through which postcards circulated in this period, enmeshing the images they contained in the nation-building process. Within this context the many images deposited in the Colonial Copyright Collection which were subsequently used for postcards can be seen as actively taking advantage of a developing means of circulation and the resulting market this provided.

As will be shown throughout this book the photograph, in a range of object forms, was bound up in various projects of nation-building and identity formation. Some of these, such as the railway, pre-date and run through the period discussed in this book while others, such as the Canadian postal service and the use of the aeroplane, were contemporaneous to the collection's creation. To illustrate the scale of the audience that the Canadian postal service allowed photographers to access through photographic postcards, in 1913 60 million postcards were sent in Canada. This is an impressive figure when one considers that the total population of the country at that point was only roughly 7.3 million.[8]

The developing Canadian postcard industry therefore had important consequences as a result of its mobilisation of views of the nation, domestically and internationally. Throughout the nineteenth and twentieth centuries these visual identities of Canada were continually under (re)construction. Within Canada, communicating new places of settlement between families and friends was important in the context of rapid mobility and change. Globally too, the postcard was integral to communication between individuals and conveying the changing status of this agrarian Dominion cum modern nation.

A new vision: Canada from the air

Communication technologies are a significant theme of this book. Chapter 3 is dedicated to the railway in Canada, while this chapter will now dwell on a large series of aerial photographs deposited by the Bishop-Barker Co. As noted in the Introduction, Harris's idea that the Canadian landscape can be understood to comprise of various 'drafts' is important to this work: this landscape, however, is a palimpsest of interlocking communication technologies and potentials. No technology supersedes the other and cannot therefore be truly seen as a progression, due to this enmeshing of technologies and landscapes. With this in mind the technologies and their agencies discussed in this work do not 'progress' temporally; instead they follow the logic of the collection and its patterns of deposit.

Amidst the large number of postcards in the collection, some mundane and many innovative, there are a few hundred that stand out: the aerial photographs of the Bishop-Barker Co. Postcards of aerial views of Canada are both enabled by, and symbolic of, a nation undergoing change as a result of modern technology. They also illustrate particularly well the way in which consumers' appetite for new postcard images drove photographers and postcard manufacturers to great lengths to find new views. As noted, the Colonial Copyright Collection includes a substantial deposit of aerial photograph postcards produced by the Bishop-Barker Co., a firm set up by Canadian pilots after the First World War. Produced, printed and copyrighted from 1919 to 1920, the postcards represent an attempt by ex-flying aces from the First World War to transfer their military skills into a postwar living. Notably the images are also some of the first examples of photographs of the Canadian landscape produced from the air and made available for popular consumption.

Between the wars the aeroplane, and the view of the landscape that it allowed, inspired excitement among all sections of society, from politicians to artists, businessmen to the general public. It represented postwar hopes and ideals that a 'great period [had] just begun', as Le Corbusier wrote in *Aircraft*. This technology no longer had just a military purpose: it represented an ability to provide people with new agency and a 'New Vision'[9] that many thought would define the rest of the century. Certainly this was the case for the architect Le Corbusier. His initial experiences of flight led him to extol how it would change the ability of people to perceive and act upon the world around them irrevocably.

The aerial photographs of the Bishop-Barker Co. were produced at a time when Canada was coming to terms with the effects and aftermath of the First World War.[10] It was a time of global change, as power geometries shifted, technological modernity continued to reshape societies and a pandemic swept across the world in the wake of the conflict. In Canada, the aeroplane and the view from above were greeted with enthusiasm after the war as they represented new, previously unthought-of opportunities for crossing and developing the landscape.[11] The alliance of the aerial photograph with the postcard served to communicate these ideas to a wider audience and increase the public scope of this excitement.

The aerial view in Canada was not reserved for visual pleasure and popular spectacle alone. In the interwar period persistent attempts were made to exploit the commercial potential of the aeroplane, with forestry programmes, the development of airmail services, aerial terrain mapping and various other schemes trialled in order to create a market for air services.[12] In some cases these were alleged to have brought significant benefit to the Canadian economy (especially from terrain mapping) in terms of resource exploitation and transportation development. However, few produced sustained income for aviators. In the 1920s the few significantly profitable avenues of employment for Canadian aviators were those provided by aerial display and aerial photography, particularly popular after the idea of the 'flying ace' had taken hold in the public imagination during the First World War. In eastern Canada the niche of aerial display and aerial photograph production was inhabited by the company of Billy Bishop and William Barker, two of the war's most celebrated heroes.

Bishop and Barker had gained renown in the war for their exploits as pilots in the British army. By the end of the war they finished as 'most kills' and 'most decorated' respectively, while tales of their daring and bravery had been communicated across the British Empire.[13] The flying abilities of both men were well known and Billy Bishop's fame has proved particularly enduring, as evidenced by the 1982 production of films such as *The Kid Who Couldn't Miss*.[14] It was William Barker's work as a reconnaissance pilot flying over German lines, however, which provided the essential skills for aerial photography. During the three years that they remained in business, the only profitable ventures the duo undertook were the displays they put on for the Canadian National Exhibition and the aerial photographs they produced for private sponsors or reproduction as postcards, either by themselves or the Canadian Postcard Co.

One of Bishop-Barker Co.'s best-known images is of Queen's University in Kingston, Ontario (Fig.1.7), one of the company's first

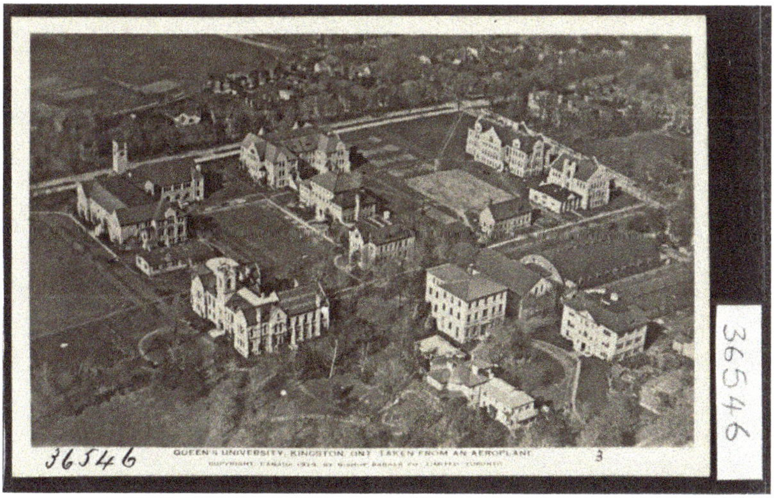

Fig. 1.7 'Queen's University, Kingston, Ont., Taken From an Aeroplane'. Copyright Bishop-Barker Co. Ltd. (copyright number 36546).

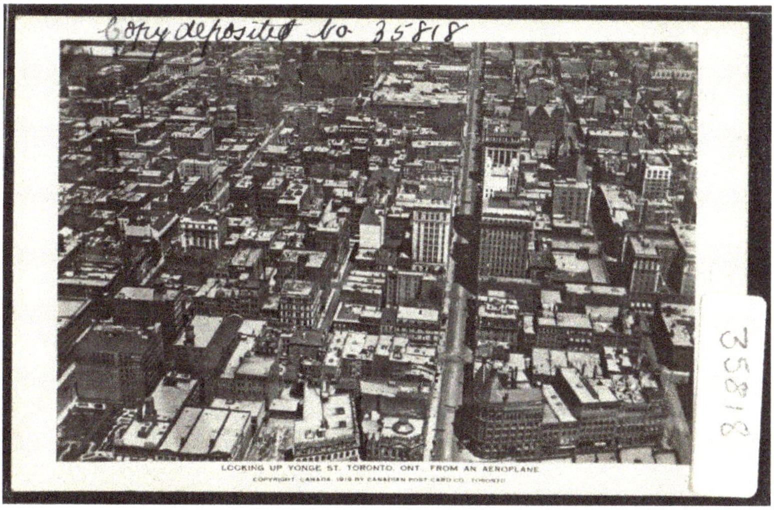

Fig. 1.8 'Looking Up Yonge Street, Toronto, Ont., From an Aeroplane'. Copyright Canadian Postcard Co., Toronto (copyright number 35818).

profit-generating commissions after its formation.[15] Evidence that this was a photograph taken for aesthetic rather than cartographic purposes – as was common in aerial photography – lies in its composition. Cameras fitted for landscape survey purposes have to be positioned, as near as possible, in the undercarriage of the plane, facing straight down to the ground, in order to reduce the effect of the earth's curvature on the image and prevent a skewing of perspective over increasing distances.[16] In the images produced by the Bishop-Barker Co. the camera is side mounted to the plane, negating the usefulness of the images for the purpose of aerial mapping. Instead the side mounting gives a co-pilot control of the camera's mechanical features, allowing the selection of shots, varied compositions and the production of photographs from different altitudes. This is distinct from under-mounted cameras: a pilot using these would have to fly at a fixed altitude so that the pre-arranged aperture and f-stop values of the camera (which could not be altered in flight) would produce viable images. As a result, the images are not suitable for measurement, but are instead intended to produce a pleasing aesthetic view of the central scene and surrounding landscape.

The camera work and picturesque composition of the Bishop-Barker Co. images are highly accomplished, especially for a field in its infancy. Neither the clarity of the images nor the altitude from which they were taken were usual for the time, with both the high quality of the work and skill levels of the pilots stemming from wartime experience. Photograph 1.7 is just one example of a technically demanding image: it involved two planes, a rapid exposure and a good eye to get the other aircraft in just the right point of the frame. The combination of these skills, honed in the theatre of war, allowed and informed the production of the new landscape perspectives produced by the Bishop-Barker Co. Thanks to the postcards of this firm, these images were no longer confined to the military or more affluent audiences, but could circulate across Canada and the world.

In all of the images taken by the Bishop-Barker Co., the elevation of the camera's lens and the aeroplane's mobility reveals the larger geometries of Canada's landscapes. Take the image of the downtown area of Toronto, for example, with Yonge Street running south to north through the middle (see Fig.1.8). At ground level the hustle and bustle of the commercial district created a claustrophobic clutter that masked the structure and underlying order of North American urban development. Yet from the air the impregnable density of Yonge Street and the rest of Toronto's downtown opened to reveal the straight lines and organisation of a regimented grid system.

In other ways, however, the city becomes no less confusing as its gigantic sprawl covers every inch of the frame; the aerial view levels the ground's relief and the scale of the scene provides few prominent landmarks to the untrained eye. To counteract this, the photograph of Queen's University, as with others taken by Bishop-Barker Co., has a highly recognisable landmark at its centre. This not only provides a striking centrepiece, but also allows viewers to orientate themselves around a relatively unfamiliar view of the Canadian landscape. Such a focus is important, given the ability of the view from above to flatten

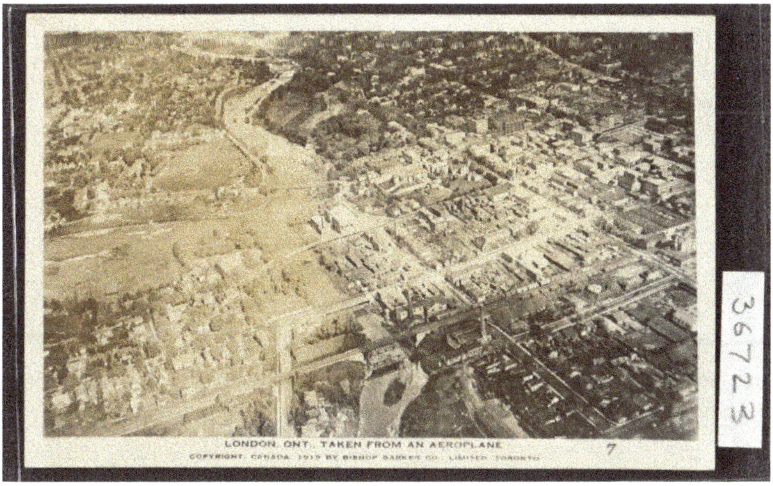

Fig. 1.9 'London, Ont., Taken From an Aeroplane'. Copyright Bishop-Barker Co. Ltd. (copyright number 36075).

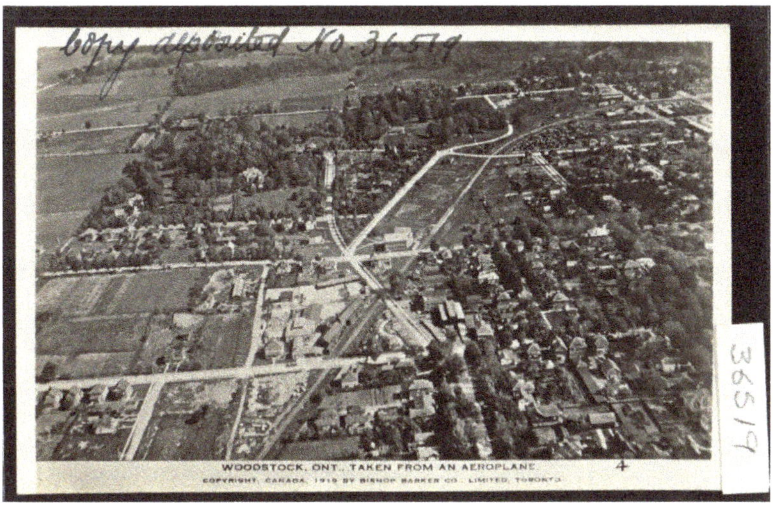

Fig. 1.10 'Woodstock, Ont., Taken From an Aeroplane'. Copyright Bishop-Barker Co. Ltd. (copyright number 36519).

topographies and mask features well-known from the ground, overlaying them in turn with previously imperceptible landmarks.[17] Artists, including members of the avant-garde, relished the view from above precisely because of its dizzying perspective and the challenge it offered to the familiar perspective of landscape (see below).[18]

Bishop-Barker Co. also used the aerial view to provide new perspectives on some of Canada's wider urban and rural geographies. The shot of London, Ontario, for example, shows the interlocking relationship between Canada's towns, industry and landscape as the view focuses on the meeting of the two forks of the River Thames (see Fig.1.9). The view illustrates London's industrial complexes set against the riverbank as well as, on the opposite bank, the residential and leisure opportunities provided by the slow, unnavigable river, with houses and green spaces running down to the water's edge. This illustrates the importance of Canada's landscape features to its urban geographies and the intertwined, sometimes contradictory, ways in which they have been appropriated for human use. While this relationship between geography and settlement was understood, the depiction of this in such an all-encompassing and grand scale of vision was new. Geographer Denis Cosgrove described such aerial views of North America as 'Apollonian' because of the god-like view provided. This term also underscores the significance of power, reflecting attempts by Canada and the United States to constrain and control the landscape in the nineteenth and twentieth centuries.[19]

Like the cityscapes, suburban images also bring modern planning to the fore. In an image of Woodstock's suburban borders, the rigid geometries carved into the landscape by rational agricultural practices become apparent from the air as the division and management of Canada's large and diverse landscapes is shown from a new perspective (see Fig.1.10). For Cosgrove, '[t]he American landscape makes sense from the air' as such views give an overview of the patterns and logics at work in the management of the landscape on a grand scale.[20] As with American photographers and the American landscape, Canadian photographers have always sought, since the advent of photography, to raise the camera higher, in order to depict more of the area around them and afford a better perception of their similarly vast landscapes. Aerial photography offered the first versatile realisation of this desire – not just because of the views on offer, but also through the mobility afforded by the aeroplane. While aerial views had been produced before, they had generally been taken from balloons or kites that were tethered and costly to move, limiting what they could capture. Now aeroplanes could capture whole areas to convey more fully the vastness not only of Canada's largest cities, but also of its formidable natural landscape.

Larger landscapes were captured by Bishop-Barker Co. by using series. An example is the nine images taken over and around the Ontario town of Brantford, produced by a roughly north to south fly-through (see for example Figs 1.11–1.13). This angle created a cross-section

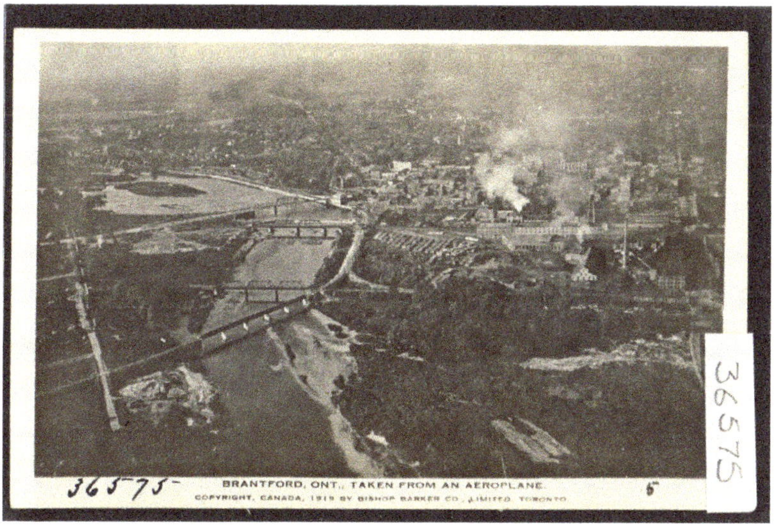

Fig. 1.11 'Brantford, Ont., Taken From an Aeroplane' [1]. Copyright Bishop-Barker Co. Ltd. (copyright number 36575).

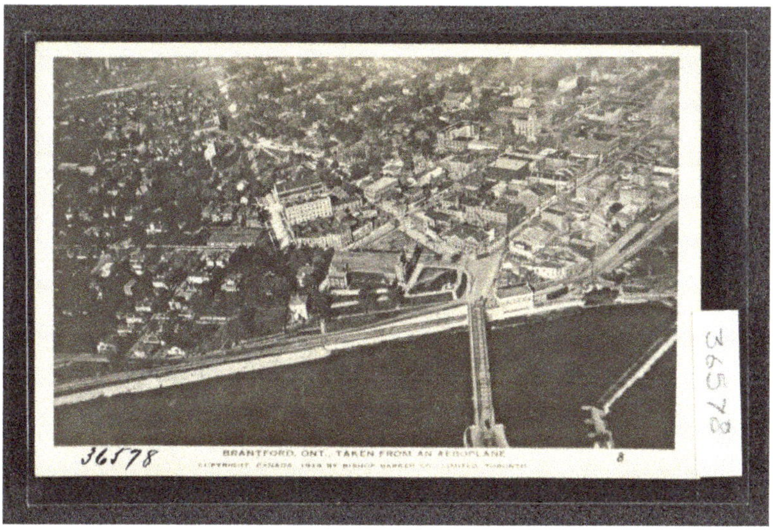

Fig. 1.12 'Brantford, Ont., Taken From an Aeroplane' [2]. Copyright Bishop-Barker Co. Ltd. (copyright number 36578).

taking in most of the town's significant features: downtown, the Grand River with its slightly abraded southern stretch and upper islands, residential areas, bridges straddling the river and the town's industry. The perspective presented across the images is one of development, progress and a technical capacity to tame Canada's landscape for the benefit of its citizens. Brantford is not a unique case, nor was it singled out for a particular photographic purpose. Instead it was photographed as part of a series of private commissions along the Quebec City–Windsor Corridor undertaken following the enthusiastic reception of the Bishop-Barker Co.'s Kingston and Toronto images. Brantford is one of the many urban and rural areas in Ontario photographed extensively (with many of urban areas depicted in their entirety) in these sponsored runs, intended for commission sale or distribution as postcard images.[21] The result was a portfolio of images from which consumers could select particular views of specific places of interest to them, including homes, leisure sites, notable landmarks and public buildings. Seen in series, the aerial view opened up new geographical perceptions of place to the consumer, unbound from routine and habit at street level and offering up the whole local area from a dizzying and exhilarating height.

The distributional reach of the postcard greatly reinforced the significance of these new aerial visions, which became highly valued and widely circulated. The postcards of the Bishop-Barker Co. presented a

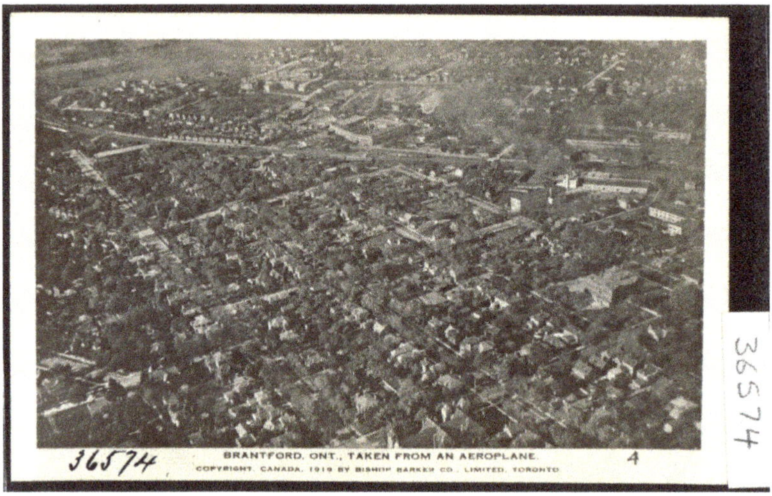

Fig. 1.13 'Brantford, Ont., Taken From an Aeroplane' [3]. Copyright Bishop-Barker Co. Ltd. (copyright number 36574).

new vision of the geography of Canada at a time when Canada's perception of itself was changing in a world of shifting political power geometries. Further, the postcard provided a format that could disseminate this view and its perspective on the landscape of Canada to an ever increasing population, not just in Canada, but globally. Such images are therefore credited with helping to secure the geographical cohesiveness of the Canadian nation state.[22]

As a result what we see is, to borrow from the analysis of Cole Harris, another layer of perspective and mobility being applied to the Canadian landscape.[23] Aerial technology would bind even more diverse spheres of Canada's landscape to the urbanised east, especially in the Canadian Arctic, through its power to survey, transport and communicate.[24] The significance of this scope and modernity is considered further in the following section, which explores the relationship of the aerial view and the Canadian National Exhibition.

Canada imagined from the air

A key national event during the time of the Colonial Copyright Collection was the Canadian National Exhibition. Formerly the Toronto Industrial Exhibition, the event became known as the Canadian National Exhibition in 1912 in order to compete with other national and international fairs. The structure and architecture of the exhibition had always changed incrementally and continued to do so after the renaming. However, the change of name marked an acknowledgement that the exhibition, and Canada itself, had become more internationally significant since the days of the first Toronto Industrial Exhibition in 1878. The idea of the exhibition as a space for the articulation of national identity in modern cities is well established during this time period. The Canadian National Exhibition was no different in articulating and disseminating an understanding of Canadian urban and modern identities, which circulated particularly through the aerial display and the postcard.

Much attention has been paid to the role of exhibitions and world fairs in the development of nineteenth- and twentieth-century modernity and its articulation to the public.[25] Tony Bennett's exploration of what he calls 'The Exhibitionary Complex', for example, shows how such fairs ordered the world for the understanding of the public, while also ordering the public to fit with the social, technological and political ideology represented by the exhibition itself.[26] In his view, the exhibition and the world's fair were therefore akin to the museum in providing an ordered, visualised understanding of the operation of the world – not just in respect to the nation, but the relationship of other nations to the host nation as well. The exhibition, as with the museum, provided visual templates for the comprehension of the order of things in the world, extensively contrasting Western modernity with the orientalism of the 'other' in order to assert the achievements of the host state.[27]

One significant difference between the exhibition and the museum, however, was the versatility of the space utilised for the exhibition. Whereas the museum provided a fixed space (and its social messages were underpinned by this fixedness), the exhibition offered a space made of prefabricated facades, underpinned by mass communication and mass production. As a result, the exhibit and its message could be changed and adapted in the face of continued developments of technology and the workings of the world.[28]

While most of this academic discussion has focused on European and, to a lesser extent, American exhibitions, relatively little work has been done on the role of exhibitions in Canada. However, as Keith Walden suggests in *Becoming Modern in Toronto*, the Toronto Industrial Exhibition and Canadian National Exhibition spanned a period of significant change. They played an important role in shifting perceptions of Canada as a rural and agrarian state to a metropolitan one, including developing an urban and modern mindset within elements of the population.[29] Walden has written about how the exhibition promoted the appropriation of modern technology within Canadian cities while also working to articulate a vision of metropolitan modernity to the Canadian upper and middle classes. As a result of this, and the canny use of the exhibition by many Canadian entrepreneurs, the exhibition played an important role in the development of metropolitan capitalism in nineteenth- and twentieth-century Canada, as testified by the later discussion of T. Eaton and Co (see Chapter 2).

Given its predominance and routine nature, it was also important for the exhibition to always have something new and 'cutting edge' on show.[30] The Canadian National Exhibition was one of the first national fairs to reopen after the First World War, in the summer of 1919. It busily set about promoting Canada's role in the war and the positive effects of the conflict on the country. In particular, its organisers were enthusiastic about the new technology of flight developed in the early part of the twentieth century and exploited during the First World War. Most importantly, the exhibition was keen to showcase the role of Canada's most celebrated airmen in the conflict, and also to impress upon visitors the wonder of the aircraft and its view from above. Further, it was keen to highlight Canada's involvement in the new technology as a means of asserting the nation's own modernity. Central to this was the by now well-established device of the postcard, used to disseminate the message of the fair in an accessible and mobile form.[31]

The Canadian National Exhibition of 1919 hosted the first display of formation flying in Canada, performed by the fledgling Bishop-Barker Co. and their associates, in ex-German air force Fokker D-VII's.[32] The company was loaned the planes by Arthur Doughty, the Dominion Archivist, who was placed in the role of Director of War Trophies in Canada after the war. This new position, along with the captured German and surplus British materials given to Canada as 'Imperial Gifts', were influential in promoting use of the aircraft in Canada.[33] The display was well received by a large, enthusiastic crowd, leading the *Toronto Globe* to headline the resulting article, '"Stunt" Flying Thrills the Crowd – Spectators at Exhibition Gasp at Feats of Daring Airmen'.[34]

Subsequent to this first show, stunt and formation flying became regular parts of the show calendar, exciting crowds keen to see the pilots'

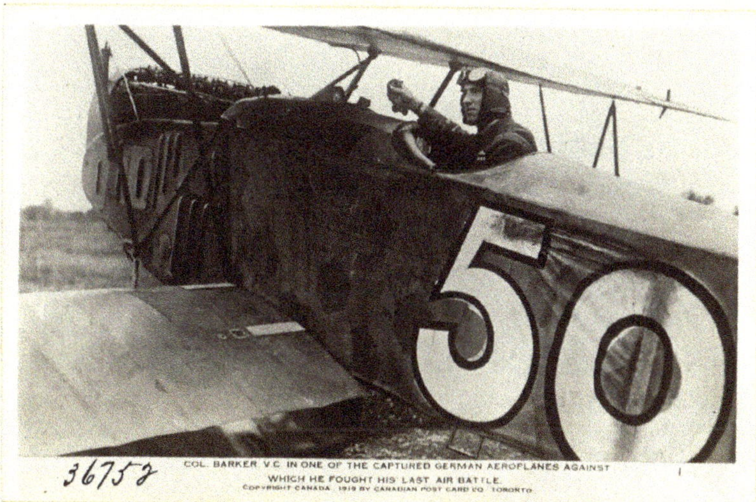

Fig. 1.14 'Col Barker V. C. in One of the Captured German Aeroplanes Against Which He Fought His Last Battle'. Copyright Canadian Postcard Co. (copyright number 36752).

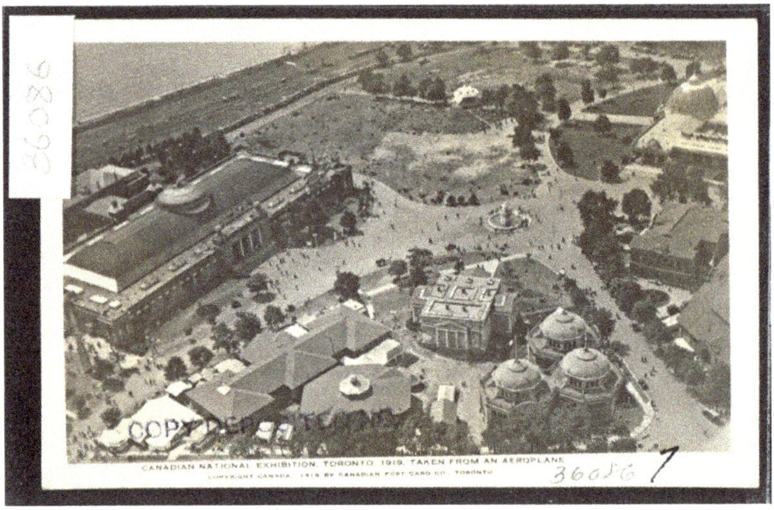

Fig. 1.15 'Canadian National Exhibition, Toronto, 1919. Taken From an Aeroplane' [1]. Copyright Canadian Postcard Co. (copyright number 36086).

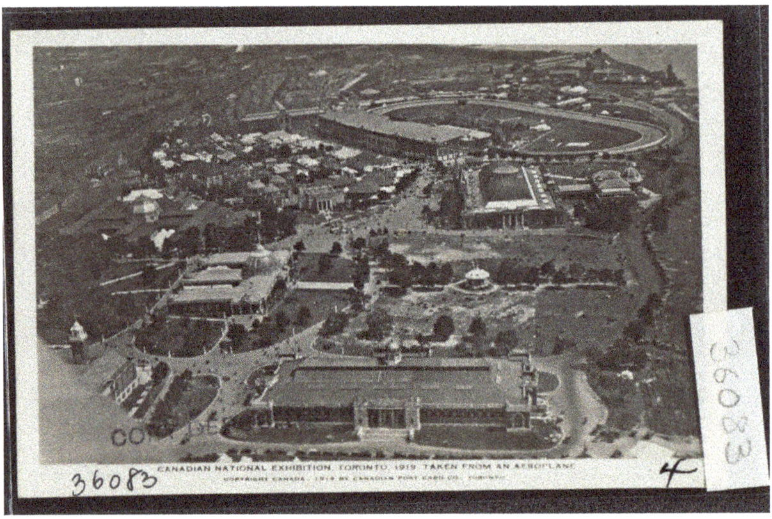

Fig. 1.16 'Canadian National Exhibition, Toronto, 1919. Taken From an Aeroplane' [2]. Copyright: Canadian Postcard Co. (copyright number 36083).

daring and thrilling manoeuvres. Enhanced by sensational media reports of iconic figures such as William Barker and Billy Bishop (both known for their alcohol-fuelled, celebrity lifestyles), as well as the availability of souvenir materials produced for the display, the technology of flight was associated with daring and innovation (see for example Fig.1.14). In short, flight represented the cutting edge of modernity.

Capitalising on the excitement for aerial shows, the exhibition organisers soon began to sell aerial postcards of the exhibition grounds, its pavilions and crowds. These were produced by the Canadian Postcard Co. and taken by the Bishop-Barker Co. As in the discussion of the images of Brantford, London and downtown Toronto, the aerial photographs were unlike any previous view of the Canadian National Exhibition grounds (see Figs 1.15–1.16). Bird's-eye views had been produced in the last 20 years, but these had only served to highlight the height and grandeur of the buildings; the logic of the overall exhibition site could not be portrayed. In these images, however, the topography of the landscape is flattened and the people visiting the fair resemble nondescript ants moving around the grounds.

In combination, these three elements – the war hero, aerial performance and photographic view – gave the visitor to the fair a sense of the wonders of a new technology and its potential for modern Canada. In the previous century Canada had tamed the landscape and achieved confederation through the use of the railway. Now the twentieth century promised a new era with the mastery of the sky. Further, all of this was depicted on the affordable, portable format of the postcard, to be taken home or sent across the world. The interlinking of the exhibition

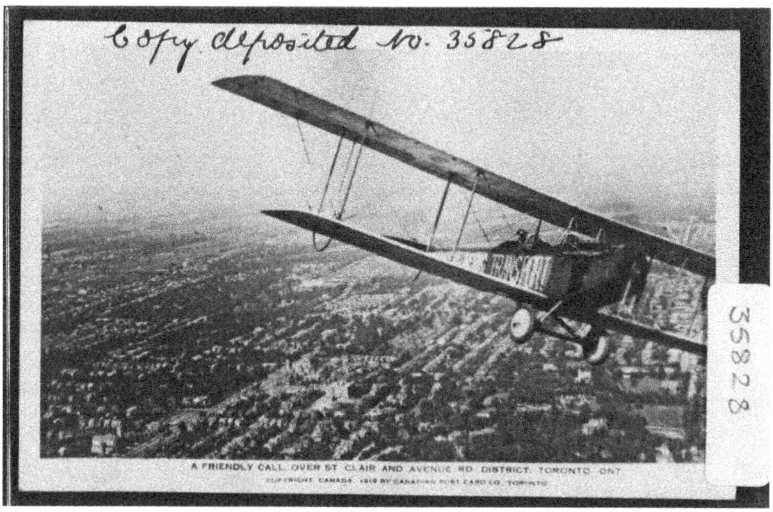

Fig. 1.17 'A Friendly Call Over St. Clair and Avenue Rd. District, Toronto, Ont.'. Copyright Canadian Postcard Co. (copyright number 35828).

message with the visual image on the postcard was a common feature of the exhibition throughout the nineteenth and twentieth centuries. Across Europe the postcard and other souvenirs were used to commemorate the understandings and messages of the world's fair, and the same is true of the Canadian National Exhibition.

The Canadian National Exhibition is just one of many worldwide examples of the mass circulation of images instigated by the postcard, an object central to the development of a globalised image world. Technological innovation created a market for the photographer to exploit, and the Colonial Copyright Collection contains myriad examples of photographs produced to satiate the appetite of the tourist, collector and correspondent. The work of the photographer then circulated through various networks to become part of complex understandings of place. For Canada, the development of technology and new networks of communication also provided an opportunity to promote the nation's own modern development. Aerial photographs in particular provided a new and valuable perspective on its landscape. With the help of institutions such as the Canadian National Exhibition, which placed the modernity of the aircraft and the spectacle of its view at the forefront of the public imagination, the postcard distributed a new perspective of the Canadian landscape.

* * *

By considering postcards and the aerial photography of the Bishop-Barker Co. in the same chapter, this analysis has done two things. It has illustrated one of the most significant ways in which the photographs of the Colonial Copyright Collection circulated in a national and global visual economy, and also highlighted the evolving frameworks of technological modernity in Canada between 1895 and 1924. The significance of the postcard and view-card lies in the ease of production and volume of circulation that these formats provided to Canadian photographers who deposited their work for copyright. These two factors gave depth to the visual economy within which these photographers were agents and allow us to perceive the potential for circulation that each of these images had.

Allied to this, this chapter shows how photographers, and the markets to which they catered, were stimulated by new technologies and visual imaginations during the early twentieth century. This chapter also marks a point where we can begin to perceive how significantly interconnected the Canadian visual economy within which these images circulated was. The format of the postcard provides a linking material thread along which many of the photographic subjects discussed in *Canada in the Frame* will flow. Furthermore, the recurrence of the Canadian National Exhibition links to the discussions that follow in Chapter 2, while the book's first considerations of the technological impact of the First World War on Canada opens the door to the more substantive discussion presented in Chapter 6. In short, while the photographers who deposited material to this collection often operated in different circles, were separated by large distances and usually did not know each other, their interconnections extend beyond their utilisation of Colonial Copyright Law.

As well as this, when viewed in parallel with the images discussed elsewhere in this book, the images of the Bishop-Barker Co. remind us of the pace of change across Canada at this time. There were myriad different Canadas available for postage, collection and communication, all linked together by this photographic visual economy. This book will focus on a number of them, including Canada's First Peoples, migrants settling in the nation and soldiers fighting in Europe, not to mention the development of Canada's railways. The form of Canada most extensively photographed and deposited in the collection, however, was the developing city, to which the next chapter turns its attention.

2
Photographing growth: Canada's cities, politics and the visual economy

Canada's cities were both the subject and the site of photographic work through the period covered by the Colonial Copyright Collection. Images of the urban landscape were designed to associate particular historical events or sites of local significance with something more general, for example civic progress, modernity or commercial society. These photographs are thus not simply depictions of places and events: they are active constructions and interventions in the sociopolitical landscape. As Trachtenberg has argued of North American photography in general, 'the history they show is inseparable from the history they enact'.[1]

The rate of photographic production and circulation within the empire and the world at large had increased dramatically by 1895, as had the public taste for photography, whether consumed in exhibits, newspapers or the home. This created opportunities within the urban economy for commercial photographers. In the Colonial Copyright Collection this is exemplified by the location of depositing photographers; individuals and businesses deposit photographs from urban locations across Canada between 1895 and 1924. Importantly, the major urban centres of Canada form a focus for the collection, with a significant proportion of deposits and the greatest range of photographers being based in Vancouver, Toronto, Montreal, and so on. These photographers turned their cameras on the landscape, people and surrounding areas that were part of the sphere of influence of the urban centre – often bound up with a visual economy in discourse with wider political, economic and social dynamics of the city.

Photographs of Canada's urban areas, where the town or city itself is the subject of the image, comprise almost one-quarter of the collection, making it by far the most significant photographic subject in the collection. This is reflected in the prevalence of photographers based in

Ontario, Quebec and British Columbia who deposited to the collection; almost three-quarters of deposits come from photographers in those provinces. These photographers tended to be based in urban areas with strong communications links (a point considered in detail in Chapter 3), and this goes some way to explain why over one-fifth of deposits come from Ontario's urban areas.

While it is important to note that the location of photographers creates a certain inevitability that they would photograph the urban areas around them, since few of us are creatively disinterested in our immediate surroundings, it is just as notable that Canada's urban areas provided a source of inspiration and a market for photographers. There are a significant number of images deposited around the turn of the century, reflecting urban booms and a corresponding growth in urban photographers. Cities as photographic subjects also reflect their general economic, political and social trends, with Winnipeg being a good example of this. The city is thus a noteworthy presence in early twentieth-century deposits, its boom attracting photographic interest. However, deposits noticeably slacken from the First World War onwards as changing demographic and economic conditions began to dampen the city's growth. The lack of images of the 1919 General Strike, for instance, also reminds us that this collection's view of Canada's cities is predominantly positive, designed to sell interesting views on postcards or other consumable media rather than provide a repository of, say, grittier reportage. However, one can only go so far in considering an absence from such a collection.

Such notable absences invite this book to consider what messages this collection does articulate about Canada's booming cities. The positive images provided depict building openings, the expansion of civic infrastructure, royal visits, the growing empires of Canadian merchants and other such topics; these are the dominant views of Canada's growing cities. In many ways such a focus correlates with the growth of photographic interest in the city detailed in Peter Hales's *Silver Cities*.[2] Hales asserts that in America the late nineteenth and early twentieth centuries saw an increased desire to depict the urban landscape as a bustling, dynamic space underpinned by development, commerce and the activities of the populous. The same turn can also be seen in Canadian photography through the Colonial Copyright Collection. With this in mind the chapter focuses on two different sorts of civic view, produced in this period at opposite sides of the country and depicting two drivers crucial to the visual economy of urban photography in this collection: the developing city and its growing businesses.

The relationship between photography and Canadian cities can be exemplified by two very different individuals and their photographic legacies. The first is J. W. Jones and his photographs of the opening of the British Columbia parliament buildings, taken in Victoria in 1898. The second is 'Timothy Eaton's' display book of views of Toronto, produced for the T. Eaton Co. in 1901 by an unknown photographer (or photographers). Between 1895 and 1924 the economic, social and political trajectories of Victoria and Toronto were impacted by markedly different dynamics, and it is in this complex situation that the photographs discussed have agency. The work of J. W. Jones forms part of the performance of statecraft in a city and province undergoing profound changes and asserting its identity in the Canadian, North American and colonial worlds surrounding British Columbia at this time. Meanwhile the 'Timothy Eaton's' photobook is an intervention in the Toronto (and even Canadian) landscape, increasingly influenced and shaped by the economic activity of the Timothy Eaton Co.

Selected from a broad spectrum of urban photography contained in the Colonial Copyright Collection, the images discussed in this chapter are not just illustrative of urban change; they were actively engaged with it. The case studies highlight political and economic aspects of urban change respectively: on the one hand, the official, ceremonial spaces of performance and display; on the other, the commercial modernity of modern urban life. While distinctive, these visions are part of wider traditions in the representation of the modern city which are not limited to political and economic spheres. In other chapters the book illustrates how Canadian photographers were involved in the wider economy of consumable image-making (Chapter 1, 'Circulations') and in documenting the broad social changes in Canada between 1895 and 1924 (Chapter 5, 'A collection of people').

Making places: photographers and urban identity

John Wallace Jones was a professional photographer and the primary partner of Jones and Co. and Jones Bros., which had photographic studios in Victoria and Esquimalt, British Columbia. Jones photographed the city of Victoria and the naval base at Esquimalt between 1888[3] and his death in 1938.[4] Arriving in 1888, Jones was cresting the wave of migrants entering Victoria who would increase its population from 6,000 in 1880 to 20,219 in 1900 (see Chapter 5 for more on migration in and to Canada).[5] Jones therefore witnessed the development of Victoria from post-gold rush colony to proud provincial capital.[6] He was also one of a number of photographers arriving in British Columbia between 1860 and the 1880s, seeking to profit from the photographic market generated by the gold rush.[7]

During his professional career Jones was commissioned to photograph many of the civic and ceremonial events in Victoria, as well as the development of its urban and naval infrastructure. Between 1898 and 1902 he submitted a series of images from around the city and the province of British Columbia for copyright in Canada; these therefore became part of the Colonial Copyright Collection. The images Jones submitted for copyright cover many subjects, including political events, social occasions, major news and also an extensive portfolio of the naval vessels and infrastructure at Esquimalt on the western edge of Victoria. However, there is evidence that Jones did not subject all of his photographs of Victoria for copyright, so those that are part of the Colonial Copyright Collection provide an interesting insight into how Jones decided on the varying values of his portfolio.[8] This in turn tells us something about the urban photographic economy at the time, and also intersects with recent work on the relationship between visual technology and national and provincial identities in Canada.[9] Druick's work on the Canadian National Film Board and its precursors, for example, explores official interest in the production of new images of the Canadian landscape and identity from the late nineteenth century onwards.[10]

Since its founding in 1843 as Fort Victoria (a trading outpost of the Hudson's Bay Company), the colony was protected by the Esquimalt naval base. The base was also situated to enforce the British claim over the area and to provide a staging post for naval operations on the west coast of the Americas, with easy access to the Sandwich Islands (Hawaii) and Asian colonies.[11] With Victoria's growth as a free port towards the end of the nineteenth century, and the continued interest of the Crown in what was now one of its most prolific new cities, the naval base across the bay was of great and increasing significance in the area when Jones arrived in 1888. Jones submitted an extensive portfolio of naval photography for copyright, with Figs 2.1 and 2.2 providing good examples of his approach to photographing the base.

What stands out in particular is the way in which Jones composes the shot to draw out the technical sophistication and beauty of the subject, be it a dry dock or warship. In these images the photographer is very much in control of the conditions; images seem to be painted on to the film of the camera. This delicacy comes across especially from the smoke in Fig.2.2; sharp and focused, it still retains its wispy quality. Jones also

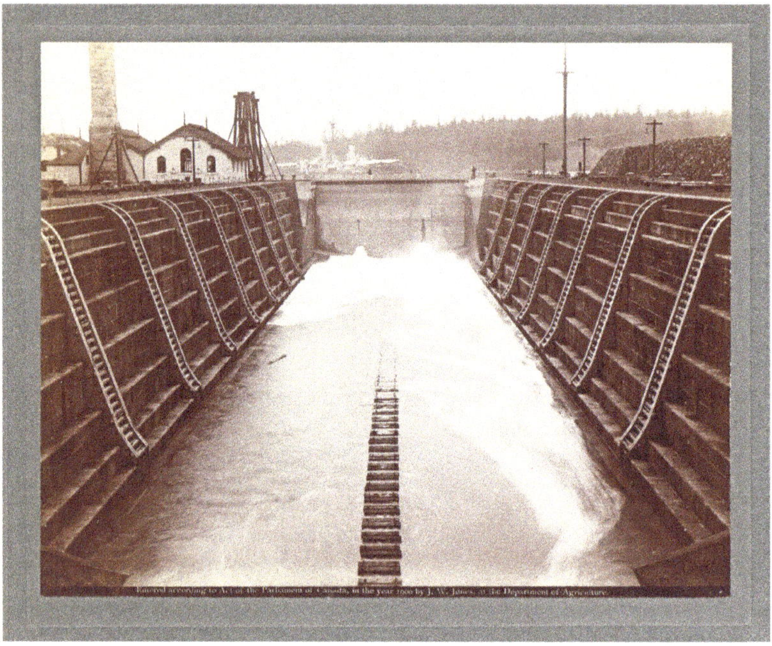

Fig. 2.1 'The Esquimalt Dry Dock'. Copyright J. W. Jones, 1900 (copyright number 12103).

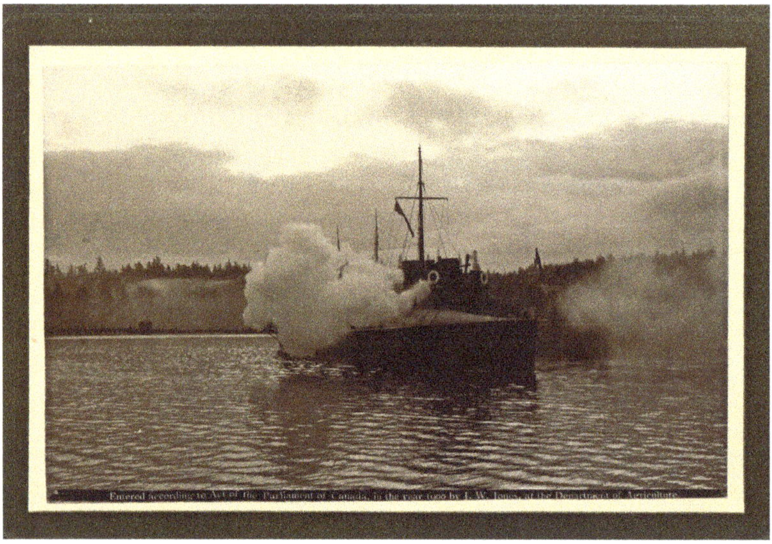

Fig. 2.2 'H.M.S. "Virago" Firing in Honour of the King'. Copyright J. W. Jones, 1901 (copyright number 11979).

captures the water delicately in both photographs, picking it out rather than blurring it. The composition of these images, in contrast to some of his other work, is considered and poised. In Fig.2.1, for example, the curved lines of the dry dock swoop down to meet with the swirling water pooling in its bottom, and the image depicts a grace that masks its utilitarian functions. Moreover, many of Jones's ships have a metallic, industrial feel that pervades the picture as a whole, generated by the effect on the water and the background light as well as the subject of the image itself (see Fig.2.2 in particular).

Jones's shots of the naval ships and yard of Esquimalt bay convey a distinctly modern technological aesthetic; rather than just tools, he portrays them as achievements of science and skill. In their emphasis on scale and majesty, these images convey an effect akin to the technological sublime.[12] The celebration of modern technology in such terms reflects a common theme in contemporary narratives of development in British Columbia, connecting to its maritime history while celebrating a new imperial era through emphasis on technological progress.[13]

It would be simple to assume that Jones and the other photographers who submitted work for copyright to the Canadian government between 1895 and 1924 were simply seeking to protect the financial value of their images by regulating their circulation within society.[14] Evidently this was a key consideration, but it was not the whole of the story. Given the selectivity Jones displayed in applying for copyright and the distinctions between his naval images and the rest of his work, the copyrighting of his naval images appears to have been motivated more specifically by a desire to distinguish their artistic significance. In short, the photographer sought to elevate his work's aesthetic qualities and to assert his creativity as a professional.[15] This was important in a period when photographic professionalism was still developing,[16] especially in a part of Canada which had only recently begun to urbanise and which supported a developing and competitive photographic economy.

While copyrighting a photograph protected the financial viability of an image by tying it to the producer (or copyrighter), it also asserted ownership of the skills and perspective that went into producing a potentially unique photographic view, composition or style. This was a potentially significant claim in a field where many professionals were trying to establish a reputation, and also carve a niche that would support further development of their practice. Given that Jones was remembered after his death as a well-known photographer whose reputation was founded in his naval work, it is likely that the copyrighting of such images contributed to expanding his reputation as an accomplished naval (and therefore military) photographer. This is a reputation that would, no doubt, also carry a considerable amount of social cachet – and that would in turn improve the photographer's professional standing in the city as a whole.

It seems that Jones's reputation as a skilled professional photographer enabled him to secure further official commissions, giving rise to another significant body of copyrighted work held in the Colonial Copyright Collection. In the same period as Figs 2.1 and 2.2 were produced, Jones photographed the arrival of the Chinese Viceroy on his first official visit to the province (1896)[17] (see Figs 2.3–2.4) and the opening of the British Columbia legislature buildings (1898).[18]

The images shown in Figs 2.5 and 2.6 appear to have been produced by Jones under the commission of the Victoria legislature, with the images commemorating the opening of the new parliament building on 10 February 1898. The perspective suggests that Jones had privileged views of the scene and, given the time constraints and logistics involved in creating these images from multiple sites, it is possible he had other photographers working for him. This being the case, it is notable that the copyright is attributed to J. W. Jones; the next part of this chapter deals with such potential absences at more length. The privileged views, something generally only conferred to the professional and official photographer, indicate that Jones was the authorised photographer on this occasion. His role was to document the event as clearly as possible in a way which could be used in subsequent publicity. The images also served to highlight its status as an historic occasion. It would appear Jones was remarkably successful in this respect, given that his photograph of the opening of parliament has still been used by the legislature in the twentieth century.[19]

Despite the jubilant scenes portrayed in these photographs, the British Columbia legislature buildings were built under a cloud of public controversy and political turmoil. Completed late in 1897, the building cost over $9 million to build, $3 million more than its original budgeted estimate of $6 million, which was already controversial. This provoked criticism both within Victoria and from outside, especially from representatives of those cities which had competed against Victoria to be capital of the province. These controversies were not solely about the parliament building itself; rather the parliament building had become a symbol of a wider power struggle to maintain Victoria's primacy in a rapidly growing province.[20] Furthermore, the character of the province was being challenged from without, as the Dominion of Canada attempted to articulate its identity in the face of cultural, political and economic

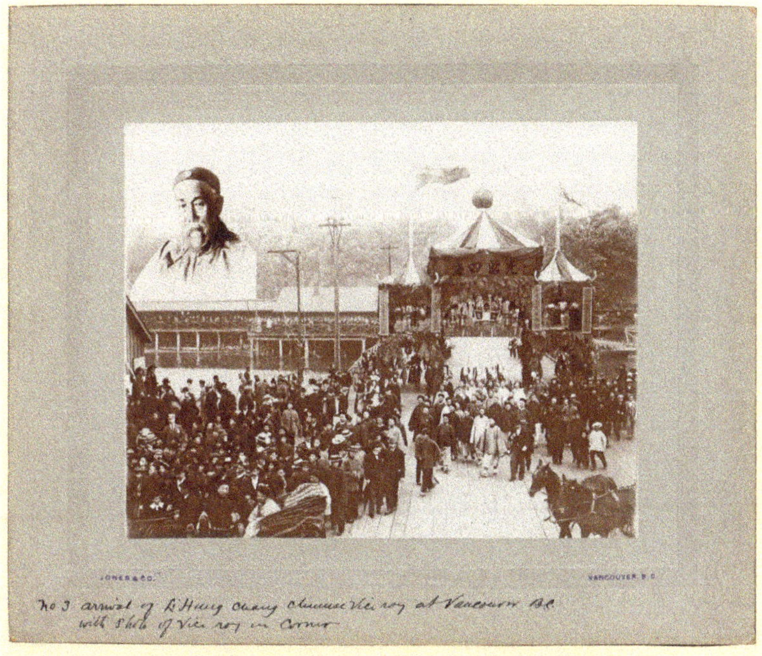

Fig. 2.3 'Arrival of Li Hung Chang'. Copyright J. W. Jones, 1896 (copyright number 8782).

encroachments from the United States. The British Columbia legislature buildings and the photographs of its opening were, therefore, significant components in these attempts to express an identity to the wider world.

Victoria was a late entrant in the field of colonial settlements in Canada and its subsequent expansion had been marked by the booms and busts of the gold rushes that occurred around the colony between 1858 and the Klondike gold rush of 1896. As a result, the town grew in a haphazard and fractured way, leading one historian to assert that, '[t]he visitor to Victoria in 1862 would have found not a city but a shacktown'.[21] By the 1870s Victoria was struggling to keep up with the rest of the province in terms of attracting new settlers and economic investment.[22] Therefore, despite winning the status of legislative capital in 1868, Victoria's reputation needed to be improved to secure its role in the eyes of the mainlanders.

These pressures led to a significant effort to tidy up the capital and create a downtown architecturally worthy of being the province's legislative centre, of which the parliament buildings were to be a cornerstone. The *Victoria Colonist*'s stern criticism of the Victoria legislature's existing

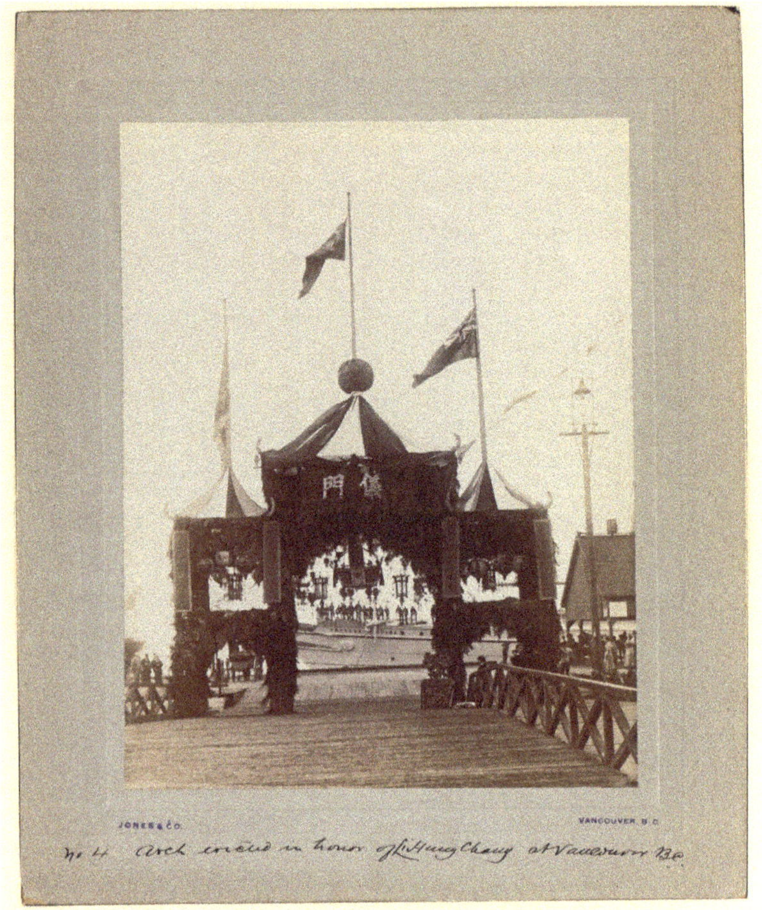

Fig. 2.4 'Arch erected in honour of Li Hung Chang'. Copyright J. W. Jones, 1896 (copyright number 8783).

architecture, called 'the Birdcages', sums up the sentiment that led to the creation of the spectacular new parliament. As the paper observed:

> Mean and insignificant public buildings are outward and visible signs of a narrow minded, sordid and uncultivated state or province. Visitors are sure to judge the whole people by the buildings they erect for public uses. Those buildings ought to be handsome as well as commodious.[23]

The paper's views mirrored many within the city. They connected to wider calls to spruce up the image of Victoria, endowing it with all

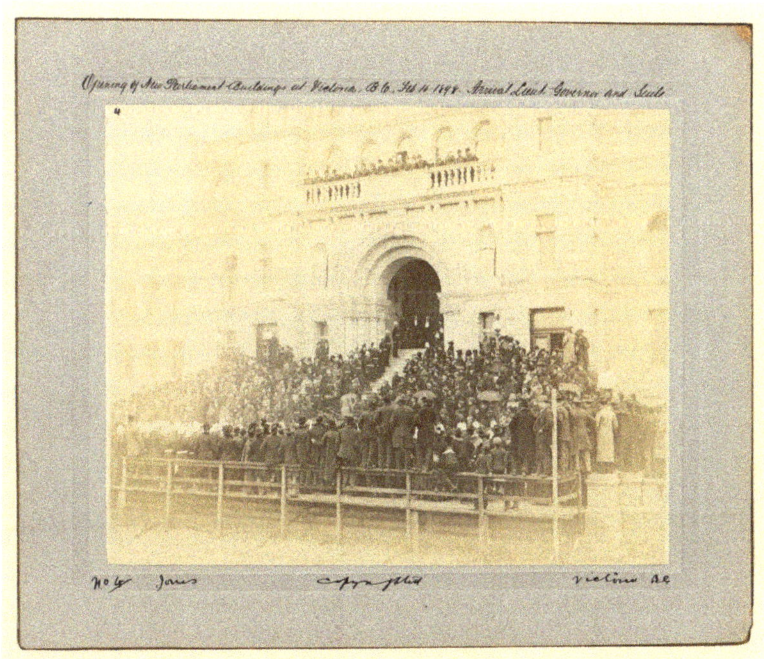

Fig. 2.5 'Opening of New Parliament Buildings at Victoria, B. C., February 10th, 1898'. Copyright J. W. Jones, 1898 (copyright number 9754).

the appearances of a proud provincial and colonial city. Such a vision was also underpinned by the colony's pride in being founded by British interests, and largely settled by them too.

The city's redevelopment was therefore inspired both by the architectural style of the British metropole and by British Columbia's history of maritime exploration and expansion.[24] This led to significant architectural and civic projects, such as the construction of an electric street lighting network that was to be, '"the first place in the far west" to follow the example of such progressive English cities as Godalming in Surrey'.[25] The parliament buildings were to underpin all of this, and were designed to articulate Victoria's goals and ambitions visually and spatially. The buildings also served as a marker of the city's achievements to the province, nation and empire around it.

Regardless of the problems with the construction of the new parliament buildings, they were successful in the rapid promotion of Victoria's new reputation as a beautiful and inspiring legislative city. The city emerged as a stately and stable capital, increasingly composed of

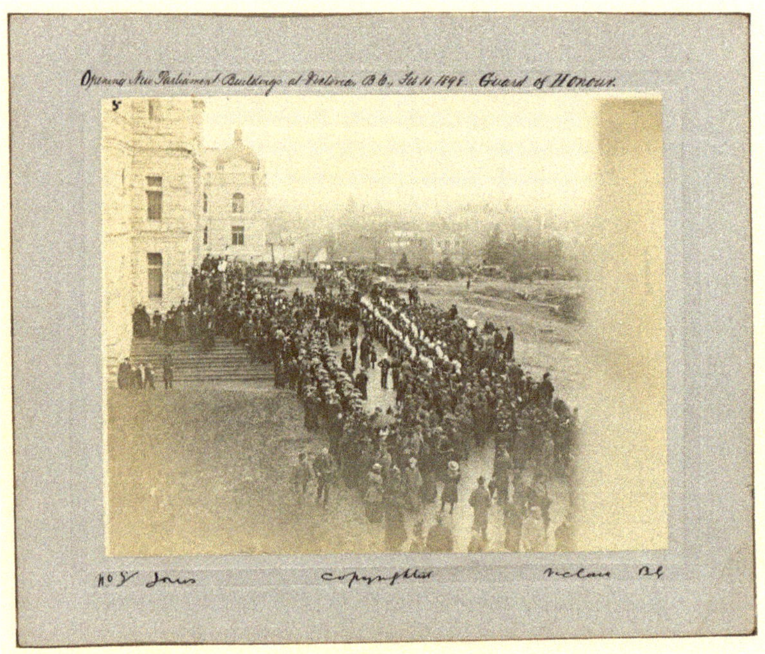

Fig. 2.6 'Opening of New Parliament Buildings at Victoria, B. C., February 10th, 1898, Guard of Honor'. Copyright J. W. Jones (copyright number 9755).

refined architecture and inspired by its British heritage. Jones's images were instrumental within this context, and Victoria's new imperial aesthetic is displayed in Figs 2.5 and 2.6: the crowd gathered to celebrate the opening is well dressed in hats and black suits, sheltering from the rain under black umbrellas, while the guards lining the steps to the front door are formally dressed in colonial military uniforms, emphasising the city's British heritage.[26] Jones's images also capture the ornate sculpture on the facade of the building itself, the grand curve of the main entrance and the quality of the masonry. Despite neglecting the building's tower, a key imperial reference, in capturing these features Jones illustrates the British imperial influences placed in the design of the building by the architect Francis Rattenbury (a recent British migrant). Jones's photography highlights the similarities between the British parliament and the new British Columbia legislature; in so doing he underscores the 'Britishness' of this Canadian colony.

It is significant that the parliament buildings of Victoria were opened at a very particular moment in a broader imperial history. They helped to define British Columbia's heritage as distinctly British, at the height of the period of invented tradition in Victorian Britain and Europe at large.[27] These links were important too in the context of resistance to increasing political dominance by the neighbouring United States and continued influxes of migrants from San Francisco during the gold rushes. The building also opened at a point where the driving technologies of the age were in flux, as the historically dominant maritime influences on the area were being overwritten by the geopolitical influence of the railway.[28]

Jones's photographs of the new parliament articulate what the building was intended to become, defining both its heritage and its future. That this was still a work in progress is suggested by some of the detail, such as the unmade ground at the forefront of Fig.2.5. These are reminders that Jones is codifying and visually defining an institution, and a set of relationships, that are still in the process of development. The government of the time was keen to stress Victoria's credentials as a grand legislative city, part of the empire and proud of its heritage as a purely British colony. In undertaking the project of building the parliament, the government announced their vision for the province, its values and destiny. The decision to memorialise the opening of the building also demonstrated an enthusiasm for the publicity potential of photography – an important consideration given the 70,000 visitors attracted to the parliament in the first two years of its opening.[29]

Jones's photography and wider body of work therefore offer important insights into the visual articulation of these city and provincial identities. His work was to become, and continues to be, part of the visual economy of British Columbia – in so doing becoming an agent in the broader sociopolitical currents of British Columbia and Canada at the time. Jones's work also shows where the paper empire and the empire of steam, ships and geopolitics interconnect. It makes a geopolitical statement on the part of Victoria while using the legislation of the paper empire to protect the value of the photograph.

Making names: photographs and brand identity

Whereas Jones presented an official, often imperial view of the city of Victoria, other visions of Canadian cities represented in the collection were more decidedly commercial. This demonstrates the multiple agendas and actors working to build Canada's new urban areas, variations captured and manipulated through photography. A primary example of commercial interests is a collection of views published by the Dominion Publishing Co. in 1901 and titled *Toronto: Album of Views*.[30] This photobook was produced under the commission of T. Eaton and Co., the largest and most profitable Canadian department store of the time – and, indeed, for most of the twentieth century. Eaton's played a highly significant role in the development of the Toronto retail economy.[31] The photobook situates Eaton and his business at the heart of a city aspiring to be a hub of both North American commerce and the British Empire, effectively in competition with better-established rivals such as New York and London.

The city on display here is very much the Victorian 'Queen City' and the 'city that works', as described by Richard Dennis.[32] In combination, the book's photographs create a visual framework through which the values of the new commercial elite could be communicated to the wider public. There are potential comparisons here with other studies of the visual representation of commercial power, in particular Schein's work on nineteenth-century representations of urban North America and Domosh's work on the iconography of skyscrapers in the early twentieth century.[33]

The focus of this discussion of *Toronto: Album of Views* is not so much on the agency of the individual photographer (compared to the discussion of J. W. Jones above) as on the effect of a particular form of urban view. Indeed, while the book is dominated by a very notable presence in Eaton, there is also an absent presence at its heart: the contributing photographer (or photographers) receives no mention, raising further questions about the photographer's role in contemporary print culture as well as the operation of the urban photographic economy of the time. Indeed, *Toronto: Album of Views* is suggestive of how, in a heated market for photographers and their products, the role of the photographer as a brand in the visual economy was fluid; it was not always directly linked to the end circulation of the photographic work. At the same time, as with Jones's photographs of Victoria, the Toronto album was designed to promote urban development. Here, though, it was commerce, not politics, that was on view.

Timothy Eaton's impact on the landscape, history and development of Toronto is notable and, as those who have written some of the many biographies about him attest, attributable in part to his force of personality.[34] Starting from almost nothing after his arrival in Canada as an immigrant from Ireland,[35] he constructed a business empire and negotiated access to the previously closed ranks of Toronto society. Eaton had a particular vision of how people should work, live and, most significantly, shop which affected not just the development of Toronto, but the development of Confederate Canada as a whole.[36] Timothy Eaton used all the technologies, forums and opportunities of the day to assert the primacy of his company. Underpinning all of this was a constant attempt to define Toronto as 'Eaton's City', a place in which the identity of the man, family and company were writ large onto the urban fabric.[37] The photobook discussed here is part of this articulation of the urban landscape, and of Timothy Eaton's wider strategy of promotion.

Eaton used philanthropy, event sponsorship, an affinity for spectacle and a willingness to embrace the latest technologies and social developments as means to assert the significance of the T. Eaton Co. as a retailer and social influence in Toronto and Canada. Advertising was a key tool here, and Timothy Eaton proved a master craftsman in utilising the new techniques and opportunities provided by a rapidly changing media and social landscape.[38] 'Eaton's Empire' was underpinned by Timothy Eaton's use of this constantly developing and changing tool of the nineteenth century.[39] In setting up his Yonge Street store, Eaton used swathes of on-site and window-based advertising to sway consumer choice away from his Queen's Street rival Simpsons and other competitors. His panache for window displays made them tourist attractions within the city in their own right, especially at Christmas time.[40]

However, what set Eaton and his company apart was his adept use of the printed advertisement in order both to draw in customers and extend the reach of his company and its client base. During his stewardship of the company Eaton introduced the Eaton's catalogue, launched at the Toronto Industrial Exhibition in 1884; this became the market leading mail-order catalogue in Canada during the late nineteenth and twentieth centuries. Eaton also was the first newspaper advertiser to pay for a 'red band' (colour) back page advertisement.

In the use of these two iconic advertising strategies, Eaton demonstrated a grasp of not just the printed form, but how to deploy it to the greatest effect. By taking risks, in that both media were untried and the costs significant, Eaton made these marketing devices almost synonymous with his brand. Monopolising forms of engagement in this way was a tactic deployed by Timothy Eaton in many forms: his philanthropy (sponsoring Toronto's most significant hospital) and even his sporting engagements (owning the most successful buggy racer of the time, Dan Patch, see Fig.2.7) operated in the same way.

Eaton's use of the photobook is a prime example of the way in which he brought together print, image and the whole package to create and

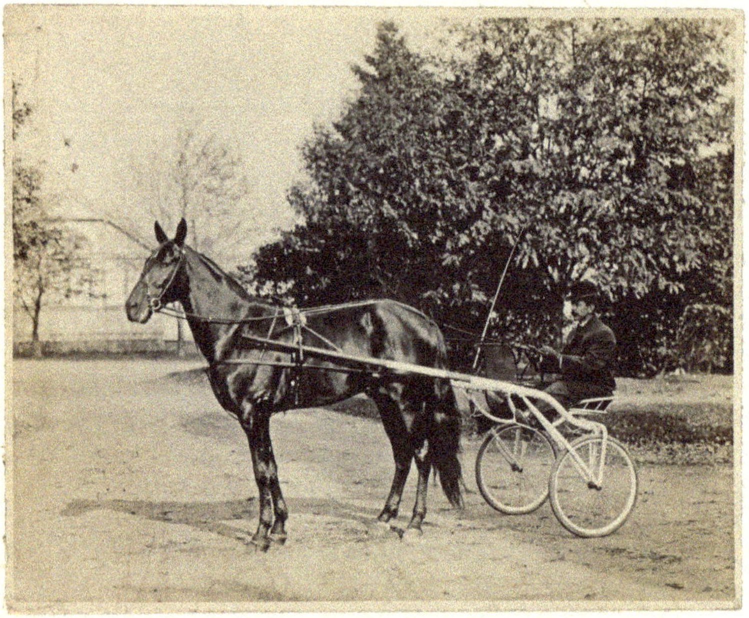

Fig. 2.7 Image of Dan Patch. Copyright T. Eaton Co., 1905.

promote his brand. Published in 1901 but copyrighted in 1900, *Toronto: Album of Views* was presented in the format of an increasingly popular consumer commodity. The book was well bound and printed on high quality paper, bearing title pages and the mark of the publisher in highly stylised characters. The contents and materiality of the photobook are significant, with both the medium and its presentation understood to be displaying photographs in order to memorialise particular subjects.[41] The publication feels impressive and provides a pleasing backdrop to the images themselves, over which the shadow of Timothy Eaton looms large when it comes to their selection and composition. Therefore the object itself gives the impression of turning the Toronto that Timothy Eaton has made into a form of urban, indeed national, heritage.

After the introductory page (Fig.2.8), the book begins with photographs of the government infrastructure of Toronto. On the first page it depicts the Ontario government buildings and on the second the city hall, completed only two years before. The photobook therefore follows the trend of its genre in portraying the legislative infrastructure of the city, and asserting its beauty and taste by drawing out its neoclassical parallels with British and European architecture.[42]

In depicting the legislative centre of the city, the photobook also provides an opportunity to place the Eaton brand, and Timothy Eaton, at its heart. Eaton used a number of tools to achieve this. Fig.2.9, for example, is an interesting departure from the overall format of the book. The image is not a photograph, but instead an architectural rendering from a semi-bird's eye view, depicting a hypothetical vista.[43] As a result, it is able to show the city hall, with completed and landscaped gardens, and the area of Queen and James Streets in the background. This angle draws attention to the proximity of Eaton's store to the legislative centre of town. At the time Eaton's store, factory and mail-order depot took up most of the city block framed by James, Queen and Yonge Streets, with shopfronts on all three streets. These are the only identifiable shopfronts in Fig.2.9 and are picked out by the flags above them.

When Eaton set up his business in Toronto, many thought he was doomed to fail, located as he was on the lower quality road of Yonge Street. Yonge Street was considered to be much less fashionable and more peripheral than Queen Street and, more prominently, King Street, the sites of most of Eaton's competitors. Despite this, Eaton's prospered, and by the beginning of the twentieth century the area of Yonge, James and Queen Streets had become far more influential in the city's consumer culture.[44] However, Eaton did not drop his guard. Despite his success, he constantly sought new ways to reaffirm the status of his store and himself within the city. As a result, the location of the new city hall was too

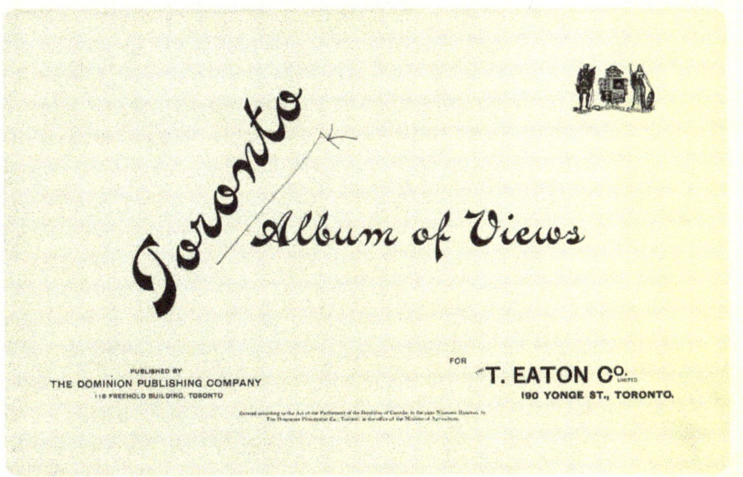

Fig. 2.8 Title page of *Toronto: Album of Views*, 1901. Copyright Dominion Publishing Co., 1900.

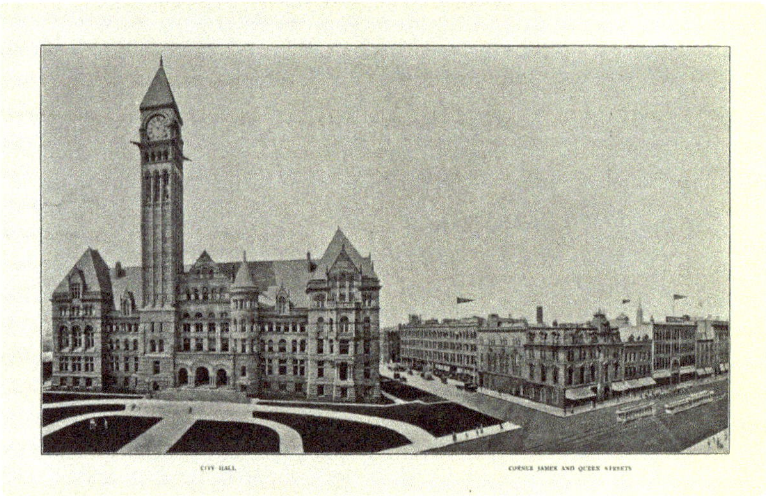

Fig. 2.9 'City Hall, Queen Street and James Street', in *Toronto: Album of Views*, 1901. Copyright Dominion Publishing Co., 1900. Flags in the image all bear the logo 'T. Eaton Co.'.

good a promotional opportunity to be missed. The image in Fig.2.9 dramatically emphasises the centrality of Eaton's, both through its compositional alignment of the two areas and its manipulation of the engraved image, in order to emphasise this spatial proximity of city hall and department store.

These spatial relationships and perceptions of the downtown geography of the city were very important to Eaton, and his attempts to place his business at its centre are not limited to this one image. The series of images which follows in the photobook is solely composed of Toronto's retail districts, depicting Yonge Street and King Street from various angles. The main entrance of T. Eaton and Co. on Yonge Street is shown in Fig.2.10. This image highlights the importance of Eaton's to the street, capturing the flags and notices, as well as highlighting the grand architecture for which the store was famous.[45] The next page depicts King Street (Fig.2.11). That this street is photographed is not surprising, as King Street was still regarded as a major fashion centre in the city, especially by those in the upper classes who determined fashion trends of the time. However, the emphasis through this ordering of images is that Yonge Street and Eaton's are the major engines of consumption in the city, and of primary importance to its structure. This point is driven home by the fact that the photograph of King Street is taken from Yonge Street, visually asserting the links between the two streets. Similarly, the next photograph in the book (Fig.2.12) depicts the corner of these two great

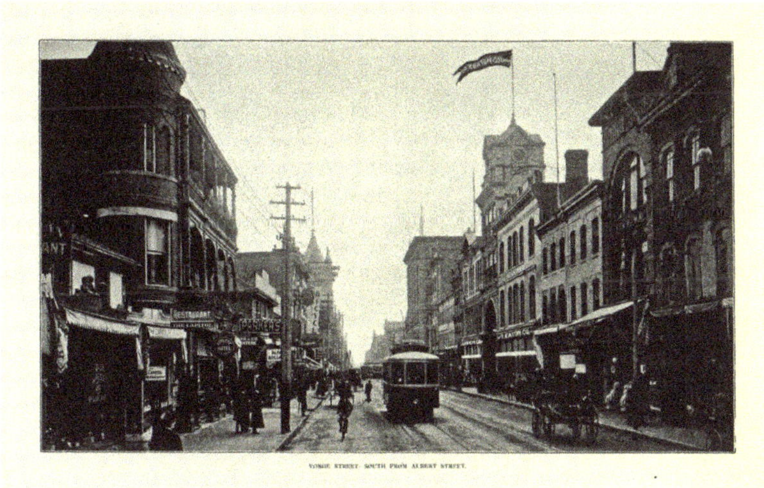

Fig. 2.10 'Yonge Street, Viewed from Albert Street', in *Toronto: Album of Views*, 1901. Copyright Dominion Publishing Co., 1900.

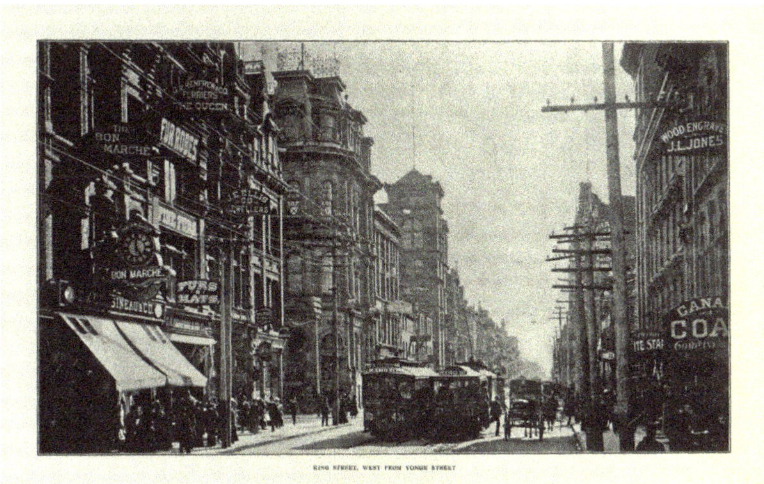

Fig. 2.11 'King Street, Viewed from Yonge Street', in *Toronto: Album of Views*, 1901. Copyright Dominion Publishing Co., 1900.

streets and emphasises their importance to the city, again, strengthening the linking of King and Yonge Streets and asserting the primacy of Yonge Street. Such a development would have been considered unthinkable when Eaton set up his business in 1864.

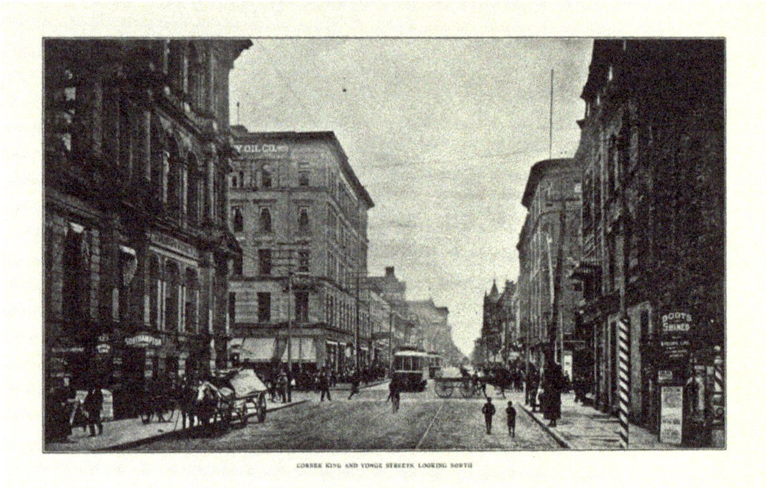

Fig. 2.12 'Corner King and Yonge Streets, Looking North', in *Toronto: Album of Views*, 1901. Copyright Dominion Publishing Co., 1900.

Later pages of the book have a format common to photobooks produced in other Canadian cities: the next 15 pages are illustrations of Toronto's educational and religious establishments, followed by its parks and well-maintained suburbs. However, even in these depictions, the shadow of Timothy Eaton and his family loom large. For example, of the two non-university seats of education depicted in the book, Upper Canada College, where Timothy Eaton's son was educated, is at the front of the pack. The school is credited with furnishing Jack Eaton with the skills and knowledge to take over the Eaton Empire after his father had relinquished control.[46] Similarly, in a montage of churches produced for the album, Eaton's own central Methodist church takes precedence. In the wider trope of urban photobooks, images of churches were usually placed to illustrate the grandeur of their architecture. This makes the primacy of Eaton's church in the photobook all the more interesting, given that it is far from the most architecturally significant. Its significance to the man is beyond doubt, however, given the centrality of church to his life and the sizeable donations he made to it.[47]

Depictions of the parts of Toronto's urban infrastructure that underpinned the Eaton family network highlight the role Toronto played as the seat of the Eaton Empire. Through these wider social and cultural connections to the city, the book illustrates that Toronto is not just a landscape the family and business act upon, but that Toronto and the family are bound together; they combine to make a better, more effective whole.

This is important as many great department stores of the era relied upon their 'local' geography to increase their significance, albeit in various ways. Harrods, London and the empire, for example, had a symbiotic relationship for much of the nineteenth and twentieth centuries: the empire supplied Harrods from all corners of the globe (a wealth of supply which underpins the store's popularity to this day), and Harrods sold the empire to London and the rest of Britain.[48]

The conclusion of the photobook reverts to depicting the significant sites of Timothy Eaton and the T. Eaton Co. business more directly. In the preceding sections the significance of Eaton's store and its relationship to Toronto's urban geography is discernible by unpicking the composition of the image. The closing images of the photobook are more overt in their assertion of Timothy Eaton and his company's centrality to the city of Toronto as they situate the business and the family within myriad landscapes of the city. For example, a whole page is dedicated to illustrating the impressive scale of the T. Eaton Co. in significant detail (see Fig.2.13). The illustration is engraved, again, and depicts a view of the block unattainable through photography. In showing the two main frontages of the store as well as the factory that lies behind them, the illustration highlights the impressive architectural achievement of a store and factory that takes up an entire city block and underscores this with the tag line, 'Canada's Greatest Store', at the bottom.

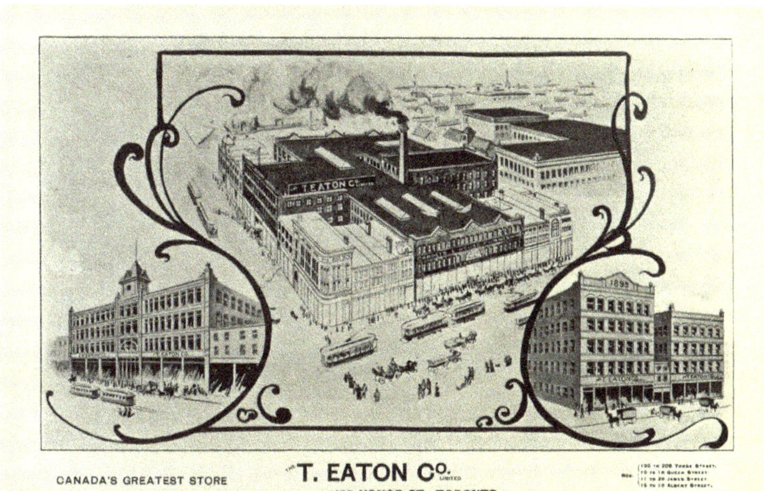

Fig. 2.13 'The T. Eaton Co. Limited: Canada's Greatest Store', in *Toronto: Album of Views*, 1901. Copyright Dominion Publishing Co., 1900.

This image is featured in a section of other impressive private architectural achievements in Toronto that takes in its best hotels and private institutions; once again, Eaton's buildings are set ahead of all architectural rivals. This places the Eaton buildings alongside hotels and private banks (the I.O.F. Temple Building is also depicted), blurring the line traditionally drawn between industry and finance and putting Eaton's space of retail and industry at its head. Here Eaton disturbs the traditional, hierarchical perception of the urban geography of Toronto by creating new juxtapositions within an established photographic medium.

The penultimate photograph in the book is of the Industrial Exhibition pavilion, the site of Toronto's famous annual exhibition where recent scientific and agricultural developments were displayed (Fig.2.14, and see Chapter 1 for more on national exhibitions). The pavilion was an impressive part of the Toronto landscape. Inspired by the Crystal Palace in London, it was designed to demonstrate Toronto's ability to host a permanent scientific fair after the city had been denied Canada's annual fair, which rotated between locations.[49] The inclusion of the pavilion in *Toronto: Album of Views* is in line with displaying the best architecture Toronto has to offer – but also emphasises the special relationship the T. Eaton Co. has with the pavilion, the Industrial Exhibition itself and, at the heart of things, the city of Toronto itself.

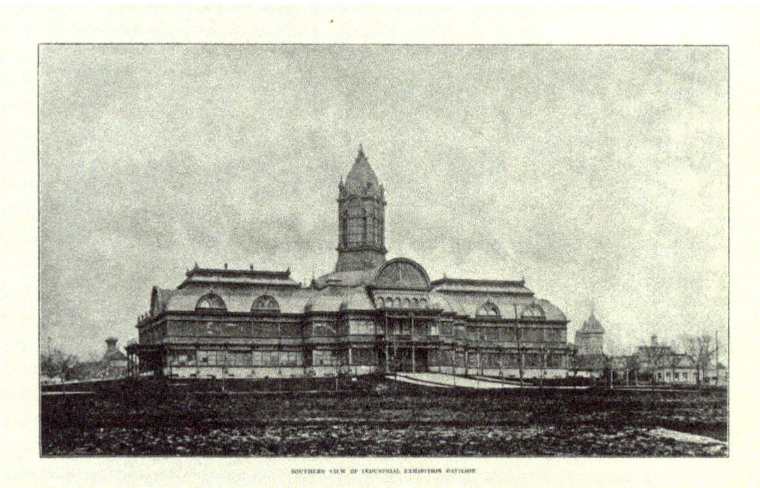

Fig. 2.14 'Southern view of the Industrial Exhibition pavilion', in *Toronto: Album of Views*, 1901. Copyright Dominion Publishing Co., 1900.

It was at the exhibition that Eaton launched the mail-order catalogue that would make his company a household name across Canada.[50] The catalogue was such a success that within ten years of its first distribution the phenomenon of 'Eaton's catalogue English', in which new arrivals to Canada would pick up the basics of their new language from the freely available publication, was well established.[51] Since the distribution of the first catalogues Eaton's and the Toronto Industrial Exhibition had a symbiotic relationship. The exhibition's reputation for fashion and modernity underpinned the reputation of an Eaton's still making its name, while the bombastic displays of an established Eaton's (particularly in competition with Simpsons) in the markets of the southern pavilion provided a massive draw to the show year after year.[52]

Toronto: Album of Views illustrates the complexity of the visual economy within which photographs and photographers were operating at the time. The photobook shows images being drawn into a broad project to display the city through the vision of one man's personality, while also asserting the links between this company and various commercial, industrial and government sites, all with a significant impact on the geography of Toronto and Canada at large. To accomplish this these photographs were commissioned to display particular and narrowly framed geographies; it is notable that when a broader perspective was needed, the bird's-eye view engraving was deployed in preference to the camera. All of these images were directed and assembled to define the geographical imagination of the city in Eaton-centric terms. The process of copyrighting the images contained within the photobook, therefore, was not merely about protecting its potential as a source of income; it was also yet another way of claiming ownership of Toronto as 'Eaton's City'.

* * *

Focusing on two exemplary bodies of work, this chapter has sought to situate urban imagery within the Colonial Copyright Collection in the wider context of the continually developing market for technologies of producing photographic views in Canadian cities. As a commercial practice, photography was commonly an urban phenomenon, reflected in the establishment of significant numbers of studios and the marketing of photographic products in towns and cities across Canada.[53] The business of photographing the city itself, and its most notable landmarks, was potentially lucrative: indeed individual photographers and companies came to specialise in this branch of work.[54] The two case studies examined here are, in this sense, representative of wider patterns and trends.

While the case studies are situated at opposite ends of Canada and in very different social and political contexts, they illustrate the significance of the photographer and the photograph as actors in the articulation of understandings of the urban landscape. These examples also illustrate that the relationships, technologies, geographies and exchanges involved in the creation of these understandings were complex. For example, the representation would sometimes be underpinned by the reputation of the photographer and their biography (as with Jones), while sometimes the photographer's vision would be appropriated by another character (as with Eaton). Images were also produced for different markets and circulated in different material forms. These factors, in turn, required the photographer to deploy a variety of technical skills, with varying degrees of success. Fundamentally, this illustrates why the Colonial Copyright Law was an important tool for the photographer or entrepreneur in the Canadian urban context. Obtaining copyright was not just a means of securing legal rights to an image; it was also a way of enhancing the authority of particular views of the city.

3

Picturing modernity: photography and the Canadian railway

The subject of this chapter has already played a prominent role in the previous one. Assessing the relationship between urban development and place-making, as in the example of Timothy Eaton's Toronto, inevitably highlights the importance of the railway. Indeed, the railway has often been represented as the prime technology in creating an integrated economy in the Canadian Confederation.[1] Furthermore, it had a profound impact on the social geographies of communities across Canada, opening up spaces and changing the relationship between people and place. In global terms, the chronology of railway development runs roughly in parallel to the development of photography, and the two technologies have a much-discussed relationship.[2] Given the myriad views it offers of the impact of the railway on society and space in Canada, the Colonial Copyright Collection provides a unique opportunity to consider Canada's changing relationship with the railway at the end of the nineteenth century and beginning of the twentieth. This chapter elaborates on the depiction of the railway through the Colonial Copyright Collection and considers the views it presents of the technology and its landscape.

As a symbol of national dynamism in turn-of-the-century Canada, there are few technologies that rival the railway in the popular imagination. Since before confederation, as well as increasingly after the completion of the transcontinental railway in 1885,[3] the railway came to stand for all that Canada had achieved in the latter half of the nineteenth century and could achieve in the twentieth century.[4] Across Canada, the United States and the world, the railway was increasingly held up as an iconic technology that could breach gaps, link spaces and realise the national and imperial endeavours of politicians and capitalists, while also increasing the potential of a truly globalised economy.[5] Symbolically, the railway and the locomotive were seen to be ushering in a new era, one of irresistible progress and unbridled ambition.

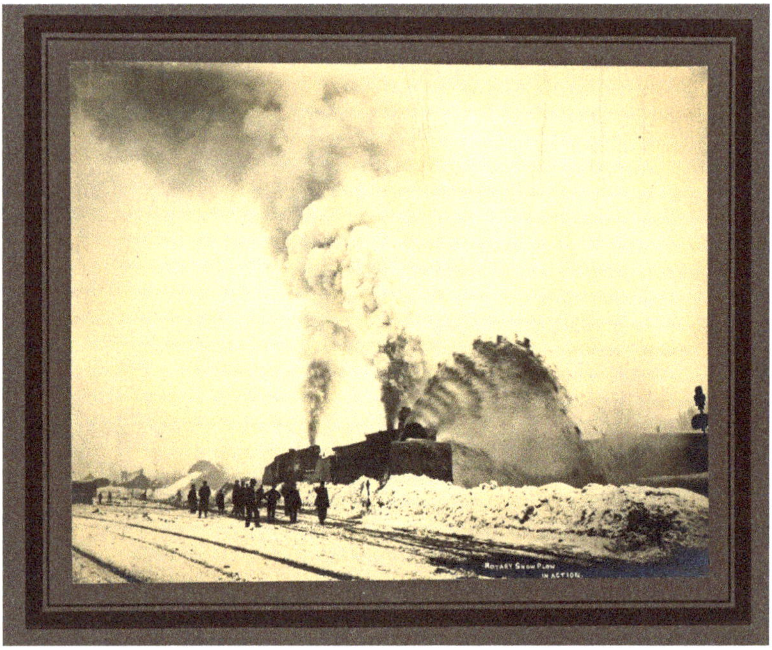

Fig. 3.1 'Rotary Snow Plow Number 5'. Copyright Byron Harmon, 1910 (copyright number 25208).

However, as the twentieth century in particular was to show, the effects of the railway were not inevitable or uniform.[6] Undoubtedly it was an engine of unparalleled change, with the construction of the transcontinental railway and the resulting explosion of branch lines changing the face of Canada forever. Yet these changes were not evenly spread across a flat, featureless plain, nor were the resulting effects uniformly positive. The railway remade places, adjusted spaces and left many Canadian nationals, not to mention new arrivals, running to catch up with the pace of change (see Chapter 5 for more on migrants in Canada).[7] Furthermore, as the railway brought new opportunities, it also brought unexpected dangers that Canadians, like others, had to become accustomed to.

These changes, mediations and articulations are pictured in the photographic record from a variety of local and individual perspectives, as exemplified by the Colonial Copyright Collection. While there are images which undoubtedly reflect the pride and wonder that many Canadians felt at the sight of the railway, they also represent more nuanced and localised responses to the 'iron horse'. In dealing with images made locally by individual photographers, this chapter will consider the view of the railway (and by extension the modernity of Canada) from a series of more localised perspectives. By considering photographs depicting different types of event from a variety of locations, the chapter will attest to the complex processes involved as Canadians tried to come to terms with their new world, and with the idea of becoming modern themselves.

The chapter begins with a brief overview of literature regarding the railway in Canada, in order to illustrate significant tropes that the photographic images reflect and reinforce. It then considers the extent to which images from the collection articulate progressivist tropes widely associated with the railway at the time.[8] Not all of the images in the collection speak directly to narratives of progress and modernity, and this chapter reflects on two specific themes represented by the camera to demonstrate this variety: the commodification of the landscape via the expansion of the railway and the horror of the railway accident. Through these two bodies of photographic work, which comprise a significant component of the Colonial Copyright Collection, it is possible to situate the culture of the railway within the complex, contested landscapes of Canada in the process of modernisation.[9]

The railway as an icon of national development

Across the breadth of historical scholarship regarding Canada there are two significant and pervasive themes relating to the development of the nation which are relevant to this chapter. One concerns the harshness of the land and its reluctance to yield to European settlement; the other explores the increasingly efficient use of modern technologies in the successful settlement of the nation from coast to coast. As examples of this, we can cite two works otherwise poles apart in terms of their time of publication, their proposed audience and their approach to historical narrative as a whole – namely, Pierre Berton's *The National Dream*[10] and Cole Harris's *The Reluctant Land*.[11] It should be noted that these are not the only works (Canadian or otherwise) that deal with this subject,[12] but the arguments put forward by Berton and Harris allow engagement with the major themes visible in the railway images of the collection.

Berton's populist historical narrative about the building of Canada's transcontinental railway is underpinned by the idea that the railway was the technology by which the whole of Canada's inner shield could finally be tamed and opened up to settlement. His account of the endeavour is monumental in tone. It is underpinned by the casting of the landscape as a hard and unforgiving obstacle to the realisation of Canada's national dream, achieved only through technological ingenuity combined with hard work and determination. Harris's more measured and methodical text also attributes prime importance to the 'reluctance' of the land itself to accept human habitation and cultivation as a crucial factor in the making of modern Canada. Throughout his book the landscape throws up obstacles as well as opportunities, while the application of communications technologies – such as waterway transport, canal building and, towards the end of the work, the building of railways – gradually subdues the resistance of the landmass.

While Berton's rhetorical style in *The National Dream* has been criticised as nationalistic mythmaking,[13] it is clear from looking at the broad scope of Canadian historical work that images of the landscape and the application of technology to master it have been very important in the development of ideas of the nation.[14] More generally, the importance of the railway in the creation of nations was a common theme in the work of many artists, writers and theorists of the time.[15] However, Berton's celebratory tone masks the possibility of further consideration of what sort of nation the railway wrought (if it even wrought one homogenous space) or how it affected different groups in different places. Indeed, the same can be said for more academic histories of Canada and/or the railway, for example Stevens's two-volume work on the history of the Canadian National rail company.[16] While much more sober in tone and rooted in compilations of historical documents, accounts such as this are prone to get bogged down in railway-centric thinking which celebrates the creation of the nation, emphasising how this could only have been made possible by the railway – without moving too far away from the 4 feet and 9 inches spanned by the railway itself.

In contrast, the work of more recent historical geographers such as Cole Harris emphasises the various 'drafts' of the Canadian national landscape that were created by patterns of living, trade and communication with Canada's urban centres (and, by extension, the rest of the world, especially Europe).[17] Harris's account illustrates how various communication and trade links persistently reshaped the economic and cultural geography of Canada, asserting with regard to the St. Lawrence Valley that '[n]ew transportation technologies, and with them changing relations of space and time, reworked the relative locations of towns along the St. Lawrence River and even the St. Lawrence Valley itself'.[18] Similarly, Harris draws out how the growing rail interconnectedness of Canada and the United States increased trade between the two, opening the door for the economic and cultural changes that would affect Canada profoundly in the twentieth century.[19]

In this context the railway supplanted the maritime vessel while mineral resources created increasing connections to the United States, creating profound anxiety and a desire to fix the political identity of British Columbia more firmly. Through his discussion of these changing geographies, Harris's account stresses how different spaces and places move to the centre or the periphery of national and regional frameworks as a result of the medium of communication. Similarly, the cultural, social and political definitions of the nation were reshaped by the prevailing mechanism of communication and the real connections it makes between places. As a result, an account such as Harris's allows the reader to consider exactly what type of nation was created in Canada by the development of the railway network and its supplanting of other forms and networks of communication.

Harris's approach has some parallels with the arguments of the early twentieth-century historian Harold Innis. In his paper *Empire and Communications*, Innis argued that global empires required modern and thorough communication networks in order to work efficiently and survive, but that these networks also undermined the culture of the empire.[20] As such, modern technology, put to work on behalf of empires, would eventually bring about their transformation. The basis of this argument that efficient communication networks link places and people creating the conditions for unanticipated changes can also be applied to the impact of the railway on economic and social geographies. That is, the railway does have a central role in the formation of the nation, but it also leads to the reconfiguration of its spaces and temporalities. The railway, therefore, is not simply a homogenising force but instead one that creates the potential for changes and unintended happenings too.

It is from this perspective that I consider the railway photographs that form a significant part of the Colonial Copyright Collection. As Berton argues, the completion of the transcontinental railway had underpinned the successful confederation of Canadian provinces and by 1895 Canada was a nation on the cusp of major economic and demographic growth. However, the railway also had significant, social, political and geographical consequences for the shape of the nation. It had rewritten the landscape and the economic infrastructure of the country: rural backwaters were now major settlement hubs, stable economic geographies (such as the St. Lawrence Valley)[21] were changing dramatically and in many areas of the country people had to come to terms with the shining artery of modernity that was running through their land and next to their homes.

There are a significant number of railway scenes deposited in the Colonial Copyright Collection.[22] As the above paragraphs stress, these deposits were made in a period of growth and change for both the railways and Canada as a whole. While the railway industry had actually struggled financially, between the completion of the transcontinental railway and the mid-1890s a great deal of political and public enthusiasm developed for the railway, as well as national pride in its construction.[23] Further, by the mid-1890s the railway was beginning to benefit from (as well as facilitate) the changes being wrought contemporarily in Canadian society. As a result, it was, once again, expanding to cover the country ever more thoroughly.[24]

The photographs in the Colonial Copyright Collection provide a series of ground-level views of this major historical transformation from various perspectives: the individual, the local, the corporate and the national. They provide significant evidence of the enthusiasm with which the railway was greeted, how it was represented by investors, constructors and owners, and some of the changes it wrought on the landscapes it cut across. However, it also highlights more unexpected repercussions of this sudden entry into modernity; the railway intersected with people's lives and homes as well as the physical landscape. The collection illustrates the impact of the railway on the lives of people in Canada in those instances when the railway relinquished its status as a symbol of progress and malfunctioned, creating the conditions of disaster.

The 'Rotary Snow Plow' photographs (Figs 3.1–3.4) are four of the most striking images of the railway and its technologies in the collection. Copyrighted in 1910 by Byron Harmon, the images depict a snow plough that operated clearing the mountain pass railways and services around Banff, Alberta.[25] The images convey a sense of the majesty of the scene and strength of the machine as the plough surges on through Canada's winter terrain, forcing it to relinquish the stranglehold it attempts to place on the landscape and Canada's arteries of communication. Compelled by steam and mechanical power, the plough forces its way through drifts and avalanches in order to clear a path for subsequent locomotives. The billows of steam and the arching plume of snow that erupts from the front of the engine communicate to the viewer the unstoppable progress of the locomotive and the plough. The message of the image is clear. The engine will progress without impediment, the locomotive will run on time and, despite the vicious Canadian winter, the country will not hibernate: it will keep moving.

Harmon's images articulate two key iconographic themes. The first is a narrative of progress. The railway and the locomotive are powerful icons of modernity, due not only to their mechanical nature but also to the way in which the mechanics of the railway and, especially, the

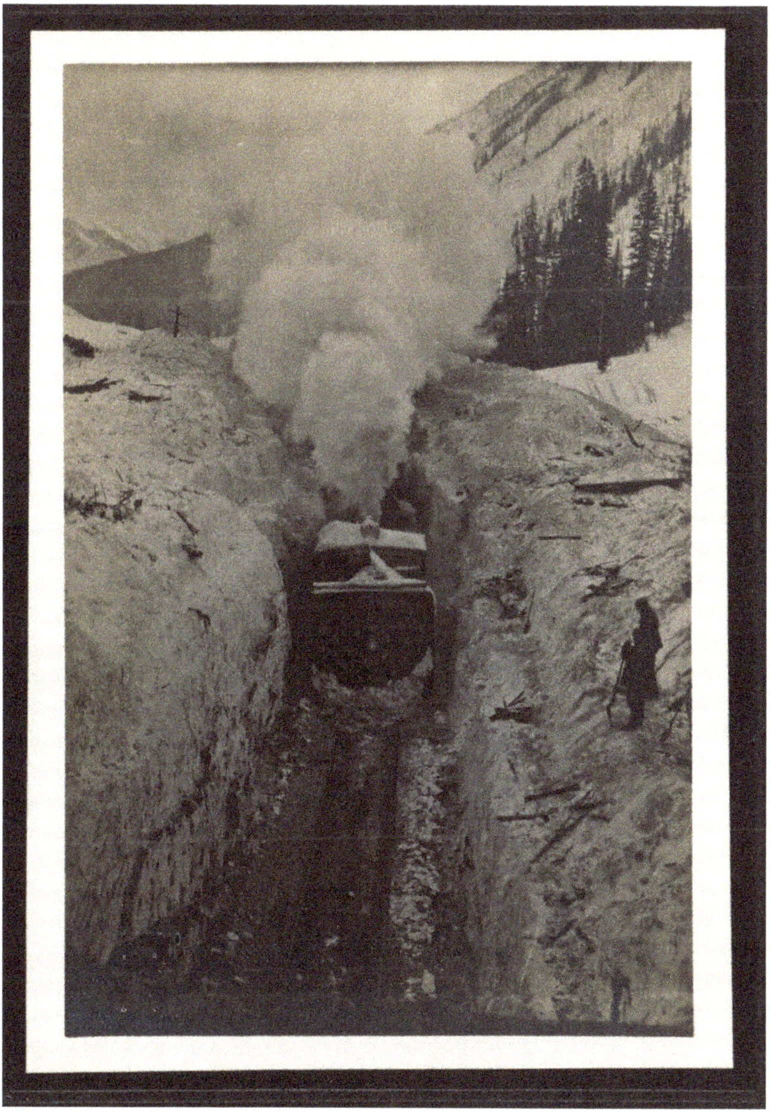

Fig. 3.2 'Rotary Snow Plow, Number 1'. Copyright Byron Harmon, 1910 (copyright number 22136).

locomotive are harnessed. The railway and the locomotive always progress; the movement of the engine is, as near as possible, constant, due to the work of the surveyor, the engineer and the labourer in levelling the landscape and laying the track to provide the least possible impediment to the engine as it steams across the country. As a result, the locomotive

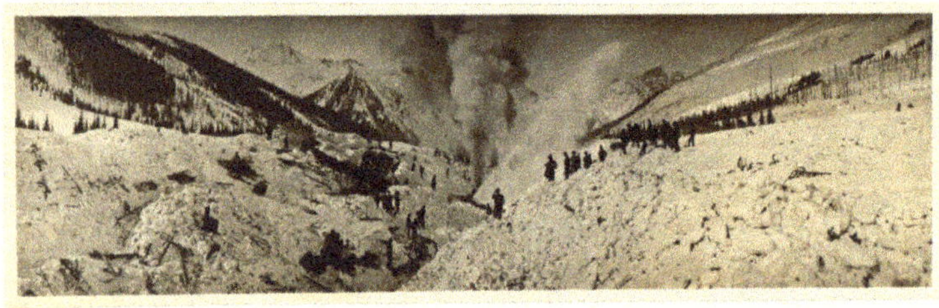

Fig. 3.3 'Rotary Snow Plow Number 4'. Copyright Byron Harmon, 1910 (copyright number 22309).

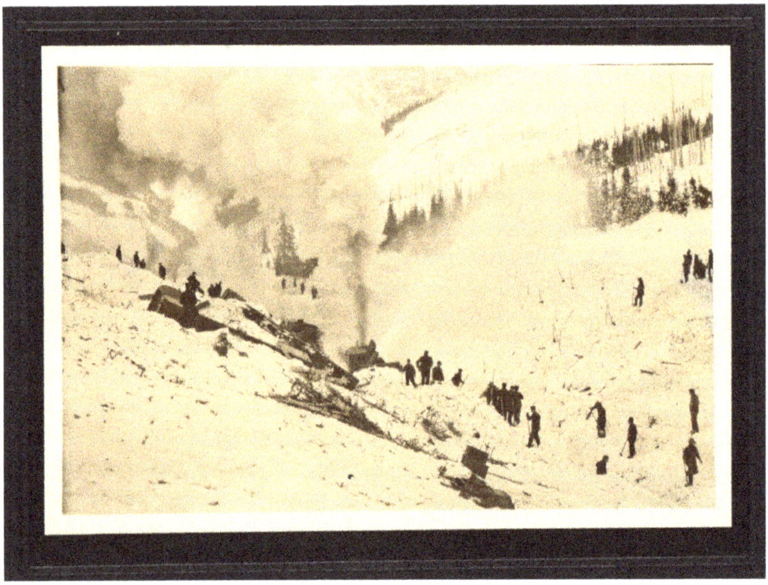

Fig. 3.4 'Rotary Snow Plow Number 3'. Copyright Byron Harmon, 1910 (copyright number 22138).

surges on across the landscape, linking places and vastly reducing once astonishing distances.[26] In these images the railway and its machinery are also seen to be physically removing the snow that various historians depict as smothering the landscape, thus conquering Canada's great physical and meteorological adversary.[27] In such imagery the railway was an exemplar of contemporary ideas of what it was to be 'modern'; modernity was progress and progress was linear. These notions are clearly communicated through Harmon's lens. Banff is part of a modern and powerful nation, one where the pulse of industry is not slackened and where progress through the application of technology is seemingly constant.

The ubiquity of snow in these images provides the second point in this discussion. In Harmon's images snow is everywhere, overwhelming the landscape and dwarfing the people placed in it. The photographer has gone to great lengths to communicate this in Fig.3.4, deploying a wide angle lens, panoramic film and considerable technical expertise to emphasise the scale of the task at hand for the indefatigable machine toiling at its centre. Canada's geography and climate, despite being the bearers of many virtues, were seen as the major factors in impeding its growth and economic success.[28] In the introduction to Berton's *The National Dream*, Canada's winter snow is deployed rhetorically in order to communicate a nation in hibernation and even bondage, restrained from achieving its goals by the conditions that smothered its interior for one-third of the year.[29] Snow is still perceived as an obstacle today, its annual fall across the country bringing out a hastily mobilised militia of shovel-bearing homeowners and snow removal contractors in the cities and the countryside, engaging in a contest of attrition with each new dump of snow.

It is the relationship between Canada, its citizens and the snow that informs the perspective portrayed through Harmon's images of the snow plough. In these images the plough is an agent of change and of progress. The force of steam and the irresistibility of the plough drive the snow from the line, clearing depots and reopening passes that once would have been closed to all travellers both before the railway and in the early days of locomotive travel. As the indefatigable engine forces its way through the overwhelmed valley in Fig.3.4, the message is just as powerful: Canada has not only drawn in its spaces and increased its openness; it has also conquered the elements. Such imaginative geographies of the landscape were influential not just in Canada, but in many other colonial projects of settlement, national development and industrialisation more broadly.[30]

The narrative of progress, both national and technological, is continued in another branch of railway photography contained in the collection and shown here by photographs of railcars and bridges. Fig.3.5 was taken in order to commemorate the opening of the railway that linked Prince Rupert to the Grand Trunk Pacific line. It depicts the first passenger train to leave the Prince Rupert depot on 14 June 1911, showing the train steaming vigorously along with its passengers in comfort. Button's image is striking both as a celebration of the opening of the

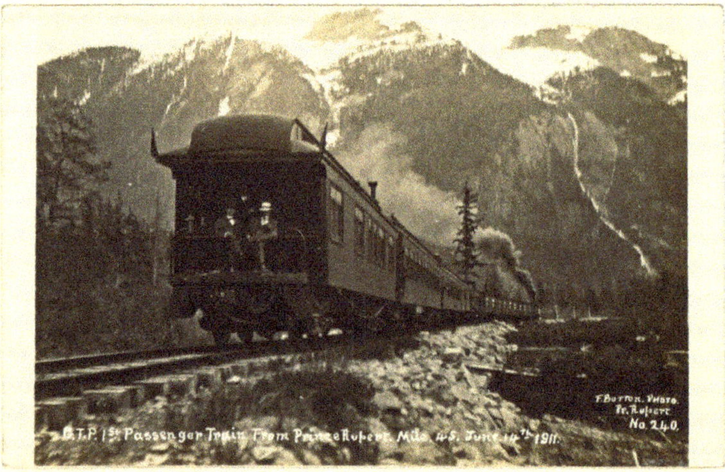

Fig. 3.5 'First Passenger Train to Leave Prince Rupert. Mile 45, June 14th, 1911'. Copyright Fred Button, 1912 (copyright number 25535).

railway and for the composition it adopts in order to portray the event. In the image we see the train steaming off into the mountains, forests and wilderness of British Columbia and the juxtaposition of the locomotive, its carriages and the landscape deserves further consideration.

The landscape that surrounds the train is rugged, even imposing; the woods are thick and the mountains are tall. It is the sort of landscape that has been perceived as a barrier to travellers and settlers alike since Canada was first encountered by Europeans. Yet now a channel has been cut and the gravel, wood and iron of the railway wind through the landscape on the most gentle of inclines, carrying passengers across the landscape with ease. As a result, a landscape that was once a barrier and would have appeared as imposing is now a backdrop, a pleasant vista for the passengers sat in comfort on the back of the train. In a landscape where once sturdy boots, adequate supplies and the strength to carry all you needed were required, a comfortable suit and a hat to keep out the sun are all that is now required for a successful journey.

In Button's image, the railway is a highway of civility, linking the hubs of civilisation, through the sprawling wilderness. Such compositions are not rare among photographs of the railway and were used to great effect by many in the promotion of the railway and the implicit taming of the landscape. One example of this is the photography of William Henry Jackson, used to promote the Baltimore and Ohio Railway at the Chicago World's Columbian Exposition in 1893.[31] As such, this image can be seen as part of an intense mechanism of promotion for the railway which had a developed and ideologically significant visual style.

The taming of extreme landscape features is also illustrated in the collection by photographs of the Nanaimo canyon and the Lethbridge viaduct – striking examples of how the boundaries of geography and nature were conquered by feats of engineering and the appliance of technology. The gorge and the valley are obstacles in two ways, the gorge representing a barrier to progress and the valley an impediment to efficiency.

Howard King (Fig.3.6) photographs the bridge and the canyon from the level of the river, accentuating the size of the cavern cut by the

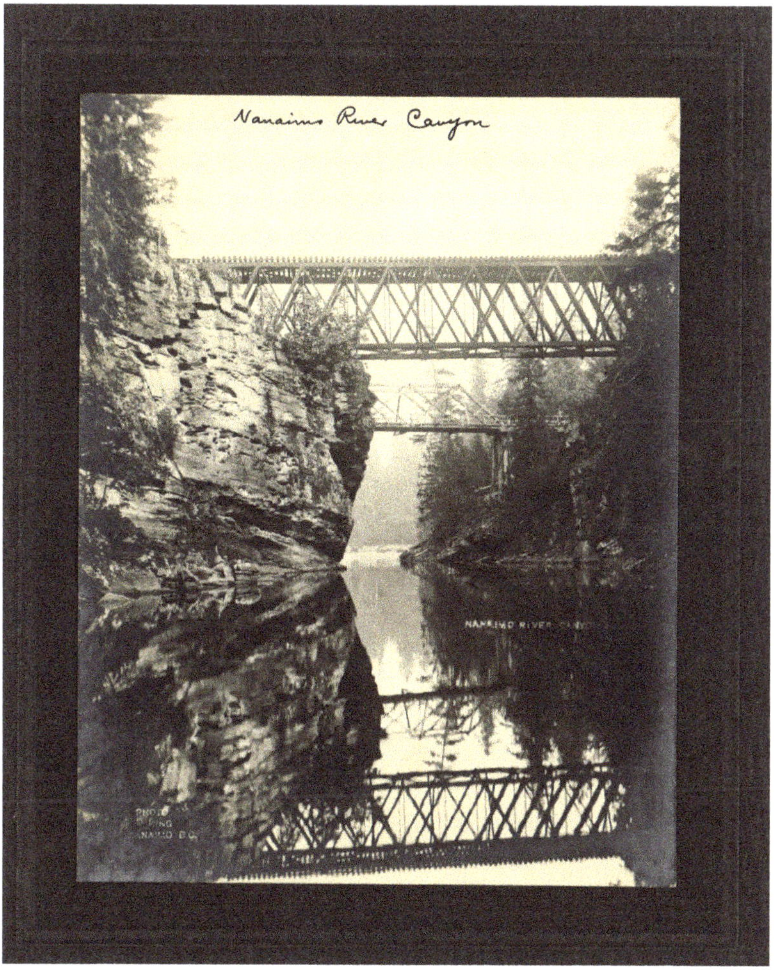

Fig. 3.6 'Nanaimo River Canyon'. Copyright Howard H. King, 1907 (copyright number 19017).

river and the relief of its walls. Further, the trees that bound it and loom in over the shot accentuate the characteristics of the bridge. It is an artery through the wilderness – and a statement that the railway will not be deterred, even when the landscape is suddenly rent apart. The ability of the railway to cross, mediate and tame even the most extreme parts of the Canadian landscape is celebrated in the image as the camera looks up in awe of the bridge across the expanse.

Arthur Rafton-Canning's photograph of the Lethbridge viaduct (Fig.3.7) shows a monument of a different kind. While the bridge over the Nanaimo canyon is depicted by the photographer as evidence of the ability of the railway and Canada to transcend any boundary, the image of the Lethbridge viaduct captures more than the scale of the endeavour involved in having the railway traverse the canyon. It is also a statement about the technological expertise deployed in the name of efficiency, another aspect of capitalist modernity. Rafton-Canning's image captures the straightening and flattening of the landscape by the railway and communicates this to the viewer in his gigantic reproduction of the scene.[32] In this respect, this image of the viaduct is a testament to the rationalising of the Canadian landscape. What was once a sloping, winding river valley has been overlain by sculpted, straight, flat lines in the name of efficiency for the locomotive.

In iconographic terms, this change has two effects. Firstly, transcending geography's barriers asserts an undoing of the natural order, with nature now subservient to society's needs and overwritten by its constructions – an endeavour underpinned by architectural and technical expertise.[33] Secondly, the production of a panorama further

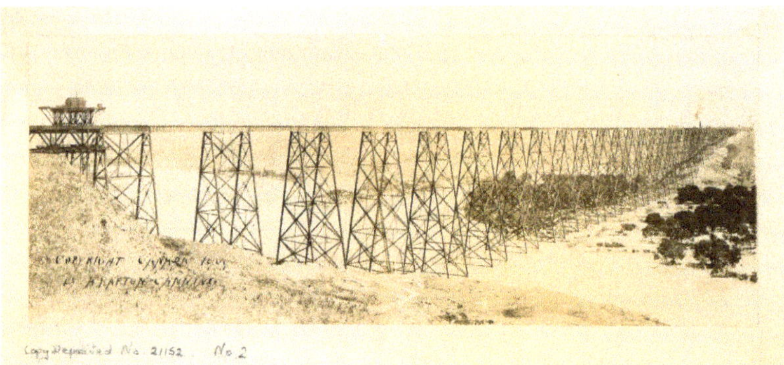

Fig. 3.7 'Panoramic view of the Canadian Pacific Railway viaduct, at Lethbridge, Alberta'. Copyright A. Rafton-Canning, 1909 (copyright number 21152).

enforces the opening up of the landscape, as the panorama was by this point often deployed in order to symbolise the accessibility of previously uninhibited spaces.[34] As a result, both visual effects combine to communicate that the landscape has been tamed and opened up; it no longer hinders human progress.

These seven photographs are representative of many others in the collection, and of a common view of the railway during the period covered by the Colonial Copyright Collection. A significant number of the railway scenes deposited in the collection highlight the civilising and taming of the landscape, contrasting the wild and inhospitable surroundings of the railway with the straight, flat, uniformity of the tracks themselves. In creating these juxtapositions the photographs shape a narrative for Canada itself: a nation that can tame its rugged contours and bend them to its will, use them to its benefit and develop into a great power.

Significant as these generic visual tropes are, they only go so far in illuminating the image world represented within the Colonial Copyright Collection. The railway's effects on space and place were neither homogenous nor ubiquitous; as Harris points out, Canadian landscapes were constantly in the process of being reshaped to accommodate new pressures and endeavours.[35] Given its localised origins, the collection reflects more than just the narratives discussed above. The camera was turned on the railway for all manner of reasons, not all of which were intended simply to celebrate the grandeur of modern technology. The next section considers the ways in which photography was used to promote the railway before this chapter moves on to depict the results of railway disaster.

The landscape open for business

The camera played an essential role in the commercial promotion of the railway. Beyond acknowledging the grandeur of the achievement of the railway, many Canadians had little experience of it and the railway companies initially struggled to generate enough use of their tracks to justify the expense of their production and maintenance.[36] The railway therefore had to promote itself to the public, generate interest and stimulate use. The following discussion focuses on how the railway companies set about establishing a relationship with the public and the importance of the camera and the photograph in this project. This continued an established relationship, as the development of photography and the railway drove one another forwards in the early days of both technologies, especially in Canada during the 1860s and 1870s.[37]

When discussing the commercial significance of the railway, it is necessary to look beyond images of the railway *in situ*. Fig.3.8, for example, is a revealing image of the Canadian Northern Railway Company permanent exhibition in Winnipeg, taken in 1912 by the Lyall Commercial Photo Company.[38] The display is spectacular, despite its small space, with trophies, trinkets and decorations adorning all the wall space and large sections of the floor. It depicts a cross-section of the technologies, locomotives, sites and commodities linked together and brought into Canada by the Canadian Northern Railway. The pictures on the walls depict the company's famous locomotives and some of the sights of the route (such as the Pacific coast), while on the wall are mounted trophies from hunting opportunities (predominantly of moose and deer) opened up by the railway's branches. Also on the floor and the lower walls are statements of what the Canadian

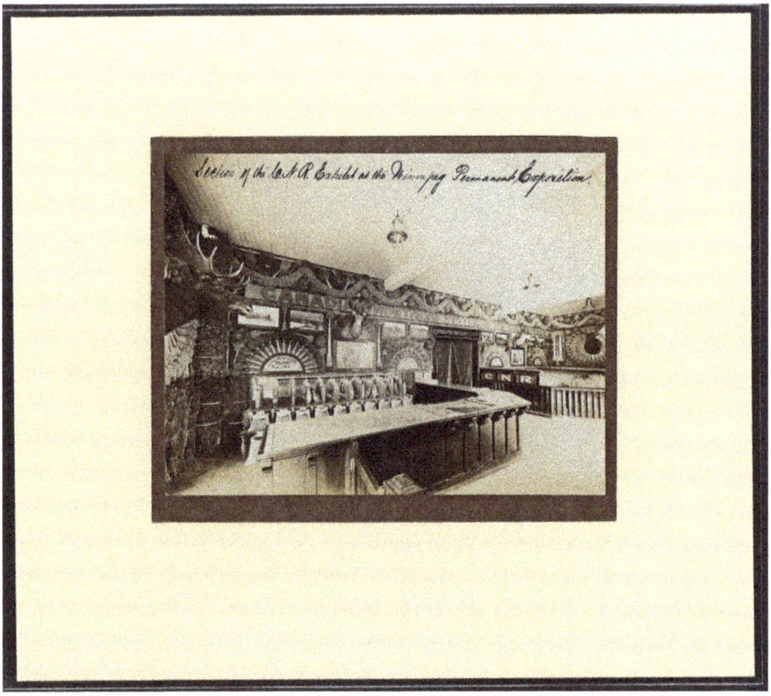

Fig. 3.8 'Section of the C.N.R. Exhibit, at the Winnipeg Permanent Exposition'. Copyright Lyall Commercial Photo Co., 1912 (copyright number 25224).

Northern Railway brings to Canada, in the form of agricultural produce and even alcoholic beverages. The sheer abundance of these products in the exhibition makes the claim that the Canadian Northern is a gatekeeper to the agricultural plenty of Canada's North West.[39]

The composition of the photograph and the decision to create such an exhibition also deserve further comment here. Forty years previously the landscape covered by the railway was untouched by commercial development, but by 1912 its spaces and produce were being represented in and transported through Winnipeg as the effects of the railway were felt. Further, animals that once ran wild in this untamed landscape were now placed on the walls as trophy-commodities, icons of nature's untapped potential in the north. The same can be said of the other products pictured: all harvested, branded and organised in order to be sold (symbolically) elsewhere in Canada or even the world. The exhibit is a symbol of what has happened to the wild spaces surrounding the railway. They have not only been tamed by its rationalising effect; through it such spaces have been changed into commodities, products packaged for export and sale.

This binding of the landscape to a corporate enterprise has parallels with the depiction of Timothy Eaton's Toronto, as discussed in Chapter 2. Here too was a landscape rearticulated for the purposes of a business and a brand. In the case of the Canadian Northern Railway exhibition, we see the landscape articulated to express the control and opportunity extended by the company, as well as to promote the sale of its produce. As in the case study of *Toronto: Album of Views*, the identity of the photographer is unknown, asserting that these are corporate productions and imaginations.

The four photographs comprising Fig.3.9 (Fig.3.9a, Fig.3.9b, Fig.3.9c and Fig.3.9d) were also taken to promote an image of the Canadian Northern Railway, but their focus and delivery are somewhat different. The depiction of two men pursuing and then riding a bull moose across a lake at first appears an unlikely vehicle for the promotion of a railway. Indeed, the only initial clue to its purpose is that the copyright to the image is owned by the Canadian Northern Railway Company. Once considered in this context, the aim of the photographs become clearer, suggesting that they have been produced and copyrighted as a result of their promotional value. The images depict two men pursuing their quarry across an open wilderness, vast, empty and no longer inaccessible. Now that the railway has opened up a passage it is a place of new potential, full of bountiful hunting opportunities to be exploited. As the animals and plants discussed in the Winnipeg image have been re-appropriated from

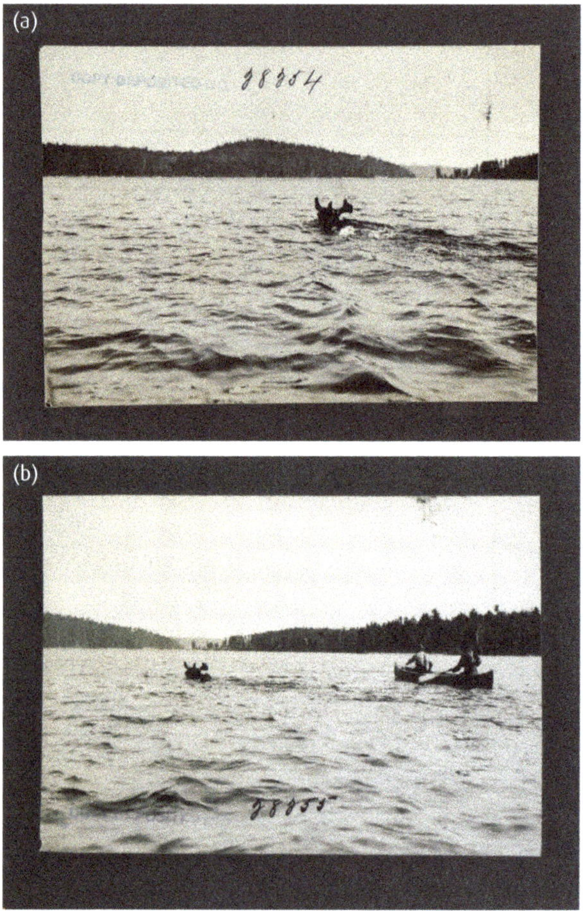

Fig. 3.9 (a) 'Bull Moose Swimming'; (b) 'Bull Moose Pursued by Canoe'; (c) 'Canoe Man Stepping on Back of Bull'; (d) 'Canoe Man Dropping onto Back of Bull'. Copyright Canadian Northern Railway Company, 1914 (copyright numbers 28254–7).

characters of the wilderness into commodities bound to the urban centre, so here the camera rearticulates the northern wilderness into a leisure space that is now accessible via the railway. The images offer the viewer a taste of the opportunities for hunting and exploration in these spaces, where even the most bizarre adventures can be catered for. This point is driven home further by other images produced by the railway company that bear titles such as, 'A Good Day's Haul' and 'Up to the Limit', which depict hunters struggling to carry their quarry home.

By considering these more evidently commercial images we gain another perspective on the relationship between the railway and the

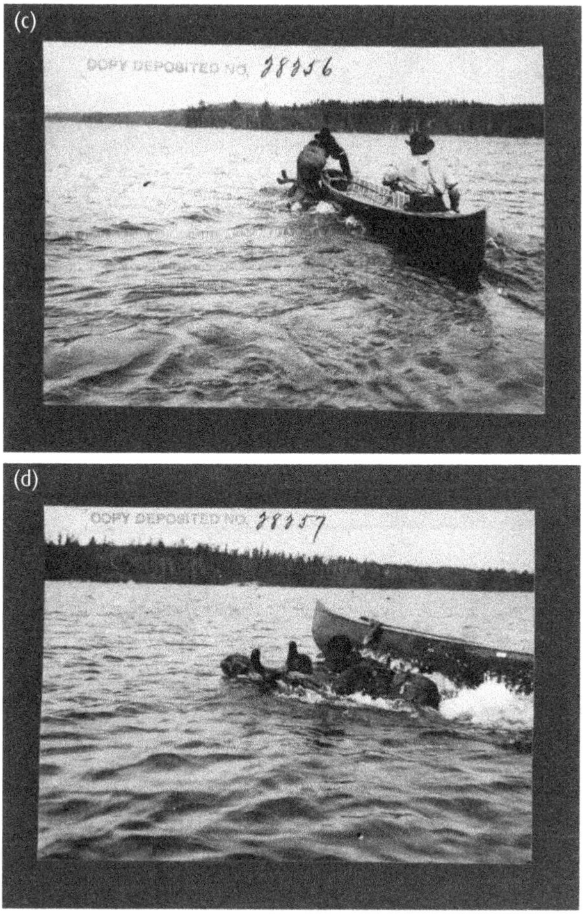

Fig. 3.9 *(Continued)*

camera in twentieth-century Canada. While the images discussed in the previous section celebrated railway technology, here we see the camera being used to articulate and promote the railway and the landscapes surrounding it as commodities. The exhibition photograph is almost a shrine dedicated to the railway and its produce: progress through technology is still the theme, but the exhibition has converted it into tangible qualities that the public can discern. In these images, the focus is not on the abstract qualities or aesthetic associations of the locomotive and the railway itself. It is rather on how the railway is benefiting Canada and providing opportunities by opening up fertile land and hunting grounds that make it more productive. The images and the exhibition, viewed as advertisements, assert that Canada is being driven forward by the railway; the country is becoming more modern, more productive and using its land more positively. Further, they assert that both the land and its produce are there for the taking. Technology, in the form of both camera and railway, has practically and visually turned the wild into a commodity, the wilderness into a tourist destination. All one needs to do is use the railway to reach it.

However, these images, viewed in the context of their dates (1912 and 1914 respectively), evidence something else about the Canadian Northern Railways System. Despite the enthusiasm that had greeted the railway and its operators since the completion of the transcontinental line, many, including the Canadian Northern, were not actually delivering on their proposed financial potential. While the photographs and public image of the railway portrayed it as unstoppable, many of its branches had in fact over-extended their reach and were running their owners into bankruptcy.[40] Indeed, despite the Canadian Northern's best attempts to promote use by the public, it was by 1914 running on empty; by 1916 it would be bankrupt and in need of nationalisation.

The bankruptcy of Canadian Northern and many other national rail network owners was a major crisis for the Canadian government. It resulted in the government buying major shares in the rail network and taking the lines under their own maintenance, creating a nationalised system that still operates today.[41] In covering this particular period and presenting many views of the railway, the Colonial Copyright Collection might be said to evidence the volatility of railway investment as much as the triumph of the railway in early twentieth-century Canada. This volatility is an inherent part of modernist projects such as the railway and is encountered in various ways, the most dramatic of which in Canada at this time was the locomotive crash.

Collisions: the impact of the railway

> To invent the train is *to invent the rail accident* of derailment.[42]

The relationship between the accident and technology is a well discussed field.[43] A dominant theme is the assertion that the 'acceptability' of new mechanical technology (objects that bestow, speed power, force, etc.) is underpinned by the ability to pass off the 'accident' as just that: an aberration, a far from normal occurrence.[44] According to the view of Virilio and others, however, the invention of technology is in actual fact *also* the invention of its accidents. As a result, the attempt simply to suppress the inevitability of the accident is indicative of a desire to mask the duality of modernity; the potential for both unbridled progress and disastrous crashes.[45] This is a theme that has been hinted at in the preceding discussion. In spite of the boosterism surrounding the railway the technology was in reality fragile and partial, carrying within it the potential for catastrophic physical and financial derailment.[46]

The Colonial Copyright Collection provides a lens through which we can perceive various sorts of understandings about the railway, both positive and negative. The following section focuses on two sets of images submitted for copyright after significant accidents on the rail network, using them to investigate perceptions of the darker, often hidden side of the railway. My perception of these images is influenced by Marshall Berman's argument in *All That is Solid Melts Into Air*, where he asserts that 'modernism', as a concept, embraces a wide variety of projects to get to grips with the experience of modernisation.[47] In this perspective it is possible to see photography as a means of getting to grips with a new technological modernity that was bringing both benefits and hazards into Canadian lives.

The images that comprise the focus of this section were taken at the site of two major train crashes, in two different places and by two different photographers. While the context (what the trains were carrying) and situation (where they occurred) of these accidents differed, both happened when the rail network was expanding again nationally. The first set of images are William Gillespie's photographs of a train crash near the settlement of Azilda, Ontario. The Azilda wreck was a collision between two trains, one carrying freight and the other passengers, outside Azilda in September 1906, and it stimulated considerable local interest.[48] The first photograph illustrates the scale of the incident (see Fig.3.10) while the second depicts a large number of individuals (including children) attending the site in order to view the accident, and subsequently posing for their portraits in front of the wrecked locomotives (see Fig.3.11).

It is the size of this crowd that interests me predominantly – a substantial proportion of what is still a small community turns out to view the spectacle that has unfolded just outside of town. Theorists of the crash have argued extensively that the public act of crowding and viewing an accident is an expression of 'eye hunger', where the dynamics of the crowd accentuate the visual stimulus at the 'spectacular centre'.[49] In the context of these images, the damaged locomotive forms a spectacular centre to the scene: an awe-inspiring object in a condition rarely seen. Similarly, the crowd gathers in order to view the spectacular event. The presence of children serves to underscore the idea of a form of 'eye hunger' being indulged; the object is divorced of some of its horror and rendered into a pure spectacle, acceptable for a child to see.

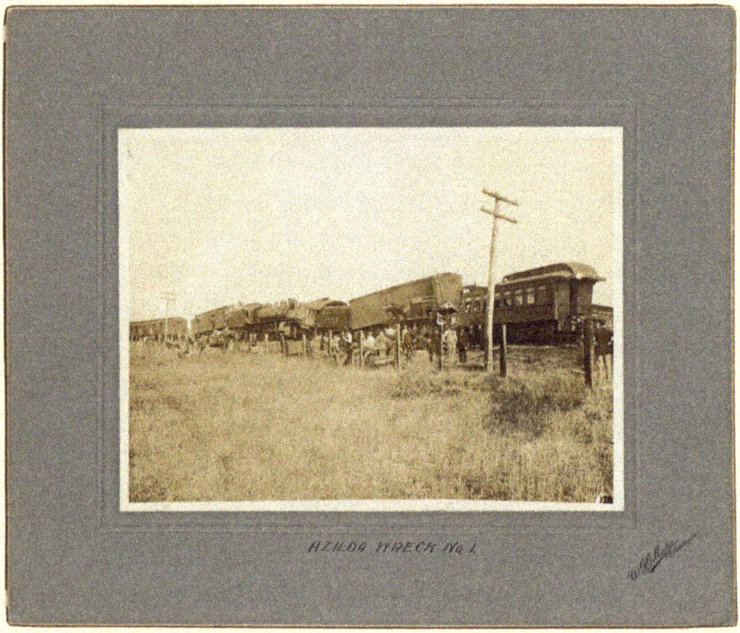

Fig. 3.10 'Azilda Wreck, No.1'. Copyright William G. Gillespie, 1906 (copyright number 17685).

While the lure of the spectacle is evident, however, it is important to consider what it actually represents. The crowd too is witnessing the scene in order to make sense of the event, and one needs to understand what it means for them and what they think of the collision of these two gargantuan objects. Similarly, the photographer is present not only to document the spectacle of the accident, but also to deploy a tool and produce an artefact that will help subsequent viewers to make sense of this accident.

What has brought the photographer and this small town together is the need to understand a new type of event – to perceive the danger of something promoted as so safe and unstoppable. The photographer thus captures not just the scene of an accident, but also the site of an investigation. Here people are making sense of an object that has changed all their lives, since Azilda was made into a settlement by the presence of the railway, but that now represents a new and previously unperceived danger. These images remind us that the railway was not just significantly re-forging spaces on the frontiers. It was remaking long-established settlements, as noted in Chapter 2, where the impact of the railway on the relative economic significance of Victoria and Vancouver was highlighted.[50] In the case of Azilda, the space has also been remade as one of potential danger, a concept at odds with the boosterist narratives discussed above.

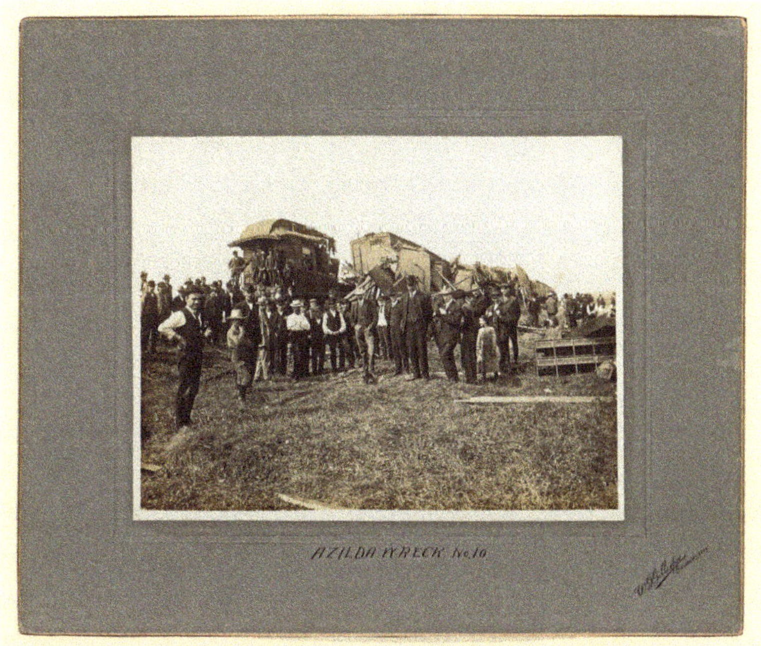

Fig. 3.11 'Azilda Wreck, No.10'. Copyright William G. Gillespie, 1906 (copyright number 17688).

It is also worth reflecting on how these photographs of the Azilda crash circulated. While they undoubtedly circulated in various forms it is notable that the images were also printed as postcards (see Fig.1.1 in Chapter 1), tying them into the networks of nation-building represented by both the railway and Canadian postal service. As a result, such a postcard, as well as showing the hunger to consume the spectacular scene of the accident, also frays the seams of these nation-building ideals. It undermines the trust of sender and receiver in locomotive technologies, and uses the Canadian postal service as a mechanism through which to circulate discordant visions of the nation-building project.

The potential of this danger is depicted more strikingly in the photographs of the Enterprise train disaster. This accident occurred in Enterprise, Ontario in June 1903, when a train ferrying artillery across country was derailed into the town itself. The Enterprise photographs are a riposte to those of the rotary snow plough and passenger trains seen earlier in the chapter, showing that this supposedly unstoppable force can in fact be halted – and exactly what happens when it is.

In the 18 images which photographer Harriett Amelia May took of the Enterprise derailment, the explosion of material is the predominant theme. The images communicate to the viewer where all the speed

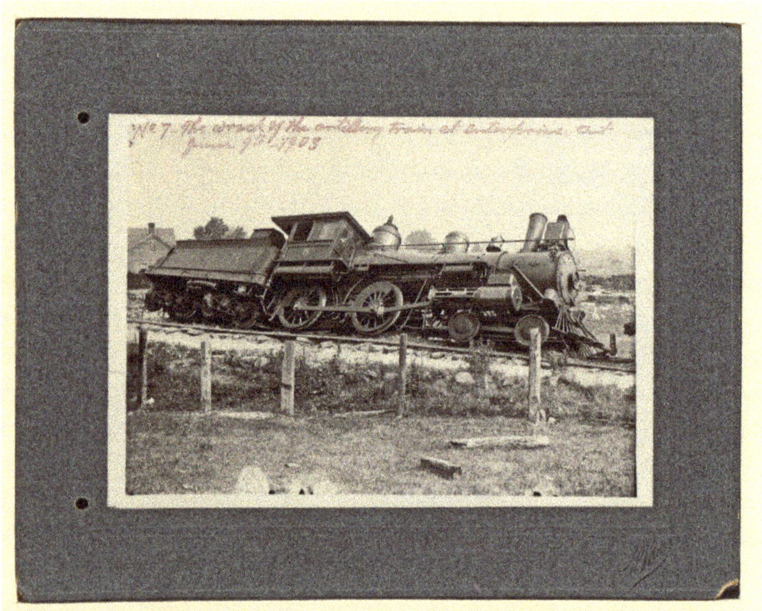

Fig. 3.12 'The wreck of the artillery train at Enterprise, Ontario, June 9, 1903 (Number 8)'. Copyright Harriett Amelia May, 1903 (copyright number 14100).

and momentum of the locomotive go during the incident of derailment, flinging the carriages and their contents in all directions away from the confinement and order of the railway line itself. The photograph with the sole military officer captures the scale of the devastation and communicates the attempt to take in what has happened, as he stands alone on the wreck, surveying the scene (Fig.3.13).

May's images are also a statement of what the image that celebrates the railway necessarily omits: the fact that this new technology brings unprecedented dangers to personal, intimate spaces, as well as opening up previously unobtainable benefits and riches from the frontiers. The photograph with the posing family provides the most striking evidence of this (Fig.3.14). The images of Harmon's snow plough and Button's leisurely jaunt, as well as those of many famous railway photographers from later in the twentieth century,[51] portray the domain of the railway, its sphere of influence, predominantly as the spaces between places (that is, the natural world of forests and mountain passes). However, May draws out the dangers of the intersection of the train with urban space and human lives. When the train acts on and within a natural setting, the interaction between machine and natural world is depicted as being without human danger; the locomotive progresses constantly and nature stands (or is moved) out of its way. Here, however, we see the locomotive smashing into the homes of those families who live in Enterprise, shattering the everyday rhythm of the place and violently depositing its machinery and cargo into a place where they should not be. The result of this is danger, to the family depicted and to the running of their lives. While the subjects are obviously posed after the event (as the family stand to have their portrait taken in their Sunday best, surveying the scene of the accident), the image still communicates how horrifying the few confused moments of the event must have been.

It is the disjuncture caused by the invasion of the railway into everyday life that poses questions here. It forces the viewer to consider the inherent dangers of technology that Virilio discussed at length almost a century after this event. The central arguments in Virilio's work, *The Original Accident*, are twofold: firstly, that you cannot invent the machine without also inventing its inherent dangers and, therefore, the accident itself;[52] and secondly, that the full potential of technology's

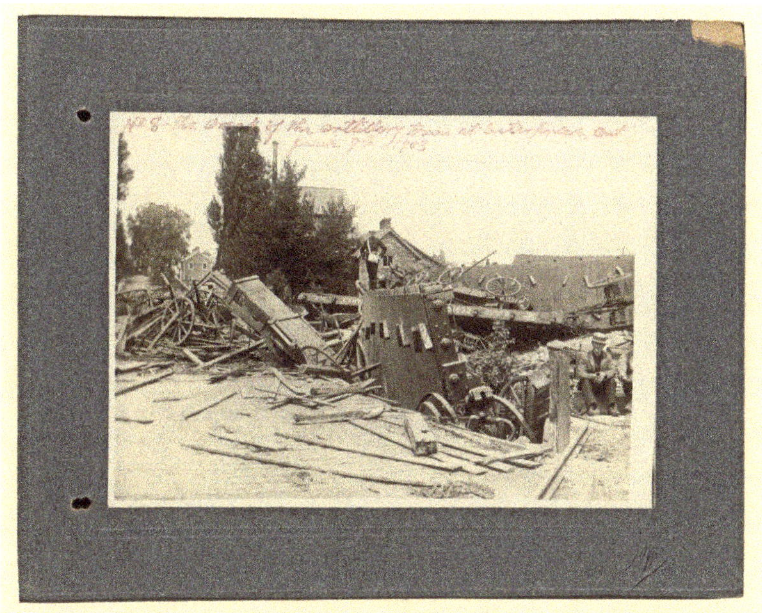

Fig. 3.13 'The wreck of the artillery train at Enterprise, Ontario, June 9, 1903 (Number 7)'. Copyright Harriett Amelia May, 1903 (copyright number 14100).

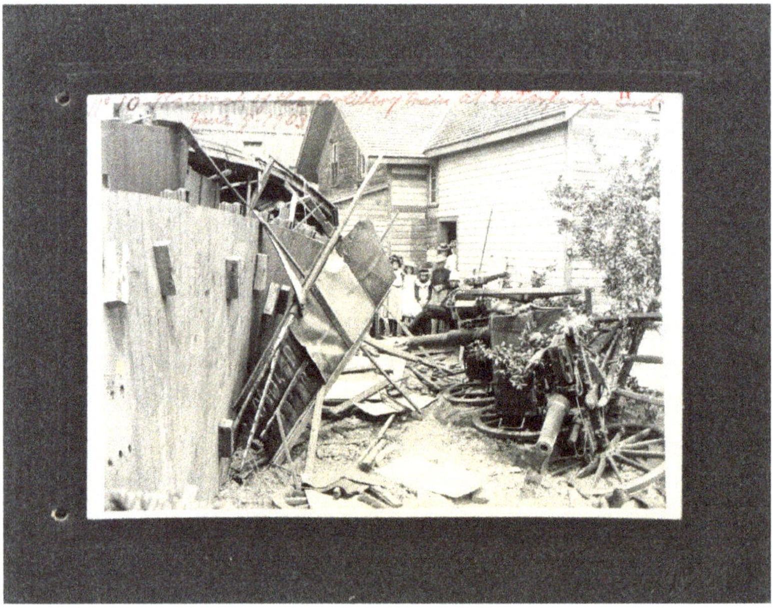

Fig. 3.14 'The wreck of the artillery train at Enterprise, Ontario, June 9, 1903 (Number 10)'. Copyright Harriett Ameila May, 1903 (copyright number 14100).

inherent dangers is realised when the technology is placed in close proximity to, or intersects with, the general public.[53] It is these two themes that the population of Enterprise is trying to understand, and that the photography attempts to communicate in the production of these images. In so doing, they assert (after the accident has revealed) that the characteristics of the railway articulated and promoted by the images earlier in this chapter are not all that technology actually brings. Instead the accident photographs (along with the chequered commercial history of the railway boom) serve to remind us that there is a politics of omission in imagery intended to promote the railway. Theorists of the accident from Virilio to Beckmann would assert this is intended to mask the inherently unsettling nature of the accident and promote the acceptability of the technology.[54]

* * *

The railway images contained in the Colonial Copyright Collection, when taken as a whole, can be read as attempts to understand the varied characteristics of the 'iron horse' and its effects, both positive and negative. The accidents and their documentation are not used here in order to discredit the images discussed in the previous sections, nor to frame them as 'untrue'. Instead they are used to nuance these more celebratory images and to establish a relationship between the triumphant, promotional and warning sets of images in the light of arguments made by Virilio and others concerning technology and accidents.

The defining characteristic of the Colonial Copyright Collection also reminds us that all these images are potential commodities in which individuals have invested time and money. Both sets of images reflect not just a fascination with the railway and its puncturing and reordering of spaces, but also an attempt in principle to capitalise on it. While the images depict different locomotives, different lines and were produced by different photographers, together they combine to form a collage of the 'substance' of the railway itself. In this sense the collection allows us to perceive photographers and publics grappling with the notion communicated by Virilio: namely, that accidents should not be seen as 'exceptionalities' but rather as 'eventualities', something that is preordained to happen by virtue of the characteristics of technology.[55] In turn, the collection's railway images as a whole present a reflection upon the price paid for technological progress across Canada's landscapes. Through the multiplicity of views, we see modernism in action.[56]

Essentially then, what we see in all of these images is an attempt by Canadians to grasp the multifaceted effects of rapid modernisation since confederation and the subsequent opening of the transcontinental railway. The railway was not alone, of course, but it did have very notable effects. Between 1895 and 1924 the national landscape and imaginative geography of Canada underwent a marked change. As the railways traversed the vast distances of the continent and obliterated its obstacles, cities became more closely linked together, settlements sprang up and the six confederate territories coalesced together to form one, increasingly independent nation. With these changes came other developments, as Canada shifted from being a nation of settlers to one underpinned by its metropolitan spaces and ideals. Networks of radio, electricity and other modern advances also sprang up at this time, largely using the railway and the paths it cut as their guides between cities.[57]

Alongside this came changes in the perception of Canada's landscape. The once unruly and overbearing force of nature was increasingly transformed into a commodity. As a result, Canada's natural wildernesses were being repackaged and rebranded for integration into Canada's and the global economy, turning once inhospitable places into landscapes of opportunity for wealth and leisure – an absolute expression of human control over nature. This repackaging was often capped by the construction of grand railway hotels in sites with dramatic scenery, such as Banff, and these edifices of modernity's expansion also became significant photographic subjects in their own right. However, this process was partial and uneven, meaning that national, regional and local spaces, and Canadians themselves, had to adapt in a multitude of ways.[58] Further, the railway also brought the risk of crisis and hazard, most violently represented at the scenes of great railway disasters.

It is particularly fitting that these visions of modernity should be constructed through the lens of the camera, a machine that offers the possibility of infinite reproducibility. The Colonial Copyright Collection offers a variety of ways of visualising these changes in the material and imaginative geographies of Canadian railway development. The first images discussed in this chapter evoke the power of the railway and its ability to reshape the Canadian landscape.[59] They are followed by images that are more self-consciously commercial, promoting railway investment and use. These indicate the insufficiency of the imagery of technological mastery to sustain the railway boom: what was also required were money and passengers. Finally the images of accidents discussed in the final section bring the other side of railway development into full view, enabling others to imagine and memorialise the experience of disaster.

In all these cases photographic imagery was not only the means of representing these geographies of progress and crisis, but was also a form of investment in itself. The fact that the raw materials of these points of view – the photographs themselves – were made locally, and their copyright protected by local photographers across Canada, gives a 'bottom up' perspective on the public imagination of the railway.[60] These images, like the railway itself, were meant for circulation.

This link between railway and image brings Part 1 of this book full circle as the media of circulation, transportation technologies and the spaces within which photographs such as these were circulated have formed the core of this part of the book. They were the spaces and the conduits through which a changing Canada was communicated and photographers travelled. During these travels and their observations of daily life the photographers who underpin this collection also captured Canada undergoing profound change. Part 2 moves on to consider how this transition affected peoples across the country, and how this was visually articulated through photography.

Part 2
Photographing Canada's Peoples in a Changing World

4
Colonialism's gaze: representing the First Peoples in Canada

This chapter considers depictions of First Peoples and Inuit groups[1] in the context of social and cultural change in early twentieth-century Canada and in the light of wider conventions of photographic portraiture. Photographs of First Peoples individuals, groups and cultural practices were frequently deposited for copyright by various photographers for a myriad of purposes. The consumer market for such images had a range of local specificities and the interaction between photographic subject, photographer, market and geography was significant. These images therefore provide important insights into the relationships between First Peoples, European settlers and the development of Canada as a modern nation.

Such images of First Peoples groups are usually considered in relation to a broader colonial project. This project, ongoing from the early days of trade and settlement, witnessed a dramatic expansion under the plans for confederation, which required a large-scale re-imagining of the Canadian landscape. This imagined landscape was one in which the First Peoples are either entirely absent or existed as spectres with a singular identity, as Canadian historian Daniel Francis has shown in *The Imaginary Indian*.[2] In reality of course, First Peoples are as distinct and individual as the various other peoples and groups discussed in this book; and in turn the colonial project varies across times and spaces.

The images in this chapter, deposited in 1900–10, have been selected partly with the intention of exploring the diversity of visual representations of First Peoples. This diversity reflected, in part, the variety of geographical contexts in which indigenous peoples became subject to the camera's gaze. The photographs were produced for consumption as souvenirs, postcards or other commemorative formats. While in many cases they represent typecasting by photographers, they are also records of individual lives, shaped by space, time and sociopolitical interactions in different contexts. These portraits differ from the landscape images of the earlier part of this book, and bring into view a new aspect of photography in the direct relationships between photographers and subjects. This interaction leads to the creation of the portraits, but the individuals concerned otherwise operate in very different social and geographical spheres. These complexities have a significant impact upon the composition of the images.

Some of the earliest experiments with photography were made through the composition of human portraits, with photographers such as Fox Talbot developing and refining his calotype process while producing images of his family around their home. This opened up the commercial potential of the new medium and the photographic portrait soon began to supplant the expensive painted miniature. Indeed, early in the development of effective photographic practices, many individuals began to undergo the laborious task of trekking up a strenuous number of stairs to reach both the photographer's studio and the good light – above the smog and gloom of the city – in order to have their portraits produced. Very soon the portrait became a widely available medium used to remember close relatives and loved ones in homes across the world.

Formal portraits come together through the interplay of many different signifiers, including the backdrop and the sitter's attire, posture and stature. All of these elements are combined in order to communicate the intended message. This method of photography is illustrated in the collection, for example through the portfolio of Notman and Sons. This company deposited a significant amount of material for copyright between 1895 and 1924, and is considered an exemplar in the field of Canadian photography and studio portraiture.[3] William Notman produced some of the earliest iconic images of Canada; his studio scenes represent Canadian life in the mid-nineteenth century in a way that still resonates today. Indeed, Notman's 'A Chance Shot' often fronts special issues on Canadian photography and is still seen as the iconic depiction of Canadian winter.[4] The reputation that William Notman built up as the major Canadian photographer meant that by the late nineteenth century he, and his sons who would inherit the business, had become *the* photographers to employ for the production of commemorative portraits.

Notman & Sons' photograph of Lady Grey in 1905 (when Lord Albert Henry George Grey was Governor General of Canada) is typical of the format of elite portrait photography in Canada during this period (Fig.4.1). Lady Grey stands clad in fur, with a snowy background used as the studio drape. The clothes worn by Lady Grey communicate the

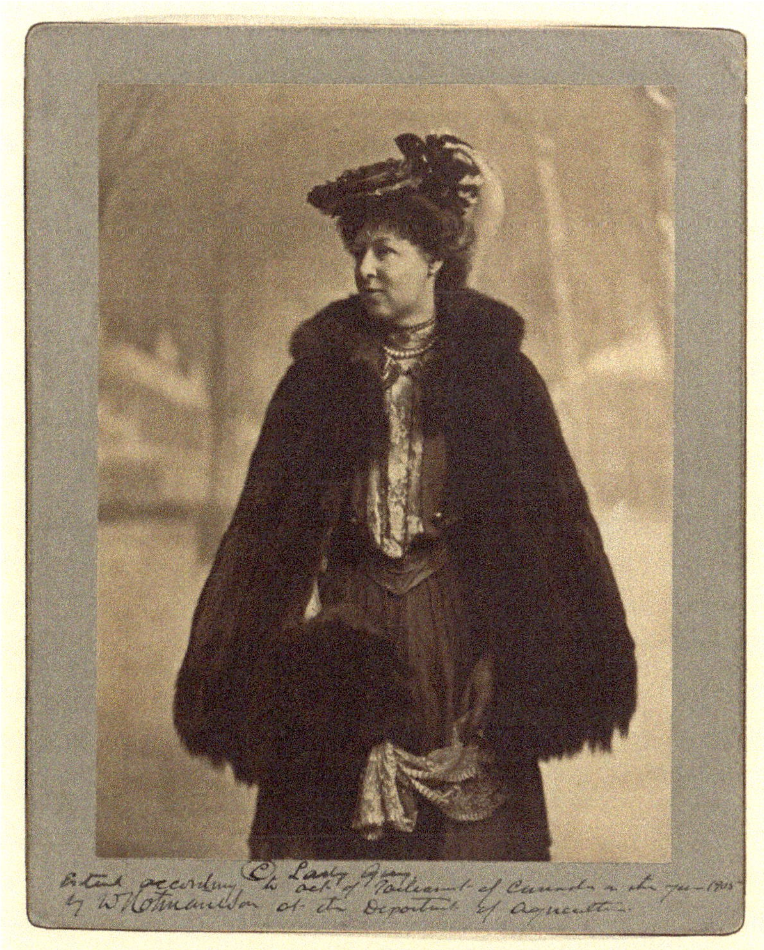

Fig. 4.1 'Lady Grey'. Copyright Notman & Sons, 1905 (copyright number 15717).

popularly understood coldness of the Canadian landscape (something frequently invoked by William Notman) and, along with her posture, also reflect her status as the wife of the governor of Canada. Shearer West notes the importance of the confluence of subject, photographer's reputation and scene in the communication of the intended message through portraiture photography and portraiture in general.[5] These factors are all present in the image of Lady Grey, and they combine to create an effective commemorative portrait of the wife of Canada's new governor.

This outline of the practice of studio-based, elite portrait photography provides both the context and counterpoint for the following discussions.

The taste for the portrait photograph and the cheapening of photographic production was accompanied by an increase in the use of pictorial and, eventually, photographic portraits in newspapers, journals and magazines in the late nineteenth and early twentieth centuries. By the early twentieth century it was the norm for a significant event to be reported in the press with an accompanying image of the individual or individuals involved sitting above the text of the article to illustrate the writing. Indeed, if an accompanying image could not be found to embed in the text, this was a cause of much anxiety to editors of local, national and international newspapers who needed a visual backdrop for their stories.

Increasingly, these publications needed to represent indigenous peoples. Canada's expansion across the North American continent in the decades after confederation was – and often is – portrayed as being benign, fair-minded and paternalistic in its interactions with First Peoples groups. This has the dual benefit of justifying the paternalistic and puritanical policies of creating reservations for various tribes in newly defined Canadian spaces and of contrasting Canada with nations seen as being more heavy-handed in their geographical expansionism, in particular the United States. This idea of a non-colonial Canadian state is still promoted today, as illustrated by Prime Minister Stephen Harper's 2009 statement to the G20 in Pittsburgh in which he asserted, 'We also have no history of colonialism. So we have all of the things that many people admire about the Great Powers but none of the things that threaten or bother them'.[6] The reality, however, as Cole Harris has illustrated, is that the Canadian government operated a particular mode of colonial expansionism in its attempts to secure geographical cohesion for the fledgling nation. While recognisably different from the geopolitical actions of other settler states, this was still based on technological supremacy, political manoeuvring, forcible coercion and cultural assimilation.[7]

In the years following confederation, and as late as the early twentieth century, geographical cohesion was an important preoccupation for the Confederate government. In the face of feared encroachment from the United States, between the 1860s and 1910s the Canadian government set about solidifying claims regarding its northern, western and central territories in a process that would have direct implications for the status of aboriginal groups, their lands, hunting grounds and culturally significant sites. In 1900–10 the main phase of this project was drawing to a close in some areas, consolidating its gains in others and awakening an interest in Canada's geographical extremes. In many ways a sense of paranoia about geographical cohesion had never left Canada and the

United States. This continued into the twentieth century, lasted through the Cold War and now manifests in the new phase of Arctic resource exploitation politics as the ice recedes in the northern hemisphere.

The images discussed in the remainder of this chapter are selected from three Canadian regions that were at different stages of integration into the Canadian state between 1900 and 1910. While they represent a small selection from the collection as a whole, these photographs reveal different relationships between settler and aboriginal groups as well as between the individual photographers and their subjects. They also provide a context for discussions involving First Peoples groups in Chapter 3 ('Picturing modernity'), Chapter 5 ('A collection of people') and Chapter 6 ('A global presence').

Tommy Longboat: race and sport in Toronto

The previous brief account of the historical development of the commemorative portrait provides a context in which the portrait of the Onondaga runner Tom Longboat can be read. The photograph was taken by the Toronto photographer Charles Aylett after Longboat's victory in the 1907 Boston Marathon. Longboat had won the race in Massachusetts in style, exploding onto the long-distance running scene and receiving the praise and indeed adulation of all in Ontario (and even some, grudgingly, in Massachusetts). However, upon reporting the spectacular win the Toronto papers found that they had no image of this runner, who hailed from the Onondaga reserves outside the city. Aylett was therefore commissioned to produce a series of images which were run in the papers and are discussed here. Another image of Longboat taken by Aylett and deposited for copyright depicts Longboat running; it is still used as part of the display on First Peoples in Canadian society in the Museum of Civilization, Ontario.

Longboat's success on the racecourse thrust his image onto the public stage. The subsequent years of his career were defined by struggles over his identity – struggles which indicate the contested place of indigenous groups in Canada both then and now. It should be noted that there is no evidence that Longboat ever publicly questioned his own identity: he was a member of the Onondaga. The assurance Longboat felt in his own identity, and confusion regarding its attempted appropriation by others, was frequently expressed by himself and friends throughout the rest of Longboat's life.[8] However, his athletic success provoked public interest in and debate over his identity in wider Canadian social circles. What is of interest here is the relationship between Aylett's image of Longboat and those public debates, and in particular what it shows about these relationships between elements of Canadian society, in this case the popular media, and its diverse First Peoples groups. This in turn reflects the importance of photographs in framing perceptions of the role and place of the First Peoples in Canadian society.

The focus here is on the role of the camera in representing a celebrity sportsman, in the broader context of the colonial contest between settlers and indigenous peoples. There is now a large literature on the history of sport as a sphere where national, colonial and gender identities are formed and contested. A central influence on this literature was the writing of C. L. R. James on cricket and its place in Caribbean culture.[9] James's account of the export of cricket around the colonial sphere to develop and underpin British values in the colonies, only for the game to become appropriated and rearticulated within local conditions and subsequently used to 'bat back' at the empire, portrays the nuanced relationships that develop between individuals, groups and nations through sport.[10] In the North American context sport also provides a sphere in which identities are constructed and contested, a process in which ethnic and racial identities continue to be significant factors.[11]

The running of races had long been a part of First Peoples cultures; it was something Canadians were brought into, as opposed to the other way round.[12] Indeed, migrant Europeans working on the Canadian land had spent much of their time since the founding of Quebec being soundly beaten, in what could be more-or-less termed marathons, by First Peoples runners. Similarly, Longboat's childhood was punctuated by many instances in which his abilities as a runner could be interpreted as a mechanism for subverting the desires of the expanding Canadian state. He regularly ran away – as fast and far as he could – from his schooling and the oppressive environment of the imposed education system.[13]

Furthermore, once Longboat began to compete in formalised races in the early twentieth century, it is clear from his own words that it was an undertaking fuelled by his desire to compete and illustrate his abilities as an Onondaga runner. It is notable, therefore, that Longboat's successes from 1907 onwards, in spite of the history of First Peoples athletes in general and the role of running in his life up until this point, garnered him the honour of being appropriated by the Canadian press 'as a Canadian'.[14] It is within this context of individual and cultural appropriation that the photographs considered here were produced in a studio by the photographer of many in Toronto society, Charles Aylett, to illustrate Longboat and his successes in Ontario's media.

In the photograph under discussion here (Fig.4.2), Tom Longboat is clothed in the garb of his trade and surrounded by the paraphernalia of

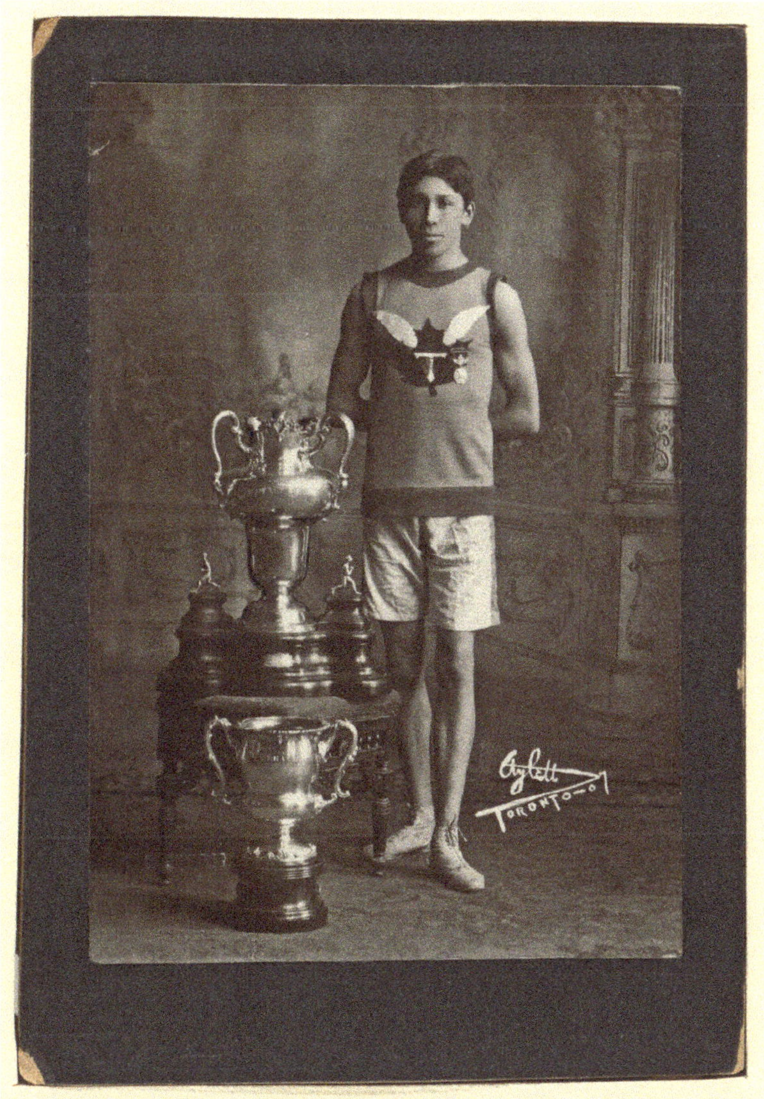

Fig. 4.2 'Tom Longboat, The Canadian Runner [1]'. Copyright Charles Aylett, 1907 (copyright number 18314).

his victories. The viewer is encouraged to see this as an image depicting and immortalising Longboat's moment of glory. The athlete stands, placed with his shoulders back, next to a stool which holds a trophy, the scale of which seems to dwarf Longboat's frame. This, it should be noted, is no insubstantial feat, given that Longboat stood just short of six feet in

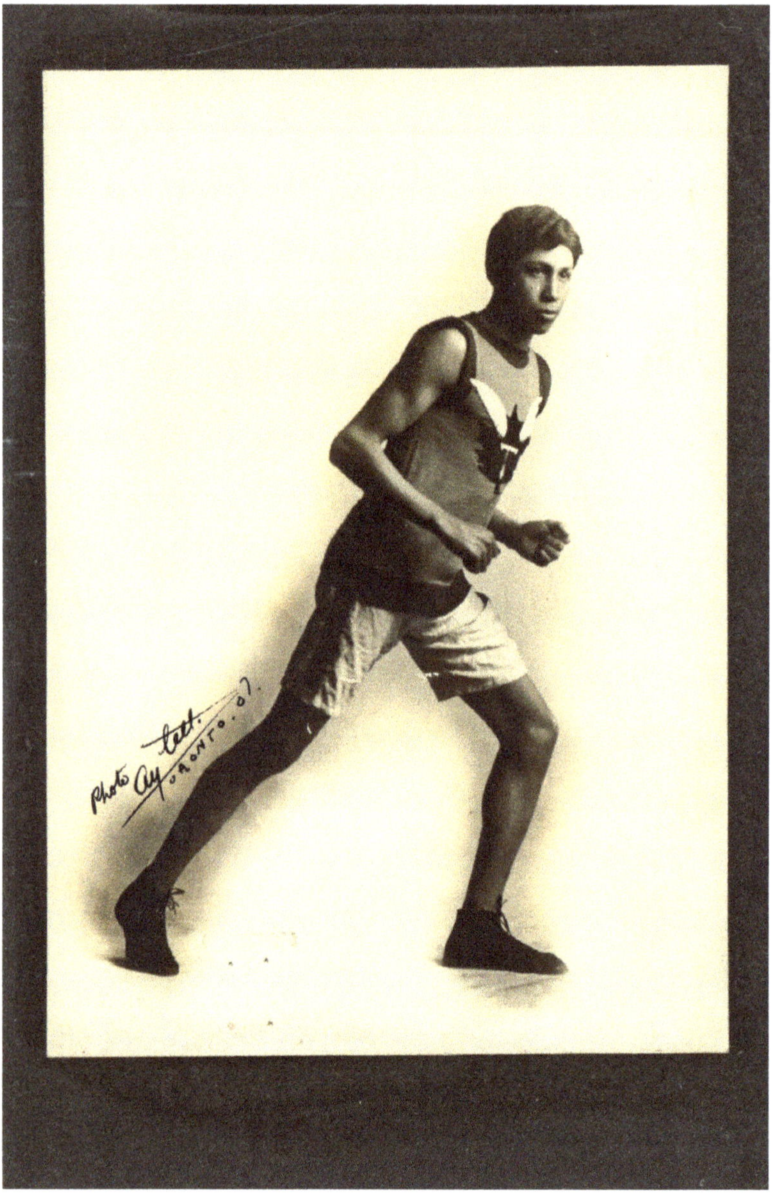

Fig. 4.3 'Tom Longboat, The Canadian Runner [2]'. Copyright Charles Aylett, 1907 (copyright number 18315).

height and weighed in at over 140 pounds: these are quite some trophies that he stands next to. The size of these awards and the gaudily ostentatious setting present a scene that to the casual view, as in a newspaper, would most successfully illustrate Longboat's success.

However, a deeper reading of the scene may illustrate something else, especially regarding the comfort of the sitter and the ambition of those who commissioned the photograph, of more substantial interest than the fleeting glare of sporting glory. To begin with, the setting may not be as appropriate for Longboat as the snowy scene in which the fur-clad Lady Grey stands. He is pictured in an ornate, decorated room, backed with dark wallpaper and punctuated by the fashionable trimmings of the time. The setting is ceremonial and distinctly formal in its aesthetic – indeed the neoclassical colonnades in the background suggest this is celebrating running in the European style as opposed to that of North America. Further, Longboat is Europeanised in his physical posture as a portrait sitter. He stands bolt upright with not even a hint of a smile on his face. This is in marked contrast to many other images that exist of him in more relaxed situations, where his posture is comfortable, with a hint of roundness in the shoulders and an easy smile. Overall, the rigidity of Longboat's posture here suggests the dominant aesthetic of Victorian portraiture, where sitters were encouraged to compose themselves as austerely as possible.[15]

In this bodily arrangement we also become aware of clues to other messages embedded in the image. To add to these physiological visual cues, Longboat also stands dressed unmistakably as a Canadian, the Maple Leaf of the Confederation daubed across his chest. There are no circles or other iconographies of the Onondaga nation. Constructing a distinctly Canadian aesthetic around Longboat in this image reflects an attempt to assert Longboat's identity as consistent with the hegemonic identity being created by Confederate Canada, which was being gradually enforced upon the First Peoples groups within its expanding geographical confines. Here in Ontario, where contact with indigenous groups had a longer history than in the western sphere within which Rafton-Canning (whose photographs will be discussed further below) was acting, the process of trying to 'whiten' First Peoples groups and assimilate them into Canadian culture had been developing for some time. Longboat found himself at the front of a new phase of this relationship. Within this phase, individuals from First Peoples groups existed in a fluid space in Canadian society – portrayed as degenerate natives when out of step with urban Ontario's thinking, but appropriated as Canadians when bringing glory to a Confederate Canada still trying to find its identity and compete in international spheres. The image of Longboat is an illustration of this position.

Essentially, as an 'Indian' Longboat was devoid of individuality, visual or otherwise. As a successful runner, however, he was appropriated as a Canadian, which required an appropriate image to be constructed through the medium of portraiture. This is best summarised by the following text from the *Toronto Daily Star*, published after Longboat's Boston Marathon victory, under the headline 'Canadian Won Big Race':

> Canada makes no bones about gaining a little glory from an Indian. In other matters than footraces we have become accustomed to leaders from the Six Nations. We give the Boston papers notice, one and all, that we claim Longboat as a Canadian.[16]

Actually, this statement was economical with the truth. The claim that 'Canada makes no bones' about Longboat's ethnicity applied only so far as he was successful. Indeed, when Longboat occasionally lost a race the media – and even many of his confidantes, including his trainer – were quick to put the defeat down to his lazy, 'Indian' ways. This continued throughout his career, often resulting in the most ridiculous and racist of statements. An example was provided in a report of Longboat's marriage to Lauretta Maracle in the *Toronto Star*.

> She does not like to talk of feathers, war paint and other Indian paraphernalia. She is ambitious for Tom and if anybody can make a reliable man and good citizen of that elusive being, Tom Longboat, it will be his wife.[17]

Such statements are significant: they reinforce the ingrained social stereotypes that affected the daily life of an individual such as Longboat as well as the production of images of his athletic prowess. Individual images do not work in isolation to create an imagined construct of Longboat as an honorary Canadian. Instead the image acts as a signifier, a visual reference point, that seeks in its composition to underscore Longboat's 'Canadian' identity and attributes and mask his status as an Onondaga. The combination of the image with reporting, text, editing and the pervading social sense that First Peoples groups should be brought into Canadian society and civilised is what actually asserts the visual trope of the image, embedding it as part of this visual-cultural exchange mechanism.

Aylett's image of Longboat can also be read in the context of the efforts of the Toronto press and wider society to remove Longboat's honorary status when he dissatisfied his audience. Many of the cultural slurs levied against Longboat during his time as a runner were borne out of cultural misunderstandings – essentially misperceptions of his running style and training regime that were interpreted as being illustrative of his aboriginal nature, especially its negative qualities.[18] It has been noted, however, that the training regimes used by Longboat are now actually widely appropriated in the stamina development procedures of professional sports persons in the twenty-first century.[19] That aside, the ability of the press to shunt Longboat back and forward between 'Indian' and 'Canadian' does illustrate the fact that Longboat cannot be a Canadian as he is Onondaga. More to the point he does not want to be Canadian, as suggested by his resistance to the state throughout his young life.

This shows through in Aylett's image. The face and features that stare back at the camera are unmistakably those of a powerful and striking Onondaga runner, as opposed to a statuesque and passive exemplar of Canadian sporting prowess. That Longboat himself should still shine through in this portrait is not perhaps remarkable within the context of portraiture. Yet within this particular image, with all its drapery and Canuck imagery, it is testament to the strength of his cultural and personal identity that it does at all. The irrepressibility of Longboat's personality was a theme that ran through his career. He continued to look after his own interests and retain his individual identity, much to the chagrin of the political bodies, press, trainers and promoters around him, all eager to 'whiten' this prodigious runner and claim him as Canadian.[20]

Longboat's resistance to all those who attempted to appropriate and redefine his own identity, even within the confines of the photographic image, is a testament not simply to the force of his own personality, but also to the potential for resistance within this colonial project as a whole. The dynamic that developed between Longboat, the photographer Aylett, the Toronto press and many in Ontario's political and athletic establishments, which led to the production of the image discussed here, is illustrative of the role these images played within Canadian society in the twentieth century and continue to play today. They are part of a complex Canadian visual culture where images are bound up in processes of performance, assimilation and resistance. Longboat's image also illustrates the complex dynamics that exist between the subject, photographer, market and circulation of an image. Each of these factors was an agent not just in affecting the creation of the image, but also in making it a depiction that can be viewed differently in various sociopolitical contexts.

By extracting these images from the archive and reanalysing them within the wider contexts of the worlds that surrounded them at the time, we can perceive how important they were to underpinning appropriations and understandings being forged regarding the role of individuals from First Peoples groups in the most settled parts of

Confederate Canada. However, we can also see that the conflicting identities thrust upon Longboat by the Canadian media, and the frustrations Toronto's society felt he visited upon them, were present from the moment Canada attempted to call the athlete its own. For, despite all the trappings of a Canadian sportsman, what looks back at us from the portrait of Tom Longboat is still an Onondaga national and the 'man who ran faster than everyone'.[21]

Modernity's vision: juxtaposing communities in western Canada

In the aftermath of the wars and reservation development programme that operated between 1870 and 1885, members of the First Peoples groups that made their settlements in the plains central to Alberta found themselves tightly restricted to reservations, away from urbanised areas. As a result, most settlers had little direct contact with members of the various groups who had once inhabited the landscapes of the Canadian west. The photographer Arthur Rafton-Canning was, in many ways, an exemplar of the migrants from various European backgrounds who came to settle in Canada and its western territories. The descendant of a Parisian family and an Englishman by birth, Rafton-Canning moved to Canada shortly after his marriage in England in 1885, attracted by the mystique of the west. He then worked for the Royal North West Mounted Police and the Edwards Bros. photographic studio in Vancouver, before eventually settling in Lethbridge, Alberta. Here he opened up his own photographic studio, the British and Colonial Photographic Co., in 1907.

By 1907 Lethbridge was no longer simply a fledgling pioneer town; it was receiving more pairs of hands and businesses, and was benefiting from the crucially important connection to the railway line which made it into a regional hub. The area that comprised the Alberta territory had only recently been brought under the full control of the Confederate government, which had to surmount geographical obstacles and a considerable amount of resistance from First Peoples in the area in order to bring the territory into the confederate scheme and continue progress toward its vision of a geographically cohesive Canadian state.

The fragmentary material archive that remains of Rafton-Canning's life indicates that it was the chance to be a genuine pioneer that caught his interest, causing him to move himself and his new family across the world. Once settled in Lethbridge, Rafton-Canning used his skill in photography to set about documenting life in the new territory and the explosion of modernity that, he hoped, was about to erupt from the soils of the western Canadian plains (see Fig.4.4). An enthusiast of the railway, his striking image of the Lethbridge viaduct spanning the landscape (Fig.3.7, shown in Chapter 3) is an example of Rafton-Canning's aspirations for the plains of Alberta: railways and towns rising out of the ground to underpin the development of a vast agricultural economy. The Lethbridge viaduct remained a source of continued fascination for Rafton-Canning. His camera lovingly documented its every step to traverse the vast gorge, illustrating this engineering marvel as an icon of efficiency, ingenuity and development.

While photographing the area around Lethbridge, Rafton-Canning also produced many images of local Blackfoot and Blood Indian groups, which he saw as the antithesis to modern progress. As a result, Rafton-Canning's images of the First Peoples groups that lived around the Lethbridge area offer a stark contrast to the depictions he created of the incoming settler society. The portrayal of the white man and First Peoples as at opposite poles of the development spectrum was far from unique among Canadian photographers. Indeed, Rafton-Canning's work is part of a broad range of photographic, literary and political works committed to this perspective, exemplified by the work of Edward Sheriff Curtis.[22] However, Rafton-Canning was one of the most notable western

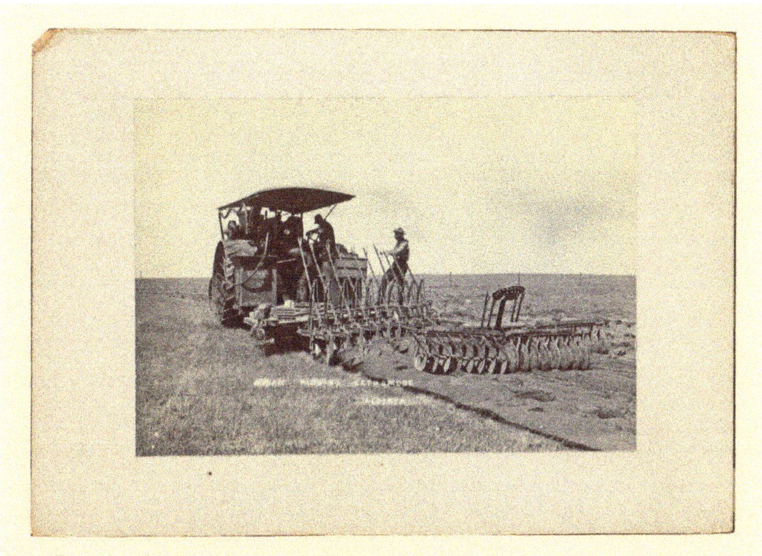

Fig. 4.4 'Steam Plowing, Lethbridge'. Copyright Arthur Rafton-Canning (copyright number 23180).

Canadian photographers, a significant voice in the locality of Lethbridge and a dedicated copyrighter of his work, such that the Colonial Copyright Collection provides a rich resource documenting Albertan life at the beginning of the century.[23]

The stereotypes constructed and disseminated, particularly through the medium of photography, have had a significant impact upon sociocultural understandings of 'Plains Indians' in the past and continue to do so today.[24] At the time they were perpetuated by settler authorities' efforts to keep the two groups separate, something Rafton-Canning also fell foul of a few times during his efforts to photograph the 'Plains Indian' groups living around Lethbridge. Further, when illustrations of 'Plains Indians' did circulate among the general public, they often pandered to a popular desire for depictions of the warlike and bloodthirsty Indian warrior dramatised during the westward expansions of the American and Canadian states. As a result, such images suggested little of the actual complexity of indigenous cultures. Although Rafton-Canning's work does not attempt to portray the Blackfoot and Blood Indians as overtly bloodthirsty and warlike killers (despite displaying a particular relish when annotating his negatives regarding the Blood Indian tribe), his photographs are complicit in portraying their subjects as members of backward or relic cultures.

'Chief Body' (see Fig.4.5) and 'Jim Snake and Crop Eared Wolf, the Head Chief of the Blood Indians' (see Fig.4.6) are two of Rafton-Canning's portraits of elders from around the Lethbridge area. Each depicts the men in their full ceremonial dress and in contact with status items, a rifle and horse respectively. While both images were copyrighted in the same year there is a noticeable difference in quality between them, with the paper on which Chief Body's portrait is reproduced being significantly lower quality than that of 'Jim Snake and Crop Eared Wolf'. Further, the visual aesthetic of the image of Chief Body also illustrates that different photographic materials were used in the production of these images.

The posing, iconographic focus and subject of these photographs suggest that Rafton-Canning was producing these images for sale as postcards and souvenirs. The market for this developed substantially after Lethbridge became a major hub in the Canadian Pacific Rail network in 1905; images of First Peoples chiefs continued to be popular with tourist markets and locals fascinated by the 'otherness' of the groups who inhabited the plains prior to white settlement. Within this market there was a desire among photographers to pander to consumer demand for images of 'genuine' 'Plains Indians'.[25] In this regard 'Chief Body' would have been a success, depicted in full dress and carrying a rifle; a teepee

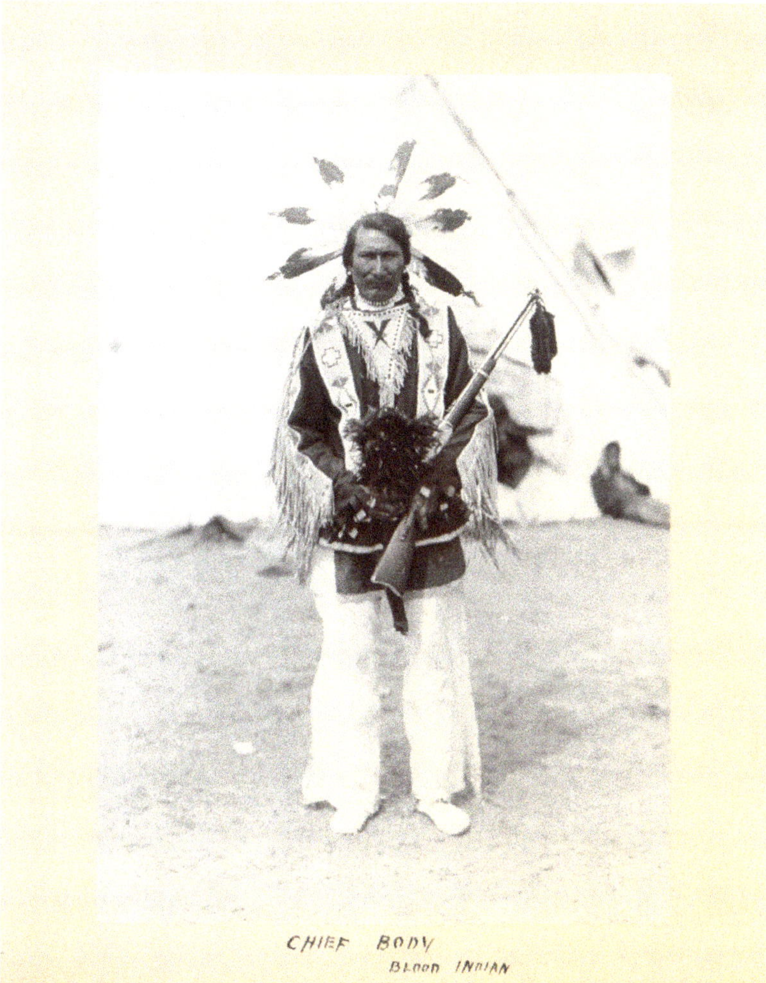

Fig. 4.5 'Chief Body'. Copyright Arthur Rafton-Canning, 1910 (copyright number 23385).

features in the background. By contrast, while 'Jim Snake and Crop Eared Wolf, the Head Chief of the Blood Indians' would have potentially had significant value as a rare depiction of the Head Chief, one would imagine that this value, if the image was sold uncropped, would have been diminished by the presence of white men (and potentially members of the Department of Indian Affairs at that) in the frame.

As well as using composition and title to emphasise that these were 'genuine' 'Plains Indians', Rafton-Canning used his documentary gaze to illustrate their supposedly primitive and simple lifestyles more widely.

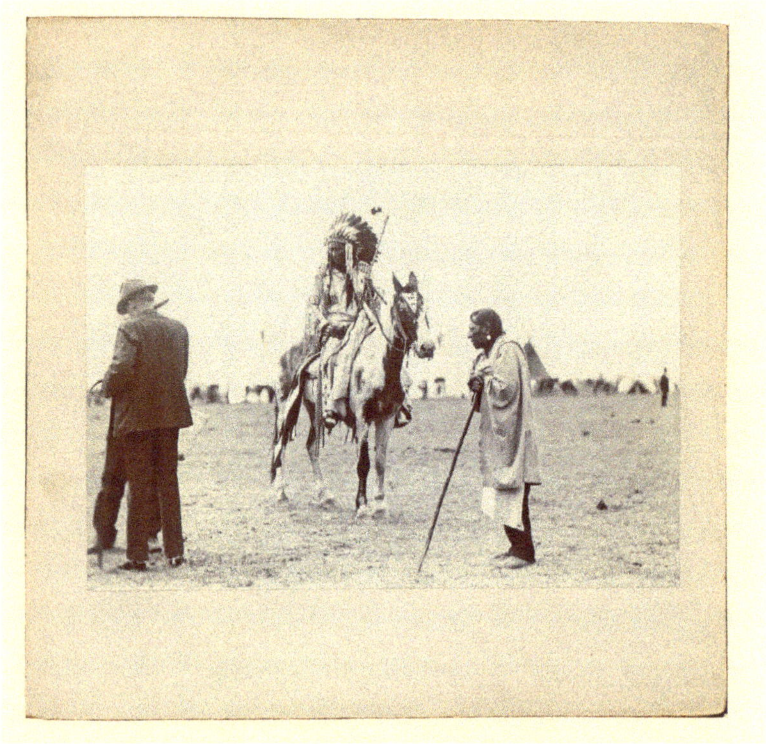

Fig. 4.6 'Jim Snake and Crop Eared Wolf, the Head Chief of the Blood Indians'. Copyright Arthur Rafton-Canning, 1910 (copyright number 22811).

The photograph of Blood Indian transportation may have been intended to juxtapose the 'backward' with the modern, and was no doubt also highly marketable to train passengers passing through Lethbridge. Again this composition foregrounds the complexity of dress and other living materials arranged around his photographic subjects. Indeed, the quality of his photography is such that Rafton-Canning's images are valued by many contemporary descendants of these groups, now attempting to piece their material heritage back together after the oppression of the twentieth century.

Yet, at the same time, it is clear that these photographs had a role to play in reproducing and conveying negative stereotypes about First Peoples. The photograph of the 'Indian Travois', for example, overlooks the significance of how First Peoples groups had adapted to the landscape of Alberta, accordingly fashioning their material culture to fit with their

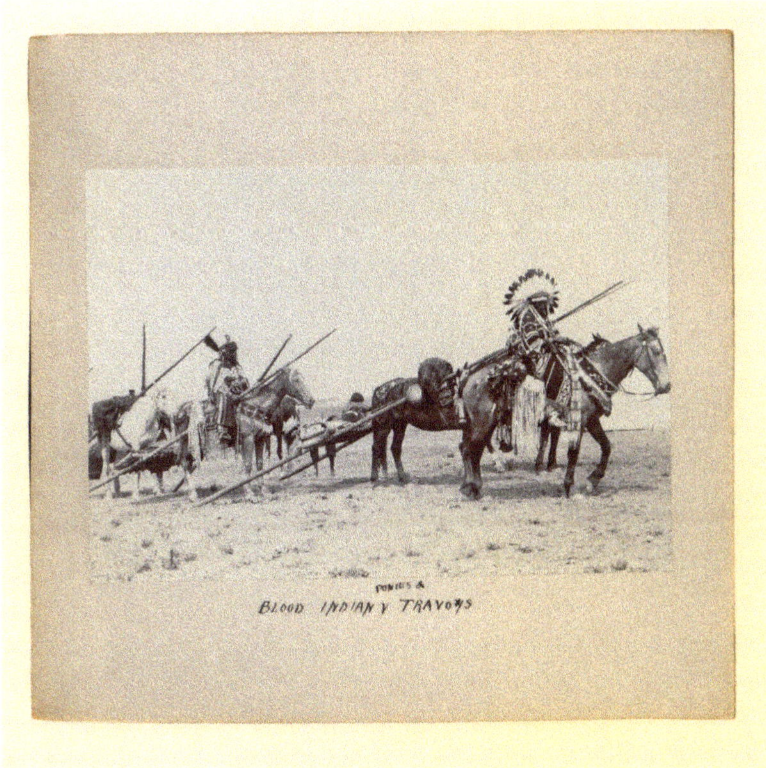

Fig. 4.7 'Indian (ponies &) travois'. Copyright Arthur Rafton-Canning, 1910 (copyright number 23390).

needs and lifestyle (see Fig.4.7). Instead these photographs, in the vein of contemporary Edward Sheriff Curtis, overlook the relevance of these items and their honed design in order to portray the Blood Indians and others as backward peoples, now out of place on the modernist plain. As a result, the work of Rafton-Canning can be perceived as exemplar objects of the tourist and curiosity photographic market that also perform as statements regarding the trajectory of western Canada and the place of certain peoples in it. The visual economy of these images and their circulation thus not only reflects the attempt to remove First Peoples people from the landscape; it also plays an active part in the process by promoting and normalising certain chains of thought.

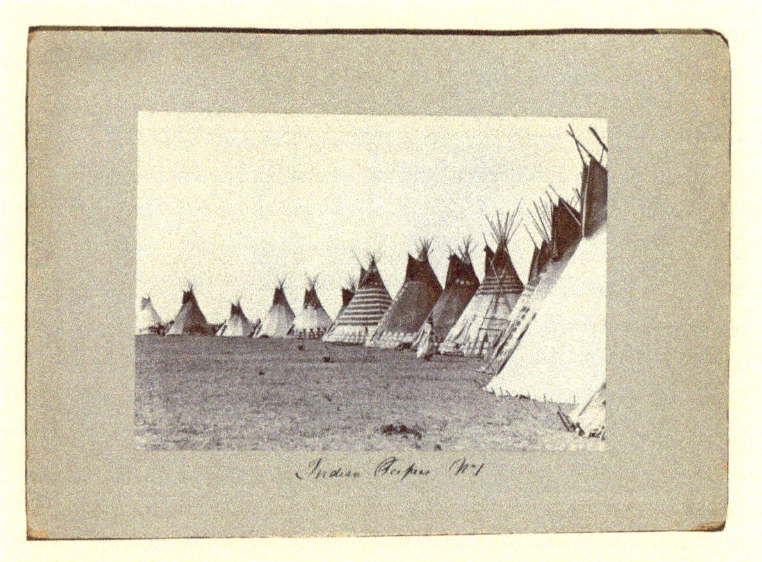

Fig. 4.8 'Indian Teepees, No.1'. Copyright Arthur Rafton-Canning, 1910 (copyright number 23387).

Looking north: photography in the Canadian Arctic

The photography of Geraldine Moodie has attracted much academic and popular attention in Canada and beyond – whether her photographs are seen as offering a distinctive perspective on the Arctic, a feminised photographic interpretation of a realm more often seen through a masculine lens or as exemplars in the art of photographic image-making.[26] The northern lands photographed by Geraldine Moodie and many other Arctic expedition members in the early twentieth century arguably portray the least incorporated part of the Canadian geographical sphere in this period. As a response to wider geopolitical pressures and the promise of mineral resources, the Canadian government co-ordinated a series of expeditions using mariners, the Royal Canadian Mounted Police and professional photographers. The mandate of the latter was to document various Arctic regions and peoples, and produce visual evidence of Canadian government control over the lands.[27]

There were various individuals involved with these expeditions in unofficial capacities. One of them was Geraldine Moodie, who arrived in the Arctic during a major state and geopolitical project. Between 1903 and 1905 her husband John Douglas Moodie (known as J. D.) was tasked with asserting and documenting Canadian control over the territories surrounding Fullerton Bay. This involved the erection of police barracks, the documentation of the local population, the extension of limited state functions (the keeping of medical records, enforcement of the law, etc.) and the use of photography in order to provide a record of the state's presence in the Arctic.

Photography played a central role in the project, providing a visual record of a Canadian presence in the Arctic and documenting the individuals already living there. In particular the camera was used to depict ill-health, malnutrition and general social conditions in such a way as to provide a rationale for the extension of Canadian welfare and support for these cultural groups, thereby extending the borders of the Canadian state.[28] Such an approach was not unique: indeed, it was part of a suite of similar projects conducted throughout the twentieth century to both project and protect the northern border of the nation state. Fledgling attempts to extend a policy of social provision north were to have disastrous consequences for many Inuit societies, and the repercussions are still being dealt with today.

The records of the official photographers involved in the Fullerton Bay expedition (such as Albert Low and J. D. Moodie) are held at Library and Archives Canada. However, Geraldine Moodie took photographs for her own professional use and copyrighted them in line with her professional practice. She had an established photographic career before arriving in the Arctic: already known for her photographs of the Cree Sundance Festival, near to the settlement of Battleford, Saskatchewan, Moodie was one of the first white settlers to be allowed to photograph this event. The images produced by J. D. Moodie and Albert Low, the ship's captain, are comparable to many other images produced in colonial anthropological expeditions undertaken in the later nineteenth and early twentieth centuries. Geraldine Moodie's images, by contrast, have more in common with a genre of intimate portraiture, appropriated by photographers from the portrait artists that preceded them, and with the practice of the photographic social study often seen in artistic photography.

Probably Moodie's most famous photograph from Fullerton Bay is a portrait of Kootucktuck, a local chief's daughter (see Fig.4.9). The photograph appears to have been intended as an art object rather than a mere illustration; even the version intended for copyright deposit exudes evidence of care and attention, being well developed and printed on high quality paper. The composition of a beautiful young woman adorned with a richly decorated costume is striking, accentuated by

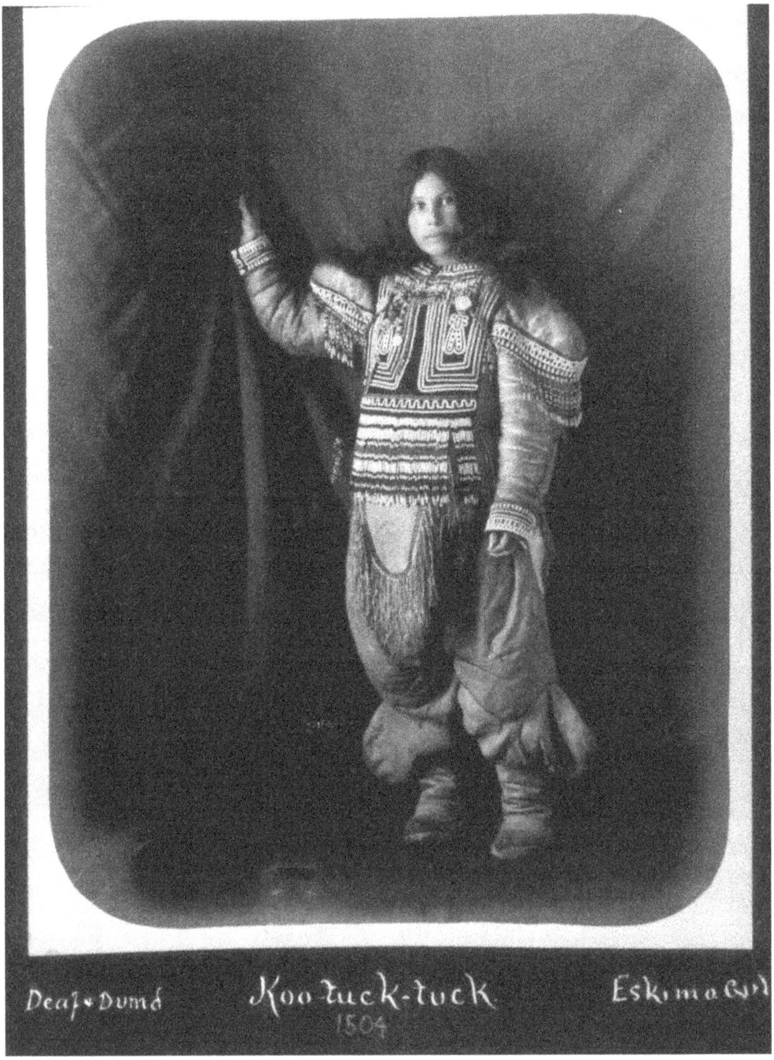

Fig. 4.9 'Kootucktuck'. Copyright Geraldine Moodie, 1905 (copyright number 16595). Courtesy of the British Museum.

the lighting and dark background. The enveloping silence of the scene (communicated by the voluminous black drapes) seems to mirror the silence of Kootucktuck's own experience as a deaf and mute woman. Moodie has positioned her subject to recreate a fleeting moment of intimacy – the closing of the curtain – that could have occurred as the sitter entered the studio, highlighting the grace of her subject and accentuating the erotic charge of the image.

The contrast between Geraldine Moodie's images and those of other photographers deploying an ethnographic or anthropological gaze is clear but not absolute. The depiction of indigenous groups as graceful and sensuous was practised by Western photographers across the globe. The anthropological image came to express Western values and stereotypes of the indigenous population in order to fulfil particular demands – in this context, for example, extending the control of the Dominion of Canadian over an Inuit group by communicating the inability of this group to care for themselves. However, Geraldine Moodie's work communicates different values and purpose, as reflected in her decision to copyright the photograph. Moodie's portraits present her Inuit sitters as strong characters with adult personalities, as reflected by Kootucktuck's sensuality, the maternal pose of Kookooleshook (Fig.4.10), or even the playful obstinance of Kiyoukayouk (Fig.4.11), whose distinctive material culture was set against a hostile and barren landscape. Like those taken by her husband, these images were composed to convey a sense of the exotic indigenous groups on Canada's frontier to those in urban Canada. Moodie's intended audience, however, were those interested in purchasing portraits and postcards rather than the readers of official reports.

The plainness and intimacy of the studio setting of these images is notable. J. D. Moodie and his colleagues felt their work was no place for a woman, so the studio was constructed as a space for Geraldine Moodie to live and work away from the actions of the official, masculine party. The provision of a separate space also allowed Moodie to form relationships with her photographic subjects different from the interactions of other expedition photographers. This is borne out by a portrait of Shenookshoo, a renowned whaler and elder in the Fullerton Bay area who had previously had a great deal of contact with Canadian whalers and explorers. Moodie's image of Shenookshoo is a striking piece of portrait photography: he stands in her studio in full hunting dress, harpoon in hand (Fig.4.12). From the confident and possessive way he holds the weapon, this is clearly Shenookshoo's own harpoon – a significant contrast to most portraits of indigenous sitters, encouraged to have their portraits taken with props which they seldom held and sat with comfortably.

In contrast to Kootucktuck, Shenookshoo is backed in white. This has the effect of accentuating his size and stature, as opposed to black which envelops and reduces the sitter. Here the aesthetic evokes the cold of the Arctic and accentuates the hunter's role within it. The stature of Shenookshoo and the gaze he returns to the camera also reflect his

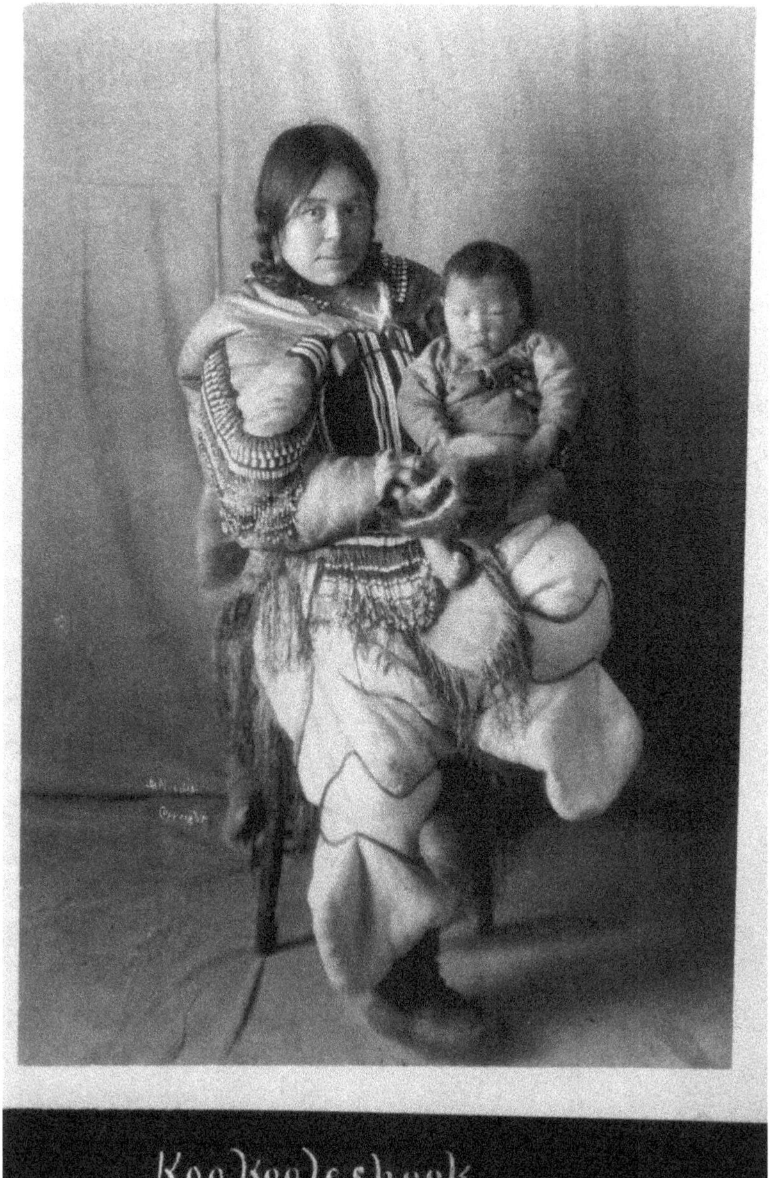

Fig. 4.10 'Kookooleshook'. Copyright Geraldine Moodie, 1905 (copyright number 16595). Courtesy of the British Museum.

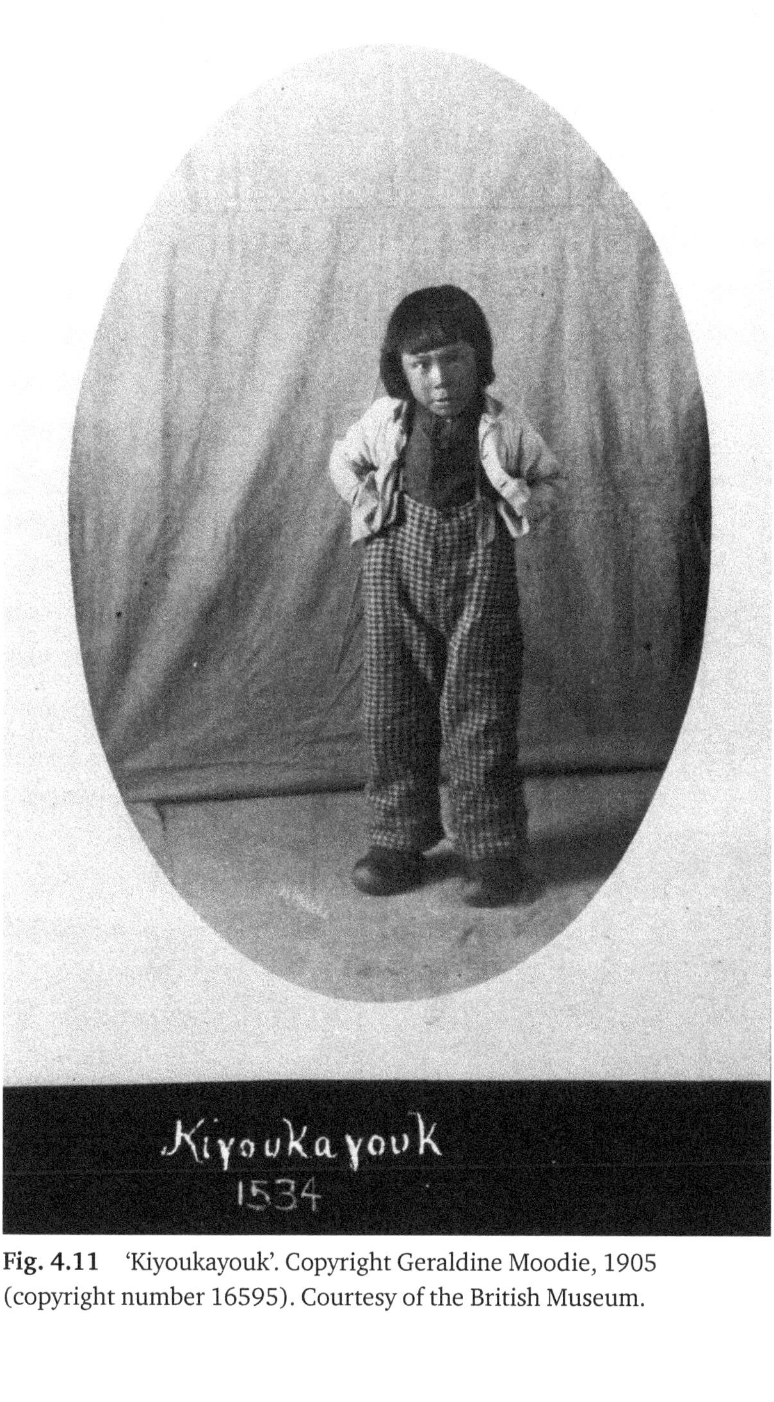

Fig. 4.11 'Kiyoukayouk'. Copyright Geraldine Moodie, 1905 (copyright number 16595). Courtesy of the British Museum.

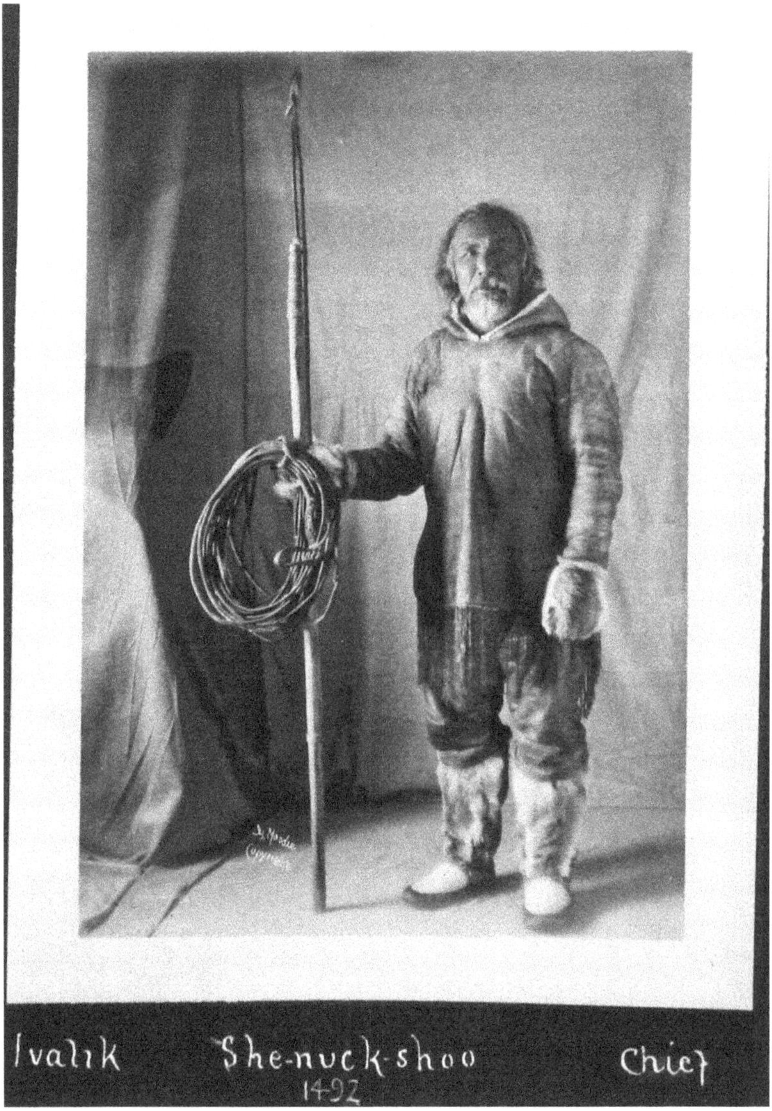

Fig. 4.12 'Shenookshoo'. Copyright Geraldine Moodie, 1905 (copyright number 16595). Courtesy of the British Museum.

authority, experience and knowledge. This contrasts to another image of Shenookshoo produced by Captain Albert Low while Moodie was in Fullerton Bay (Fig.4.13). Low's version presents 'Old Harry', the name he used in dealings with whalers around the Fullerton Bay area and by which Low might have known him on earlier visits to the Arctic as captain of a

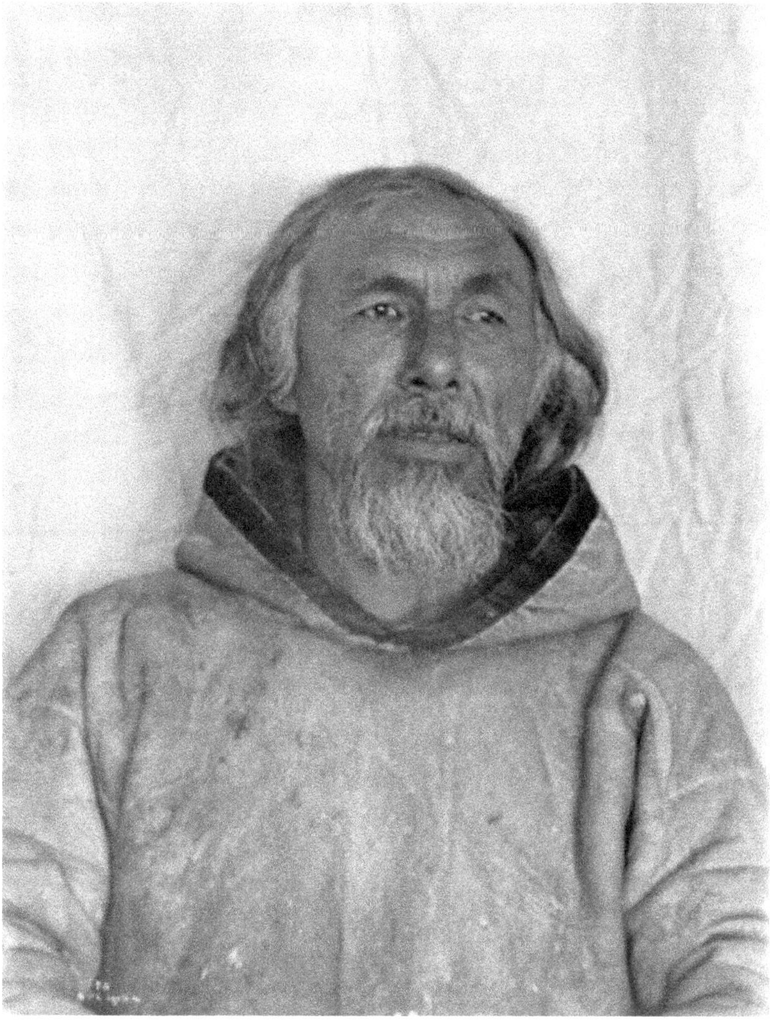

Fig. 4.13 'Old Harry', Albert Low, 1905 (no copyright details). Courtesy of Library and Archives Canada.

whaling schooner. The image immediately carries a different meaning, reinforced by the perspective: 'Old Harry' is depicted in a seated, head-focused portrait, as opposed to the full body one produced by Moodie. This compositional format was used on all but a few occasions by Low, reflecting the way in which images appeared in the reports of the expedition. Notably Low produced one full-body image during this trip: that of his Inuit wife 'Shoofly' (a name given to her by Low and his crew rather than her real Inuit name).

The importance of the studio to the creation of Moodie's work, both as a space where she could control variables and, possibly, build relationships with sitters, is underlined by later copyrights of Moodie's. The two photographs seen in Figs 4.14 and 4.15, copyrighted in 1907, are the only two Arctic photographs taken outside the studio that are copyrighted by Moodie. The depiction of the barracks suggests the importance of this space in the remote landscape. It reminds the viewer that Geraldine Moodie was present in the Arctic as part of an attempt to extend the control of the state – not just to Arctic spaces, but to the very bodies of the Inuit Moodie was photographing.[29]

The women photographed in Fig.4.14 show Moodie's continued interest in Inuit women, their material culture and homes. Notably, however, the images are also of lesser quality and have more of a distanciated gaze than the studio shots. The more distanced view in Fig.4.14 further underscores the importance of the studio as a space of practice for Moodie. This image has a different feel to those created in the

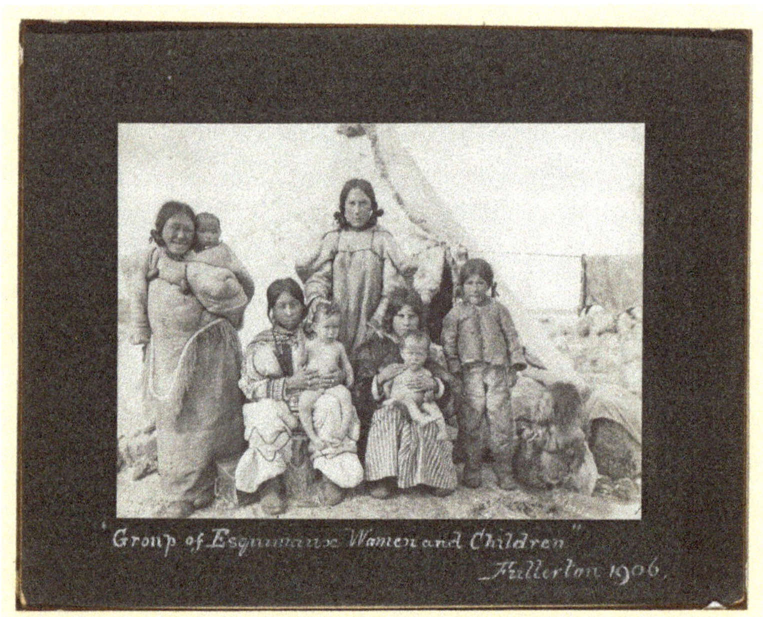

Fig. 4.14 'Group of Esquimaux women and children Fullerton'. Copyright Geraldine Moodie, 1907 (copyright number 18546).

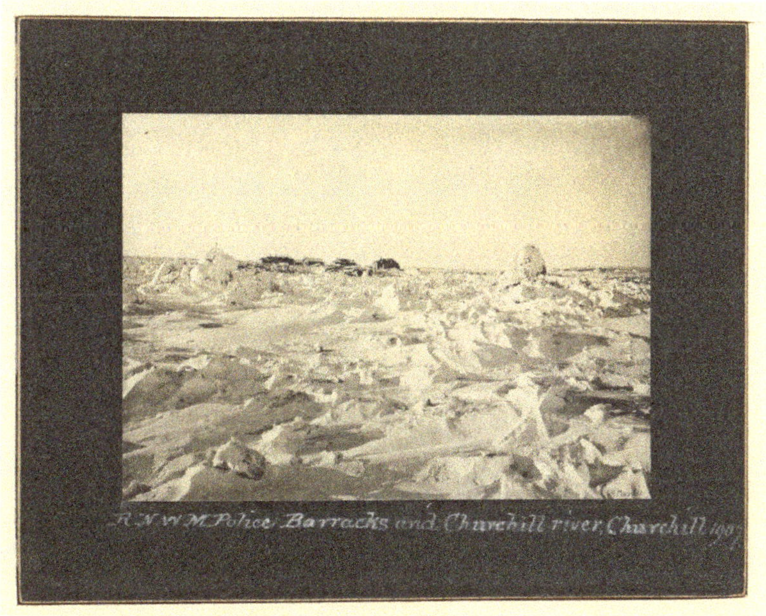

Fig. 4.15 'RNWMP Barracks and Churchill River'. Copyright Geraldine Moodie, 1907 (copyright number 18547).

studio; where these were carefully staged and provide insights into the sitters, the image produced outside of the studio feels as if it was hastily arranged – almost grabbed. It is an attempt to record a scene quickly, paying little attention to individual agency and difference. That the studio portraits operate differently suggests this space allowed Moodie to build a rapport with her sitters. It is also likely that this relationship, the dialogue and the confidence it inspired allowed the sitters to contribute to the formulation of the image – a situation strongly suggested by the characterful portrait of Kiyoukayouk and hinted at in portraits such as that of Shenookshoo.

Picking up the discussion of Shenookshoo, the different images show how the biography of the photographer affects the composition of the image. Geraldine Moodie's perspective came from the qualitatively different interactions she had with her subject, both by virtue of being in Fullerton Bay for different reasons than the official photographers and by her status as a woman. These interactions were further influenced by the different space in which the photographs were produced. This is also illustrated by the different titles given to the individual in the portrait, Shenookshoo and 'Old Harry'.

Importantly, each portrait also has a specific purpose informed by the photographers' biographies. Low's image is constructed to convey the character of the head of the community while focusing on his age. This is significant to the broader project of the expedition, as other photographs of the male members of the community taken by Low tended to emphasise their ill-health. That is not to say that Moodie's images are any less problematic: while they may provide an appealing contrast, they are nonetheless partial, designed to convey cultural exoticism and appeal to a consumer market in Canada. As such, these images illustrate the different ways in which photographers approached the same communities. They serve to highlight the plurality of visions about these communities and their individual members that would subsequently circulate in urban Canada.

* * *

This chapter has illustrated some of the complex dynamics which affected the representation of First Peoples groups – not only between 1895 and 1924, but also over a longer and continuing period. The influence of factors such as the increasing ubiquity of the camera, the demands of the market, the biographies of the photographer and the requirements of specific genres, including portraiture and anthropological photography, is evident in many photographs within the Colonial Copyright Collection. In addition these images contain traces of profound geographical difference: in the spaces in which an image was produced, the events playing out in that place and the agency of the photographer and subject. The images discussed in this chapter need to be seen in the context of wider photographic tropes regarding the depiction of First Peoples groups or of indigenous peoples in other colonial spheres. Yet engaging with the specific geographies underpinning the production of the image can produce deeper readings. The relationships involved in the production of these images also vary from place to place, highlighting the diversity of interactions between colonists and native peoples.

Canada between 1895 and 1924 was a place of change, in which individuals and images were increasingly mobile and geographies were being continually shaped and remoulded. The Colonial Copyright Collection, offering up a collage of partial views, provides evidence of how these processes were being perceived and consumed by individuals across the nation, while also presenting glimpses of how they were affecting many communities and individuals too. Since this time, and since the images were deposited for copyright, Canada has continued to change. This has not diminished the significance of the images, but rather suggests new contexts in which they can now be read and used.

These discussions have also highlighted that the interaction with, and depiction of, First Peoples groups across Canada was never undertaken in isolation of broader happenings in the country's development. Sporting events, conflict, settlement and many other issues affected how First Peoples groups interacted with Canada and how Canadians viewed them in return. With this in mind, this chapter is not the only location where the depiction of the First Peoples is discussed. Chapter 5 turns its attention to the photographing of the 'Last Best West', and the images discussed in the present chapter speak very strongly to the complex photographic perspectives analysed in the coming pages. Chapter 6 too pays attention to how the image of First Peoples was drawn into the First World War. In both these chapters, then, the complexity of Canadian society, its visual economy and the record of the Colonial Copyright Collection are clearly apparent.

5
A collection of people: migration, settlement and frontiers

People drive the Colonial Copyright Collection: photographers submitted to it, consumers bought the photographs and people are photographic subjects. People were also the driving agent of change and development in Canada during the late nineteenth and early twentieth centuries, a period that saw profound population growth and demographic shift across Canada. Chapters 1 to 4 of this book have touched upon this change showing some of the sites in which it acted (cities), the technologies that facilitated people's movement (railways and postcards) and some of the consequences of this change (such as increased competition for land and the marginalisation of First Peoples groups).

In this chapter an emphasis is placed more squarely on the demographic development that Canada went through. We have already seen how the technologies that drove this change both fascinated and profited photographers, as the railways and postcard have done, but it is also clear from the Colonial Copyright Collection that the demographic change associated with filling in some of Canada's last uncolonised spaces was also a fascination to Canada's many photographers. During the timespan of the collection camera workers document the development of new towns, the arrival of new populations and the work people set about, as well as casting an anthropological eye on migrant communities.

'Migrant' is a word that needs to be approached carefully in this chapter, lest it mask the complexity of the flows of people that characterised Canada's western development – and, for that matter, the development of Canada itself. All colonial settlers in the west are considered to be migrants, even those from Anglophone and Francophone families long-settled in Canada's east and far west. The Métis of the Red River settlement and mobile First Peoples groups could also be considered to be migrants, as well as being long-established groups of people whose needs and lifestyles were at odds with – and were displaced by – the coming wave of colonial settlement in Canada's west, as shall be shown later in the narrative.

Crucially, those Anglophone and Francophone settlers who would take to western settlement laid claim to particular types of colonial identity, one of the dominant colonial power (that of those settlers nominally understood to be of 'British' heritage) and one of Francophone settlers, the latter descended (directly or symbolically) from the first Europeans to settle what is now known as Canada. Both of these groups, despite being migrants themselves, often had strongly held and conservative views of how the west should develop. As a result, those newest Canadians – a diverse group including, to name but a few, Eastern Europeans, Northern Europeans, Jews, minority Christian groups and even African Americans, and who British and French Canadians termed 'migrants' – were often expected to conform to expectations or be regarded as 'other'.

Within this chapter the term 'migrant' is therefore a slippery one, being applied to different groups in a variety of contexts but bound by their presence in a particular space. It is important to be mindful of this, and of the differences between groups, as the chapter progresses because the people caught up in this description were aware of their cultural distinctiveness too – a situation that fascinated Canadian photographers whether they were established, itinerant or newly arrived migrants.

This photographic work is conducted in one Canadian space above all others, 'The Last Best West', which underwent dramatic development in the wake of the completion of the Canadian Pacific Railway.[1] In its early section the chapter looks at who was moving in Canada, what drove this new wave of migration and the photographic impulse that went with it, adding further depth to the discussion of the railway in Chapter 3. At its heart this section considers how the resulting communities reshaped the landscape of the west and the photographic visual economy that resulted from this diversification and social mixing. This movement was often at the expense of those who already lived in Canada's west, an inevitable consequence caused by the 'filling in' of 'The Last Best West', a land that was actually never empty. Finally the chapter considers the 'Canadianness' of these individuals and groups, questioning whether what we see in some parts of the collection is a representation of 'other' Canadians or a developing visual representation of a multicultural Canadian west.

Drivers of 'The Last Best West'

'Pioneer' is a word that comes up a few times in the list of titles for the Colonial Copyright Collection. As a title for photographs marking the first

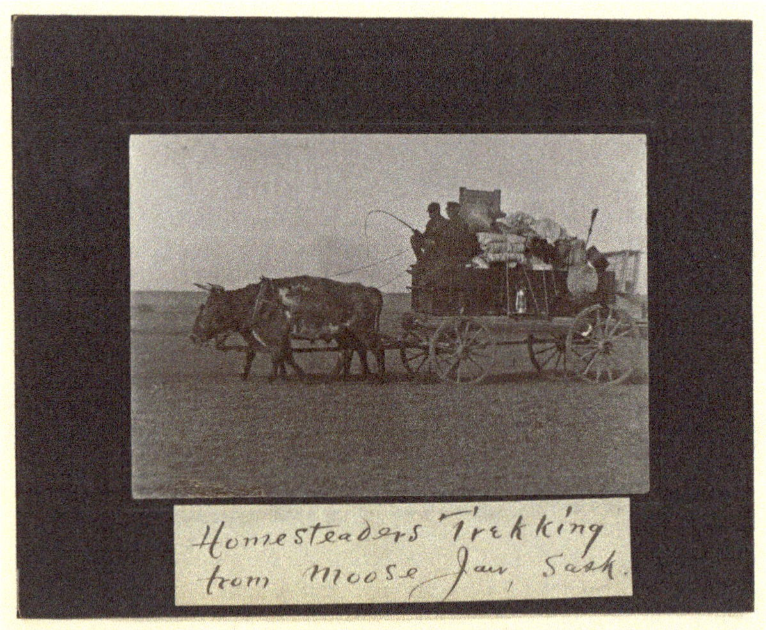

Fig. 5.1 'Homesteaders Trekking From Moose Jaw, Saskatchewan'. Copyright Lewis Rice, 1909 (copyright number 20797).

days of settlements or commemorating foundations some years down the line it is an evocative and powerful word attributed to individuals and groups photographed in Canada's west and northwest. Another word that jumps out of the collection is 'homesteader' – and indeed one of the first images from the collection I ever saw is here reproduced as Fig.5.1, part of a series on the Moose Jaw homestead rush. This series of photographs, copyrighted by Lewis Rice in 1909, captures a moment in Canada's life that is, in a globalised popular narrative, more often thought of as being an element in the development of the American prairies (see Figs 5.1–5.3). It shows the family unit packing up everything and heading off for the promise of land in the west, in the manner of Tom Cruise and Nicole Kidman in *Far and Away*.

And indeed this kind of migration was predominantly part of the American story for much of the nineteenth century, to Canada's misfortune and underpopulation. This began to change in the late 1890s, so the Moose Jaw homesteaders photograph represents a later record of this general trend. The homesteaders captured in these photographs

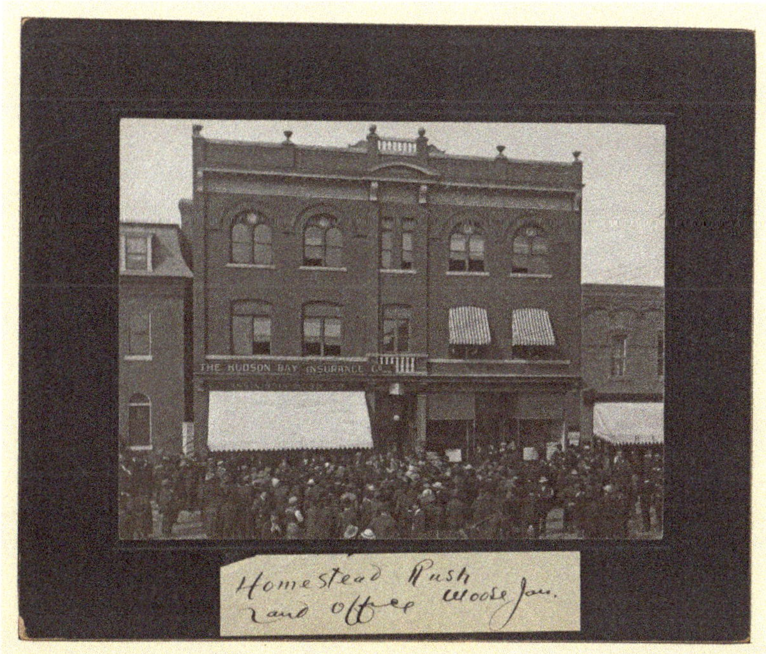

Fig. 5.2 'Land Office, Moosejaw, Saskatchewan'. Copyright Lewis Rice, 1909 (copyright number 20795).

are the result of the administrative and technological opening up of Canada's west and a shift in the prevailing attitude of migrants towards the United States. By the late nineteenth century there was a developing impression that the lands of the American west were filling up and that the best opportunities had gone – an impression that coincided with the new marketing techniques applied by Clifford Sifton during his tenure as head at Canada's Department for the Interior under the Liberal government of 1896 onwards.[2]

In short, then, the collection serendipitously starts being developed right at the start of Canada's migration boom. From 1896 onwards total numbers of migrants rose year on year, reaching seven million people by 1907 and continuing to rise until the First World War restricted movement and therefore numbers. Canada's demographic trends were shifting profoundly during this period; by 1911 almost 50 per cent of people lived in urban areas across Canada, with boom cities such as Winnipeg proving to be major sites of settlement and economic drivers of the Canadian west.[3] The effect of this change can be seen in the photographs of the Colonial Copyright Collection, as towns celebrate their founding, population

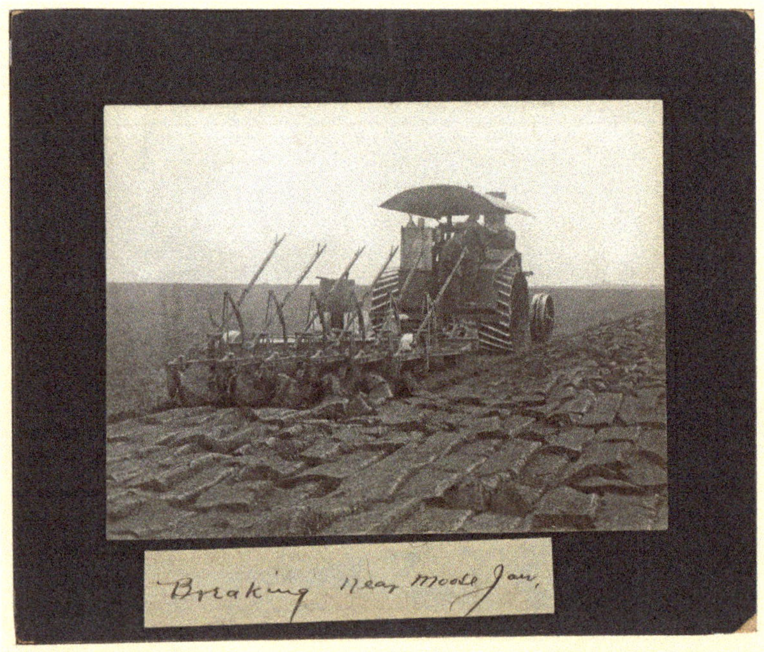

Fig. 5.3 'Breaking near Moosejaw, Saskatchewan'. Copyright Lewis Rice, 1909 (copyright number 20796).

increase and the development of new infrastructure while also providing markets and sites of operation for photographers and photographic businesses.

Photographs in the collection of areas such as Medicine Hat are illustrative of some of the many urban areas that underwent rapid development during this period. They also show the civic pride that developed in its turn, a level of care and attention that belies the haste of foundation and speed of growth. Drawing from this a number of photographers and photographic companies inhabited an economic niche by travelling around and producing photographs of these new areas. Of particular note is the photography of the Winnipeg Photo. Co., who went around various new settlements in western Canada photographing major points of infrastructure, such as post offices and railway stations. These photographs were then put together in montages and placed on ornamental backings, as Figs 5.4–5.6 show, providing a further example of the pride and performance of civic identity that went with these spaces.

Photographs such as those of the Winnipeg Photo. Co., however, like many of those in the T. Eaton photobook discussed in Chapter 2, are

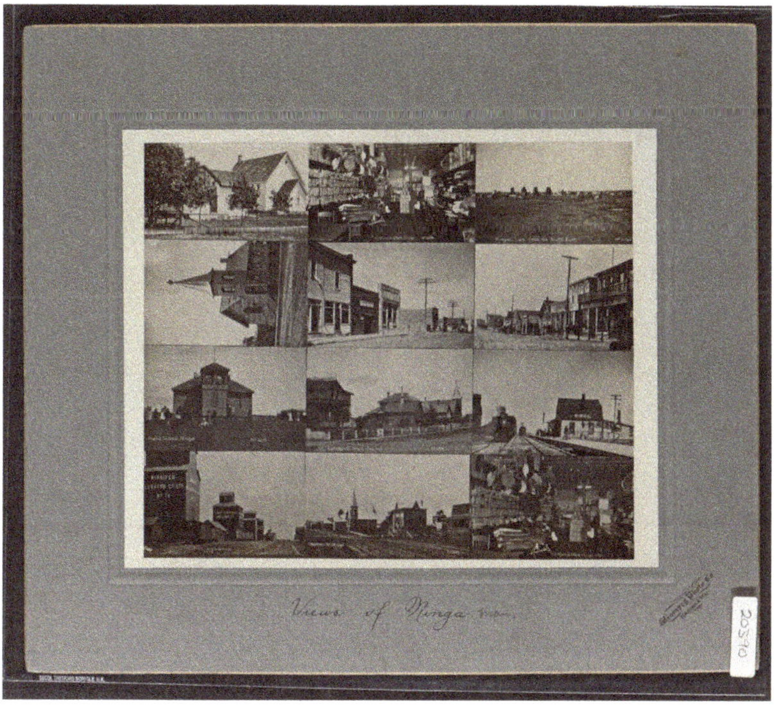

Fig. 5.4 'Views of Ninga, Manitoba'. Copyright Winnipeg Photo. Co., 1909 (copyright number 20390).

noticeably devoid of human life. They are ornaments adorning the rapid expansion of Canada's west, constructed to show the beauty held in their rapid construction. The real pride, however, can be seen in photographs of those settling Canada, the pioneers mentioned above and illustrated in work by Lewis Rice (Figs 5.2 and 5.3). Across the collection we have messier photographs, with unruly groups, mud, dirt and lived-in buildings filling the frame. There is, then, a disjuncture between the occupied frontier and the ornamental one; the former, while attempting to create a new order and liveability, is also human and untidy. This separation is common in the photography of urban spaces, but it is often symptomatic of deeper disjunctures. On the Canadian frontier this performative veneer of pleasing aesthetics not only masks a messier polity, but also a group of people from all over the world, rapidly thrown together, who had to learn to get along, as will be shown in the conclusion of this chapter.

Through the photographs of pioneers and rapid urban expansion we can thus begin to perceive a visual record of how the aims of the Canadian government began to be achieved in the Sifton years. Canada's

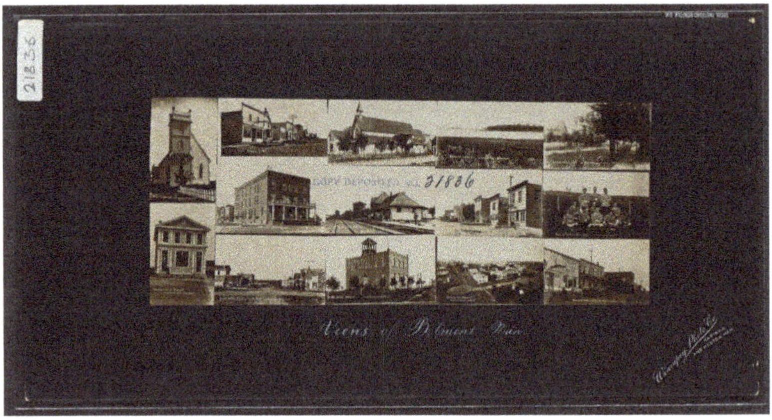

Fig. 5.5 'Views of Belmont, Manitoba'. Copyright Winnipeg Photo. Co., 1909 (copyright number 21836).

west was indeed filling up. This is not to say that previous Confederate governments had been disinterested in encouraging migrants; indeed MacDonald's government made the Canadian-ising of the west a priority. Instead the shift in fortune for the Liberal government illustrates how, in the early twentieth century, the prevailing socioeconomic currents that influenced migrants shifted in favour of Canada. Besides the changing opinion of the possibilities to be found in the United States, some of the other reasons for this shift can be found in the previous chapters of this book. It is important, therefore, to look at not only who came, but also why.

Canada's frontiers were always different from those of its neighbour, the United States. Creating a nation out of the bounds of colonial exploration and entrepreneurship meant that Canada's development post-confederation was about filling in spaces in between places – often with a desire to fulfil this goal before its geopolitically expansive neighbour could fill these gaps in itself. Technology was always a fundamental tool for the knitting together of Canada's spaces; telegraphs, railways, postal networks and the camera itself were all tools which facilitated this process. During the course of this book technology's potential benefits and perils have been the subject and driver of various chapters. Here, once again, we must turn our attention to the role of technological modernity in Canada's dramatic spatial and demographic changes.

The discussion of the railway in Chapter 3 illustrated its importance to the development of Canada and the place it held in the imaginative psyche during the time in which the Colonial Copyright Collection was developed. As such, its significance to the development of 'The Last Best

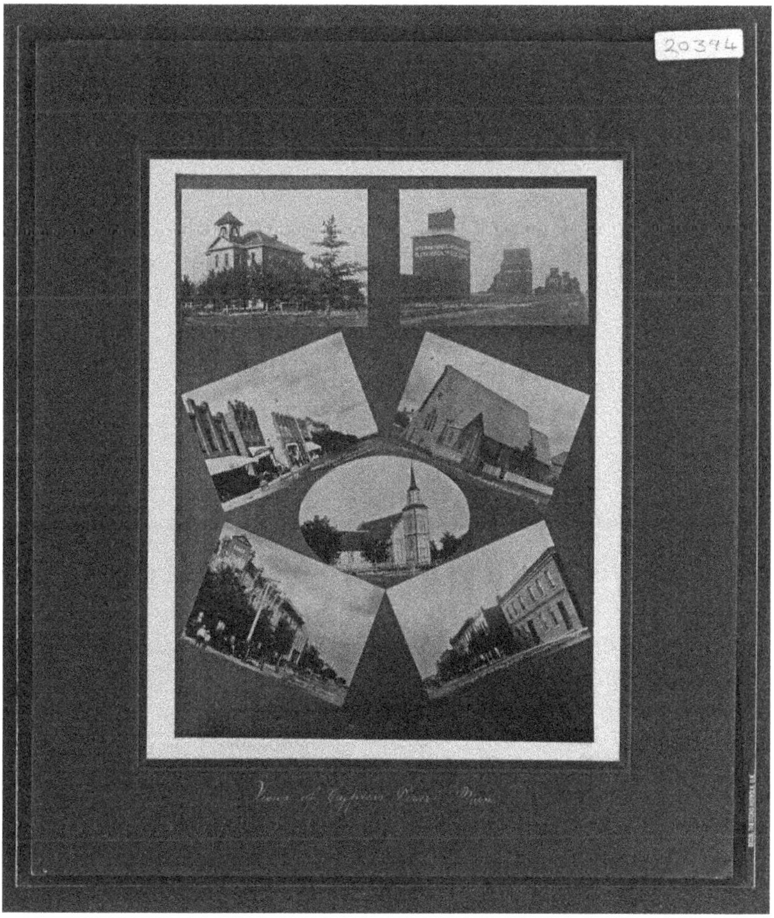

Fig. 5.6 'Views of Cypress River, Manitoba'. Copyright Winnipeg Photo. Co., 1909 (copyright number 20394).

West' also needs reiterating here. In Eagle's *The Canadian Pacific Railway and the Development of Western Canada*, the role of the railway not just as a transporter of migrants but also as an owner, administrator, renter and seller of land is made clear.[4] As can be seen through the analysis of the photography of Arthur Rafton-Canning in Chapters 3 and 4, the railway was not just a tool for opening up spaces, but also for claiming them as part of this Canadian national project as well.

The theme of taming the landscape is also worth considering again with regard to another element of the photographic documentation of the west's settlement. As Knowles has pointed out, the impact of technological innovation was felt not just in terms of getting people out to the west; it was also significant in order to allow the reforming of the west into an agricultural landscape.[5] Innovations in agricultural equipment had a profound impact on the west, as tools such as tractors opened up the possibility of profitably farming large areas, using a much smaller body of people to work the land. Photographs in the collection are a testament to this, showing both these tools at work and the fruits of their produce. They are smart and advertorial, while the tone is positive and enthusiastic for the potential of the union of technology and land. It is notable too that the tractor and other heavy farm machinery, such as that in Fig.5.3, are some of the most photographed technological subjects in the collection.

However, the potential of this technology is inherently limited by capital, as farm equipment and the amount of land required to make it technically viable are financially expensive. This would mean that the ability to purchase and use this equipment in the west was limited to persons already established in Canada or, possibly, across the border in America.[6] To put it another way, the technology was not easily available to many making the journey from Europe, least of all those coming to Canada on Sifton's subsidised packages.[7] What we begin to see, therefore, in the prim settlements, technologically modern farms and small-town parks photographed and deposited in the Colonial Copyright Collection is a very Anglo-Canadian version of 'The Last Best West'.

In the mind's eye of many in the twenty-first century it is possible that the sort of landscape, lifestyle and culture being opened up by all this technology was something akin to the portrait in Albert Edward Brown's 'Topping a Bad One' (Fig.5.7). This photograph evokes Canada's 'Last Best West' and articulates it as a Canadian western frontier, with the same plains, ranches, cowboys and heroic drama that feature in the popular imagination of the American frontier. Both the American and Canadian west are visually articulated through the depiction of the big horizons captured in this photograph, but socially the two spaces are markedly different. The way Canadian settlement in the west was mediated by its engines of social change – in that companies, railways and government played an active role in influencing who came and where – distinguishes it from the American context. Similar drivers were in play in this context too, but the forces behind them, such as American politics of independence and an emphasis on entrepreneurial economics, to name but two examples, were different. The end result would therefore never be exactly the same as in the Canadian context. As a result, while Canada's urban development and the settlement of new people increased year on year, these were individuals marked by the agency of Anglophone Liberal

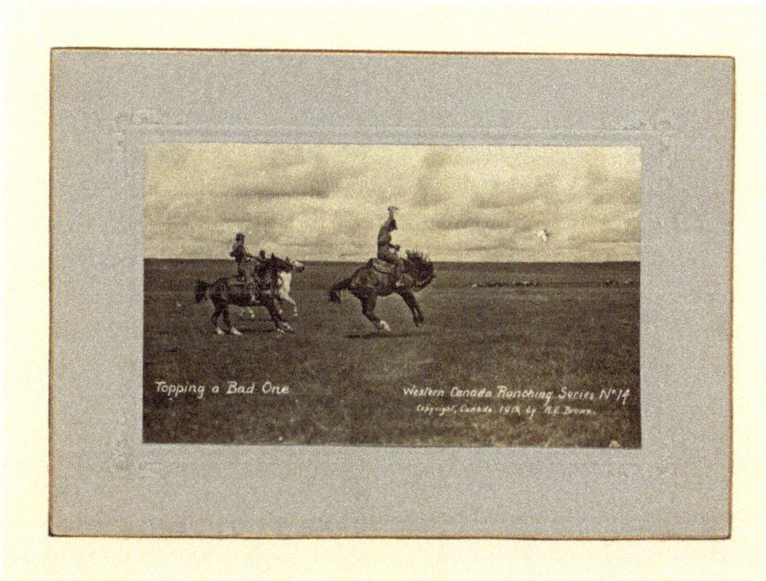

Fig. 5.7 'Topping a Bad One'. Copyright Albert Edward Brown, 1912 (copyright number 25366).

politics, the Canadian Pacific Railway, mechanised farm technology and many other factors.

The story conveyed by the photographs analysed so far is perhaps one that would be recognised by many with a grounding in Canadian history. In this respect, it is significant that an element of Canada's photographers did articulate their contemporary surroundings in a way that would be expected by viewers today. However, this is far from the whole story. Western Canada did not undergo a profound spatial, technological and demographic change without its sociocultural balance also shifting. All recent writing about the development of the west is at pains to illustrate the profound changes brought by the addition of American, British and European migrants to Canada in large numbers.[8]

This too did not go unnoticed by photographers, particularly with regard to those migrants who did not fit in with the Anglo-Canadian identity many were keen to establish and maintain. It is therefore important to understand how the photographer's lens was trained on those 'other' Canadians, whose differences in appearance, culture and religion framed them on the margins of Canadian society, as well as those they displaced. In doing so we are reminded that the 'filling' up of western Canada was not a benign process, but one defined by displacement, conflict and competition.

Canadians contesting the frontier

Miriam Elstor's photographs of Ruthenians settled in Alberta are a fascinating insight into both the ethnic and cultural diversity of the Canadian west and how Canadians sought to understand this new mix of people. Ruthenians were one of the many Eastern European groups who migrated to Canada in the late nineteenth and early twentieth centuries. The reasons for their leaving were diverse. In 1895 Dr. Josef Oleskow wrote to the Canadian Department of the Interior, stating that, 'a great number of Galician agriculturists of Ruthenian (Slavic) nationality desire to quit their native country, due to over-population, subdivision of land holdings, heavy taxation, and unfavourable political conditions'.[9] Since the 1990s there has been a large amount of writing about the ethnic diversity of migrants from Austria, the Ukraine and other parts of Eastern Europe who were part of a large-scale migration that began in the 1890s, focusing on their agency in and effect on the development of twentieth-century Canada.[10]

Elstor's photographs are part of a larger range of work in the Colonial Copyright Collection where photographers focus on migrants in and around their communities. The photographs Elstor copyrighted in 1911 are taken in and around Mundare, a small settlement in central Alberta some 70 km from Edmonton (see for example Fig.5.8). There are only a handful of photographs in total and they focus on the look, material culture and lifestyle of the Ruthenians who settled in the area. Elstor's work does not appear anywhere else nor at any other time in the collection, but it is striking how similar her emphasis on family and material culture is to the work of Geraldine Moodie, discussed in Chapter 4. Like Moodie, Elstor's photographs focus on the details of people's lives and cultures in order to draw out the material culture and intimate views of individual lives.

It is noticeable that Elstor's photographs are all taken *in situ*. There are no studio shots, and therefore there is not the strong sense of people entering a space unique within the area in order to be photographed (compared to Moodie's personal studio in the Arctic during this time when Canadian interaction with the north was often state-driven and intensely masculine). Instead Elstor's photographs seem to be taking advantage of the potential of the rapidly improving camera technologies of the 1910s and onwards. Elstor has taken the camera onto the streets of Mundare and out to the homes of people beyond the settlement. However, despite the difficulties of taking portraits in a non-studio environment, Elstor's photographs are clear and well composed.

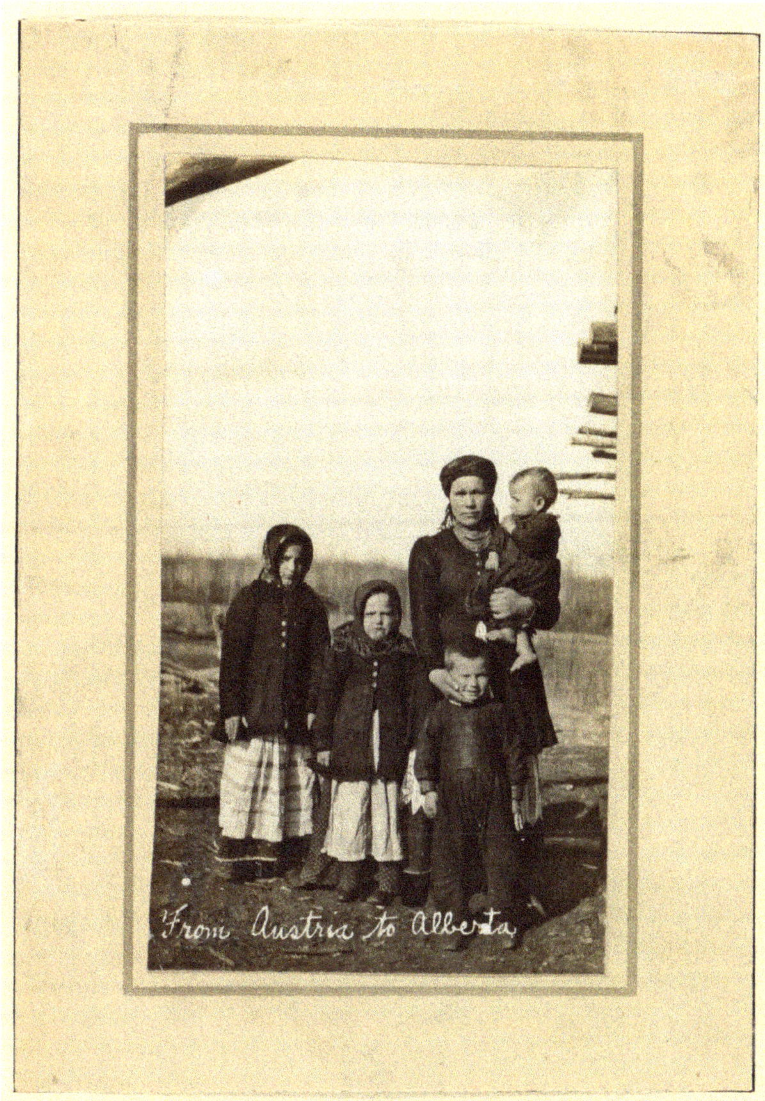

Fig. 5.8 'From Austria to Alberta'. Copyright Miriam Elstor, 1911 (copyright number 23665).

Family, dress and home are the focus of Elstor's photographs. As with Moodie's images of Fullerton Bay's Inuit community, the difference and 'otherness' of the group is apparent, illustrated by Elstor's fascination with Ruthenian dress and structures for the caring of children. In 'Ruthenian Woman in Best Attire' (Fig.5.9) Elstor's fascination with the dress is apparent by her positioning of the subject in a rather simplistic, illustrative pose. Indeed the female subject's turned face is reminiscent of many expressions of 'are you done yet?' that have been expressed to cameras over the years. Elstor's photograph of the child in a roof slung cot also displays this fascination with domestic life, as evidenced by the fact that the cot is occupied, possibly at Elstor's request (Fig.5.10).

However, in focusing on these differences and on the 'otherness' of the photographed subjects these photographs also illustrate a parallel cultural familiarity and Elstor's awareness of this. Family, home and dress are as important to these new Canadians as to those Anglo-Canadians who would see themselves as the more dominant social group. She also emphasises the role of these new Canadians as functioning and integral parts of the farming communities that will underpin a settled western Canada. A photograph entitled 'Breaking the Sod' and another called 'Street Scene, Mundare' (Fig.5.11) add depth to a series of photographs that pay more attention to the home life of Ruthenians. They take the focus away from a potentially isolated home life and show settlers working the land, illustrating the importance of family in this and the Ruthenians' dynamic use of the land, as well as being part of the small urban community on their doorstep.

The degree to which Elstor's photographs were posed or constructed in dialogue with her subjects is unknown. As a result, we cannot be sure how much of the actual life of these Ruthenians we are seeing in these portraits or if they are simply an imagined version of them. However, it is worth noting that in either situation our conclusion as a critical viewer would be the same; within these frames we perceive the differences and similarities that migrant groups brought to Canada. They were, unmistakably, visually and culturally 'other', with practices and habits distinct from Canadians around them. Yet they also had many practices and ideals similar to the milieux of established Canadians, of which they were now part. Farming the land was their aim and family was important, while home and appearance were things to be appreciated. In short, however they were composed, we can see in Elstor's photographs the foundation of a group who would become a fundamental part of western Canada, and of Canada as a whole.[11]

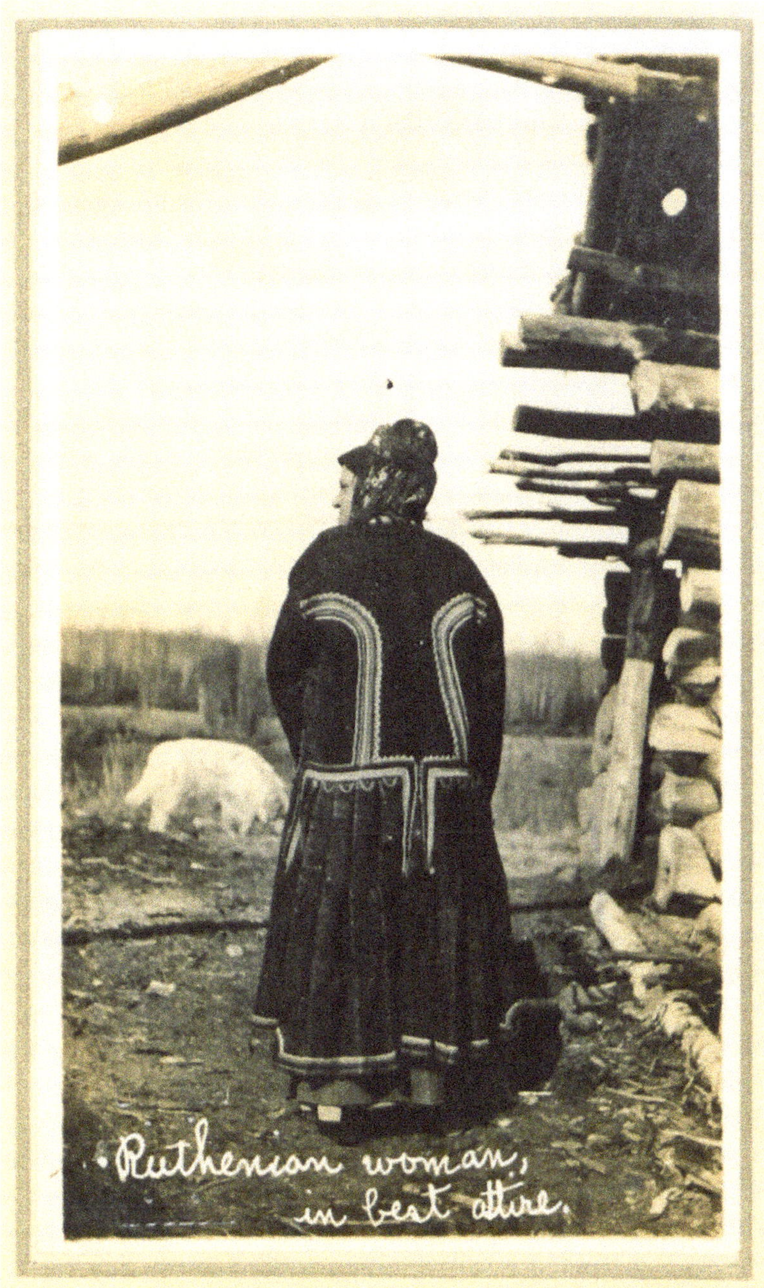

Fig. 5.9 'Ruthenian Woman in Best Attire'. Copyright Miriam Elstor, 1911 (copyright number 23691).

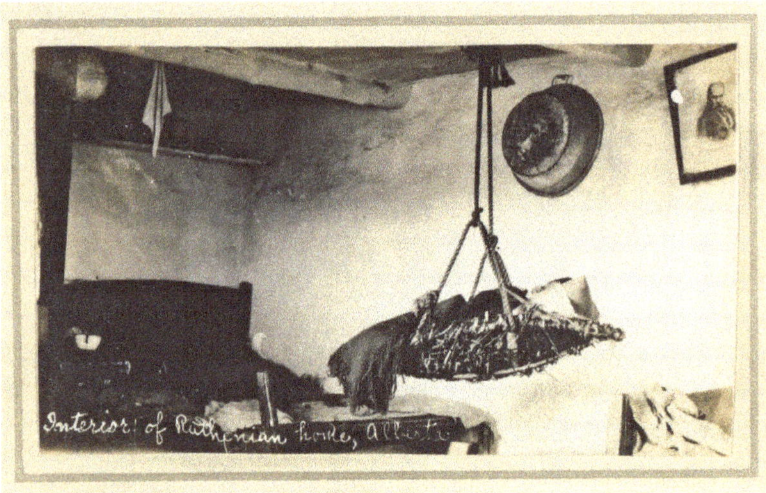

Fig. 5.10 'Interior of a Ruthenian Home'. Copyright Miriam Elstor, 1911 (copyright number 23666).

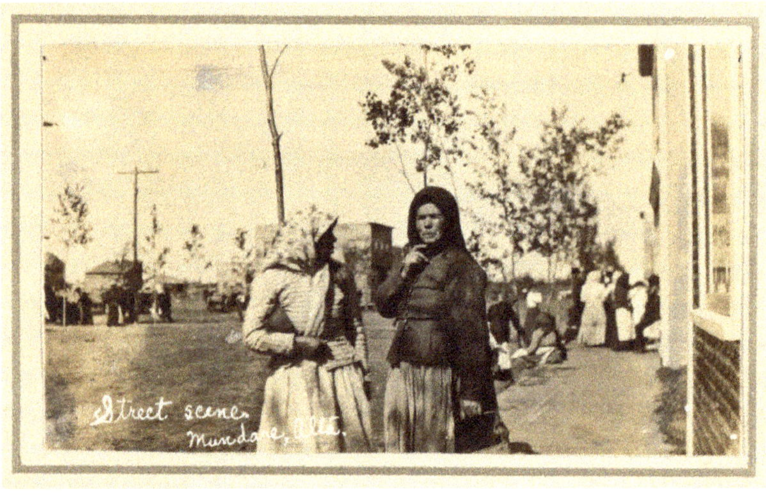

Fig. 5.11 'Street Scene, Mundare'. Copyright Miriam Elstor, 1911 (copyright number 23667).

Other groups of migrants are also photographed fitting into and building their place within Canada, as Elstor's Ruthenians are doing here. Of particular note are the two photographs of the construction of a Mormon temple at Cardston in 1917 (Figs 5.12 and 5.13). As Knowles has noted, the Mormon settlement that was founded in 1887 was successful and well regarded, not least because of the knowledge of irrigation that was brought with the community.[12] The two photographs in the Colonial Copyright Collection taken by Walter Herman Best in 1917, 30 years after the initial Mormon settlement in southern Alberta, represent a moment of huge significance. Mormon life revolves around the temple and its completion, in such a short amount of time after the initial migration, illustrates the success of the group and how it has established itself within the Canadian landscape. It is the capping, or 'topping-off' in building parlance, not just of a religious space and monument, but also of a migration.

It would be easy to view these photographs in isolation and assume that the cultural diversity and hybridisation of western Canada was therefore unproblematic. However, there were many lenses turned on migrant communities within Canada. Race, religious difference and

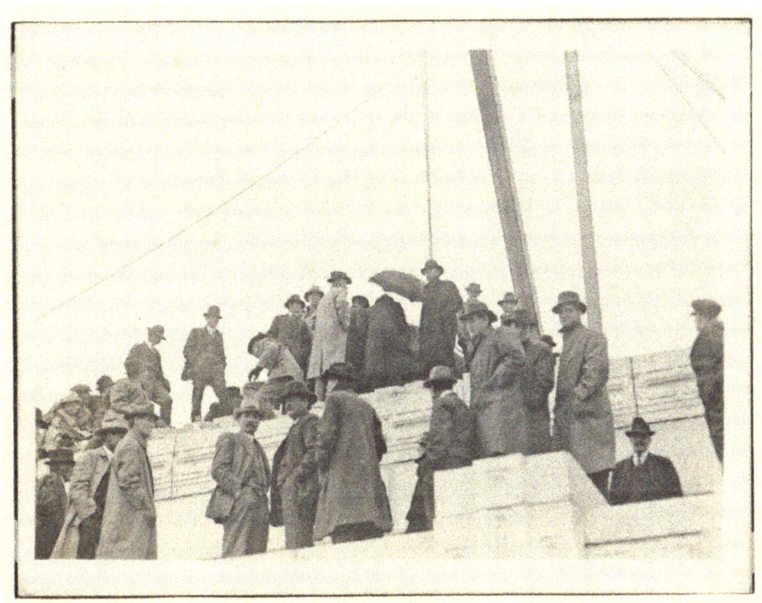

Fig. 5.12 'Laying the Last Stone at the Mormon Temple, Cardston [1]'. Copyright W. H. Best, 1917 (copyright number 33442).

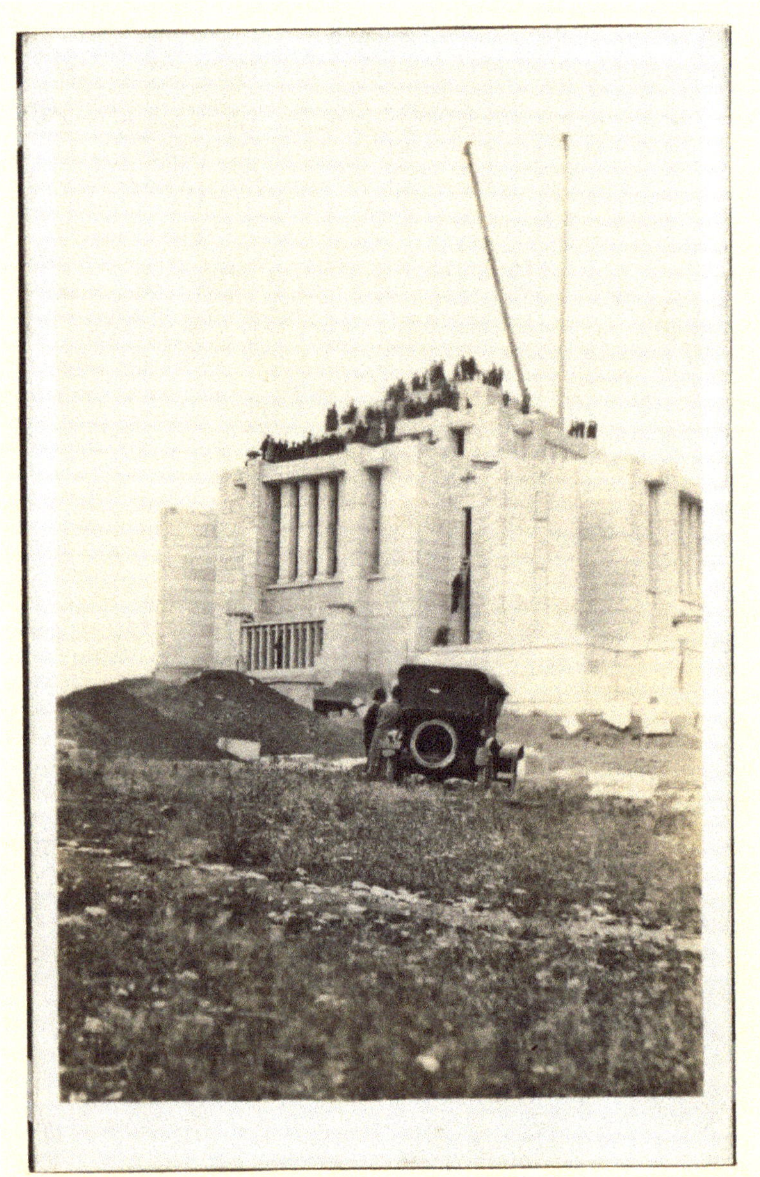

Fig. 5.13 'Laying the Last Stone at the Mormon Temple, Cardston [2]'. Copyright W. H. Best, 1917 (copyright number 33443).

ambivalence towards Canadian nationalism and British imperialism were some of the many ways in which migrants from a variety of places could find themselves being treated as insurmountably 'other'. Again, the Colonial Copyright Collection and the photographers who deposited to it focus their gaze on these situations, not only in the west but also across Canada.

The significance of race in the west, and in Canada in general, cannot be ignored and is important for this discussion. As authors such as George Elliot Clarke and Charmaine A. Nelson have noted, black Canadians have long found Canada's predominant culture to be white and burdened with significant prejudices regarding blackness and the place of black individuals of any descent in the country.[13] Clarke has discussed the long presence of black Canadians in Canada, be they Caribbean slaves brought as cargo, enslaved people working in Canada's urban areas in the eighteenth century or the many other migrant groups, such as the black Empire Loyalists who settled in Canada between the eighteenth century and the present day.[14] Both Clarke and Nelson observe that these groups are largely invisible in Canada's history, in the same way that many black Canadians are still socially and politically invisible today. They argue that such invisibility has been caused by a white-dominated society 'forgetting' the significant elements of black history which have played out in Canada's Provinces and that such processes continue today. Both authors also argue that white Canada has actively undermined the presence and cultural status of black Canadians, an action illustrated by photographs deposited in the Colonial Copyright Collection.

In *Only Farmers Need Apply* Troper notes that the migration of black Americans to the Canadian west was effectively stymied by the Immigration Branch, who specifically focused on restricting the movement of this group to take advantage of opportunities in the west.[15] There is a long legacy of resistance to black migration from America to Canada, even during the period of the Underground Railway. Of particular note are the difficulties faced by black Empire Loyalists who moved to the maritime provinces in the wake of American Independence, usually after fighting and sacrificing a great deal for the British cause.[16] In this case and others over the following century race, social practice (particularly around religion) and economic competition fostered deep divisions between black migrants and the white communities surrounding them in Canada.

In *Strangers at Our Gates* Knowles illustrates how black migrants from America were identified as potentially bringing the conditions of

America's 'negro problem' with them. Commentators hoped that the climate of Canada's west would be unappealing to black Americans, thus leaving the west as a space for the cultivation of white settlers. As Schama's[17] account of the black Empire Loyalists shows, however, black migrants to Canada, while finding the climate less appealing, found it no barrier to success. Instead it was the social and practical impediments put in place by racist members of local authorities that caused people to leave Canada's Maritimes.[18] It is noteworthy, then, that the Canadian Immigration Branch performed a similar function during the twentieth century.

The social and cultural underpinnings of this racist resistance to black immigrants are illustrated by a series of photographs in the Colonial Copyright Collection. Copyrighted by the Atkinson Bros. of Toronto in 1898, these photographs contain portraits of nude black children with titles such as 'All Coon Look Alike To Me' (Fig.5.14) and 'Alligator Bait' (Fig.5.15). That the photographs and captions, 'Alligator Bait' in particular, mock their subjects and position their race as being reason to solicit a terrible death underscores their purveyance of a form of normalised racism. This is further underscored, again, by the copyrighting of the images, which illustrates that both images and captions were socially acceptable, and that the photographers thought the photographs would also sell on the public market.

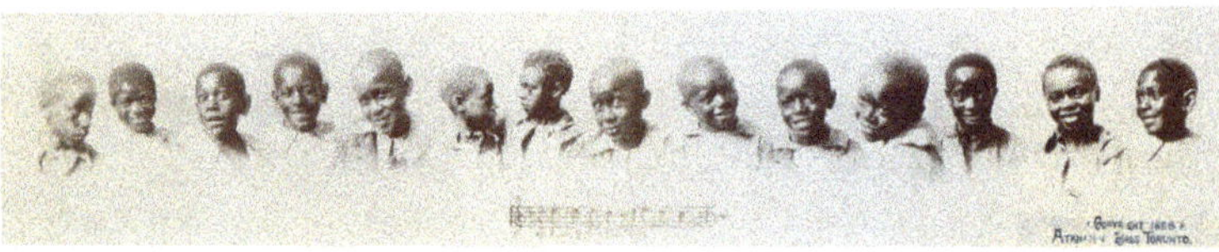

Fig. 5.14 'All Coon Look Alike to Me'. Copyright Atkinson Bros., 1898 (copyright number 9796).

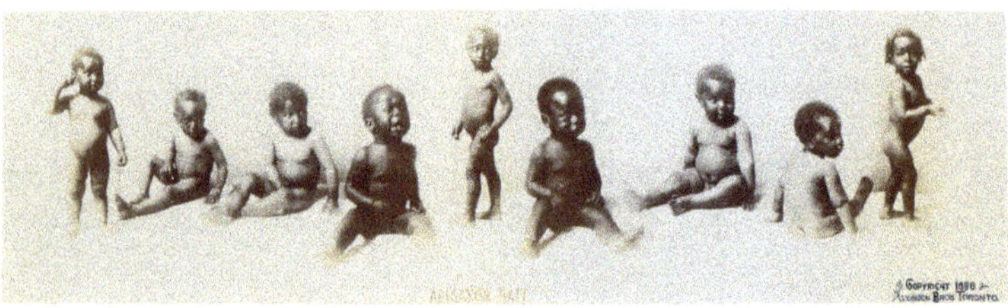

Fig. 5.15 'Alligator Bait'. Copyright Atkinson Bros., 1898 (copyright number 9797).

This should be placed in context of the later work of Atkinson Bros. In the early twentieth century it would seem the Atkinson Bros. were purveyors of picturesque views, printing postcards and compendia of views, including *Souvenir of the Canadian Northwest: Containing 50 views of the principle* [sic] *places from Winnipeg to the Pacific coast*.[19] Through this we can see that the photographic studio specialised in the production of trivial souvenir photography and that they had an eye for markets. The Colonial Copyright Collection is full of romantic ephemera, pictures of dreamy-eyed children, playful cats and romantic views; the style of the Atkinson Bros. photographs is noticeably similar to these images and their 'humour' suggests that the images were designed for sale on the same market.

As such, the photographs are an illustration of the racist attitudes and social issues that may have been faced by black migrants wishing to settle in Canada. That the Atkinson Bros. were obviously mobile photographers with a later history of working in Canada's west and north would also suggest that they understood these communities and were aware of the broad context of racism in Canada's provinces. Such a prospect makes these photographs an uncomfortable reflection of elements of Canadian society at the time.

Black American migrants were not the only ones who faced marginalisation and discrimination in Canada during the boom years of migration. The analysis of Elstor's photographs of the Ruthenian community around Mundare illustrates a community viewed as developing into a cohesive part of modern Canada. However, this was not the case for all migrants from the east of Europe; by the end of the First World War migrants from Eastern Europe were treated with a new level of suspicion. Yet even before the First World War and Russia's Bolshevik Revolution, some from this large and ethnically diverse community experienced more prejudice than others.

A particularly notable early example is the treatment of the Doukhobors. Initially this community had a positive experience of Canada, leaving behind persecution in Russia via the active engagement of the Canadian government. The Doukhobors were not only encouraged to come, but also given entitlements to their own settlements and permission to abstain from elements of Canadian politics that were abhorrent to their culture, in particular war and conflict as the Doukhobors were pacifists.[20]

The photographs here show the entry of the Doukhobors into Yorkton after their long and interrupted migration from Russia. Taken in 1902 by Thomas Veitch Simpson, the images cover the arrival of

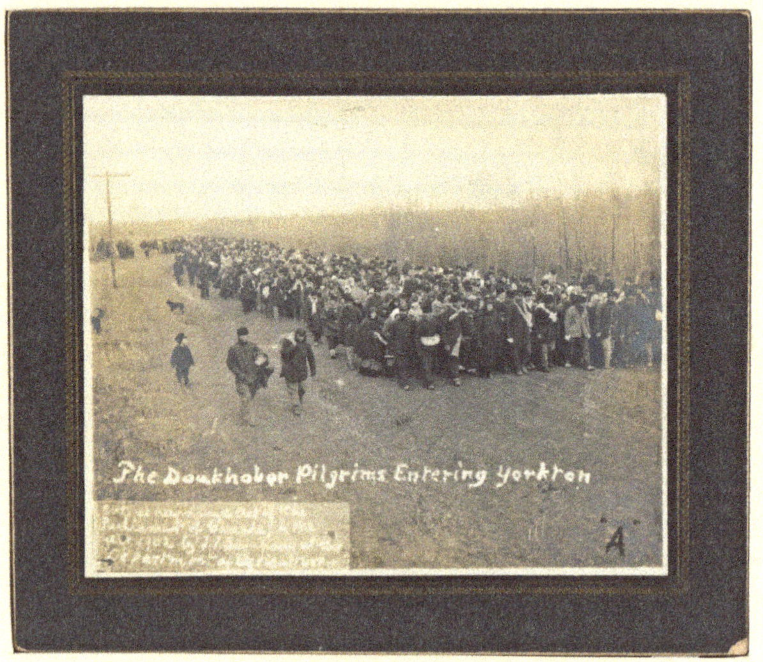

Fig. 5.16 'Doukhobor Pilgrims Entering Yorkton'. Copyright T. V. Simpson, 1902 (copyright number 13519).

the Doukhobors, here termed 'pilgrims', at Yorkton (see e.g. Fig.5.16) in a series of five photographs. Simpson was a migrant himself; he had arrived in Canada with his family soon after his birth in England, and had become an amateur photographer who practiced as a veterinary surgeon in Yorkton.[21] These photographs constitute the majority of his deposits and therefore illustrate how significant he thought this moment was for Yorkton, as well as suggesting he felt others (such as newspapers and magazines) may have also had an interest in the event.

Simpson's photographs illustrate the mass of people who were part of this migration as well as the toll the journey has taken on the migrants themselves; one photograph (Fig.5.17) is titled 'Doukhobor Pilgrims Carrying their Helpless'. The photographs themselves are noteworthy as an historical record, but the quality of the camera work behind them is poor, suggesting that Simpson captured the images in haste and with less care than would be ideal. The rest of his portfolio in the collection, while lacking in the quality found elsewhere, supports this theory as they are noticeably more studied.

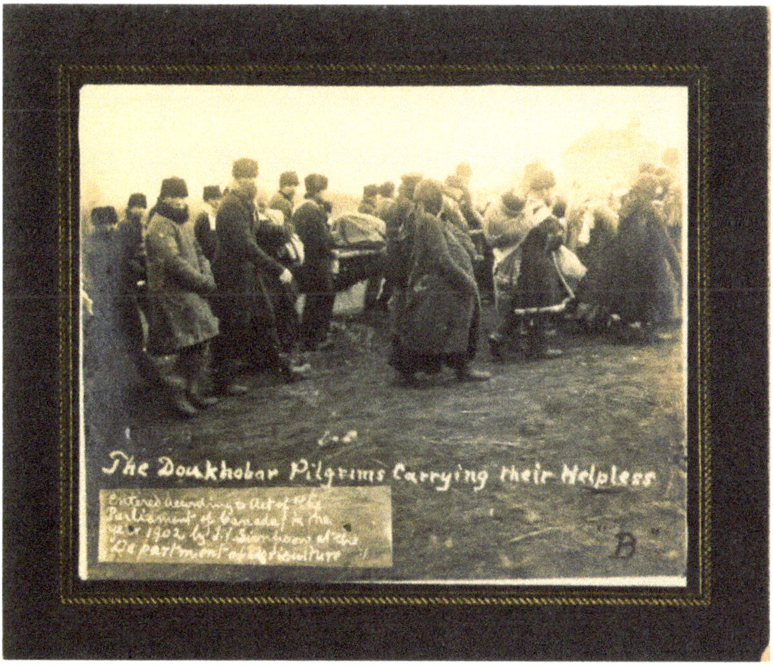

Fig. 5.17 'Doukhobor Pilgrims Carrying their Helpless'. Copyright T. V. Simpson, 1902 (copyright number 13520).

Overall Simpson's photographs convey a sense of scale and reflect the potential change this group could bring to Yorkton. However, they do not display this overtly in their composition, except in two instances. Entitled, 'Doukhobor Pilgrims Leaving Yorkton to Evangelise the World' (Fig.5.18) and 'Doukhobor Pilgrims Refuse to go Back to Their Villages', the photographs themselves convey little of the significance of events, instead continuing to show a large group of people in motion. It is Simpson's captioning of the photograph that conveys as much about what he *imagines* to be happening as what actually is. As a group the Doukhobors were escaping persecution in Russia and had been well received in eastern Canada on their arrival. However, their desire to live in a group and the perceived scale of their numbers seems to intimidate Simpson, and it is hard to imagine him being alone in this view.

In Simpson's images, then, we begin to see the troubles that would continue to affect the Doukhobors in Canada. By the time Frank Oliver, who replaced Sifton at the Department of the Interior in 1905, was

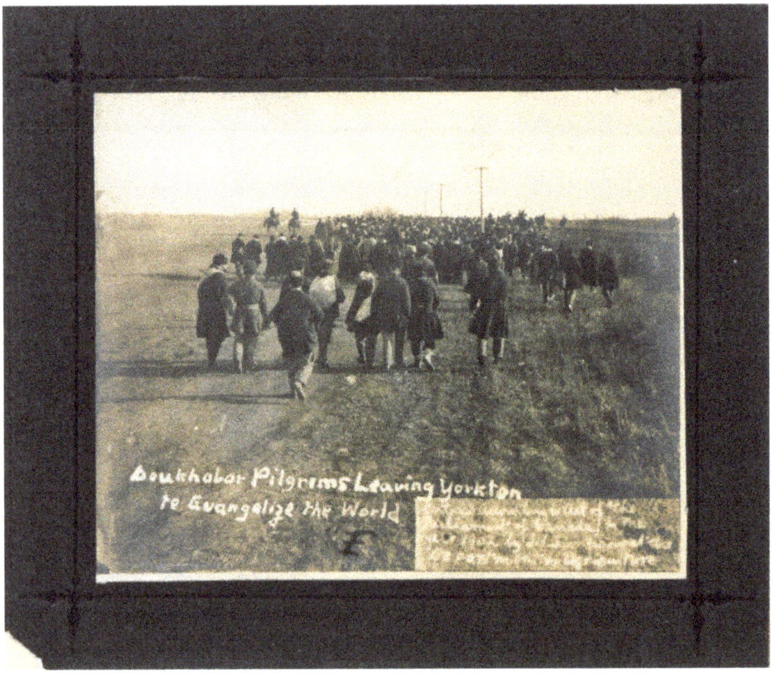

Fig. 5.18 'Doukhobor Pilgrims Leaving Yorkton to Evangelise the World'. Copyright T. V. Simpson, 1902 (copyright number 13523).

in charge of immigration policy the Doukhobors were being hounded for their refusal to swear an oath to the Crown – an act Oliver used as grounds to remove the lands and homesteads granted to Doukhobor migrants during Sifton's time in office.[22] The fear of people such as Oliver and, given Simpson's captions, we may assume those in Yorkton and surrounds too, was that the Doukhobors would not only fail to assimilate, but also that they would try and spread their religious and political beliefs into the Canadian west. This was felt even as far as the United States, where papers such as the *Los Angeles Herald* ran articles about the attempts of the Canadian state to constrain the proselytising of Doukhobor groups.[23]

This climate of fear and mistrust would lead to the Doukhobors eventually moving to British Columbia in order to live on land bought by their leader Peter Verigin (Fig.5.19). Yet even this did not end the troubles the Doukhobors faced. Verigin himself was killed in a train explosion on part of the Canadian Pacific Railway, the cause of which remains unknown to this day. The story of the Doukhobors serves to

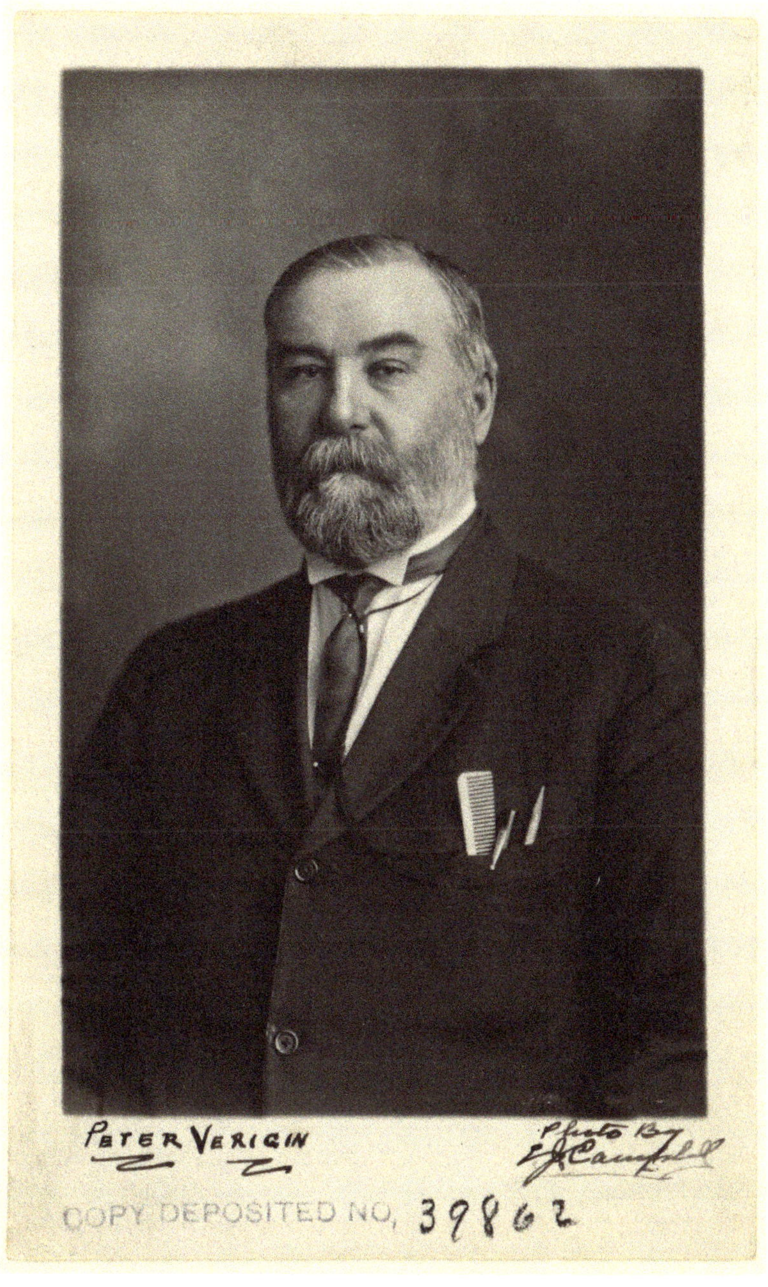

Fig. 5.19 'Peter Verigin'. Copyright E. J. Campbell, 1922 (copyright number 39862).

illustrate how difficult life could be for groups with distinct cultures and beliefs who wished to move into the west of Canada. Expected to assimilate and become Canadian in a narrow, Anglo-Canadian way, this was often too much for communities to bear. In short, the idea of a diverse, multicultural Canada was still some way off.

It is important to note that one should also view the photographs in this chapter in the context of those discussed in Chapter 4, which took the depiction of First Peoples groups as its focus. As photographers such as Rafton-Canning sought to claim the landscape and others in this chapter sought to imagine its Canadianisation, it is important not to forget the huge cost of this borne by the First Peoples communities who used to inhabit this land. The inability of the westward expansion of Canada to co-exist with these groups in a functional way is, therefore, not just a tragedy for the people who already inhabited this area, but also to those distinct cultures that were to try and occupy it after the conflicts of the mid-nineteenth century.

Similarly, consideration given in previous chapters to the railway and its relationship with photography highlights another area of confluence between this chapter and the themes considered in the rest of the book. Brian Osborne has argued that railways facilitated the flow of migrants around the country while the camera was deployed at the point of their departure to manage their transit and settlement.[24] The remaining records represent a desire to control this population and an anxiety about how it would assimilate into Canadian society; when compared to this work, the railway photographs of the Colonial Copyright Collection also demonstrate the interconnectedness of the core photographic subjects deposited for copyright between 1895 and 1924. This again illustrates how the visual economy of these images – and Canadian photography more generally at the time – were intimately bound together and could be used to myriad ends, especially as Canadians wrestled with the anxieties arising from a changing society.[25]

What we have seen in this chapter, then, is that while there were many factors which needed to come together in order to form the western provinces of Canada, they were, in the short term at least, a series of communities with very narrow social barriers. This was all to change; some of those groups who were part of this migration would assimilate into society, and also redefine what it meant to be Canadian in the twentieth century.[26] Others would be less fortunate, be they the cultures embedded in these spaces before Canada existed or those strongly defined groups who wished to be part of these new opportunities, but could not satisfactorily assimilate to others' expectations.

***

This chapter has illustrated the complexity of not only migration to Canada's west, but also to Canada as a whole by considering the ways in which it was visualised by photographers. Race, ethnicity, religious background and culture were significant factors in Canada between 1895 and 1924, as they had been in the long narrative of its prior history. The Colonial Copyright Collection provides a fascinating insight into this history and its articulation by Canada's photographers. It is, in many ways, a shocking collection. Photographs such as those by the Atkinson Bros. provide a vivid reminder not only of the strength of racist feeling in parts of Canada, but also its social, and commercial, acceptability. On initial impression there is something quite bland about a copyright collection, its creation inspired by the implementation of law and commerce. However, reading between the lines opens up fascinating and shocking insights, as is the case with the photographs of the Atkinson Bros.

Likewise, reading between the lines of the photographs of Miriam Elstor provides a more pleasant insight into the impression some Canadians had of their new neighbours, along with hints at the development of a multicultural Canada. Clearly these people were regarded as different, and they were certainly treated by Elstor and presumably others as being something of a novelty. However, there is also the suggestion of some sort of affinity between different peoples, a suggestion that they are not as different as superficial judgements might make out. The photographs of the Mormon Temple, for example, depict a celebration not just of religious spectacle, but also of the successful establishment of a new community, whose roots and culture are now sunk into the soil and etched onto the landscape.

The collection also reminds us of what drove this movement of people and provides equally striking reminders of those whom the technology of modernity and colonisation drove out of the way. It is these accidents of legislation, the bringing together of disparate materials with something to say to each other, that make the story of the Ruthenians, black American settlers, trains, tractors and Blackfoot Indians inseparable. It is also a reminder of how the meaning of a photograph is never fixed. Instead the photographer's composition and initial meaning is always reshaped by captions, archival situations and reinterpretations by new viewers and new media.

Photography is also a tool – in this case, to tell stories about people who are new to Canada's lands. In Chapter 6 we will see it being used to tell a story about Canada's role in the wider world. However, it is important to remember that such globalised image production and circulation has a role at home as well – a role that cannot be divorced from the story being told in these photographs. Crucially, as Canada diversified through the settlement of the west, there were those who sought to reinforce its core values and to reassert its Anglo-Canadian-ness. To them the extension of the state and its involvement in imperial wars were just one theatre in which to perform and assert this identity.

6
A global presence: photographing Canadians going to war

Writing in the twenty-first century, Canada's role in foreign conflicts appears a significant and established one. As both a peacekeeping force and an army with an increasing role in direct combat, as in Iraq,[1] Canada's military forces and senior figures are known the world over. There was a time, however, when Canada's military was less well recognised, especially as an independent fighting force. This is despite the fact that Canada's colonial forces did play significant roles in eighteenth- and nineteenth-century continental conflicts, including the Seven Years War, the War of Independence and the War of 1812. However, their fighting roles outside of North America were limited until later in the nineteenth century.

From the South African Wars onwards,[2] however, Canadians and people living in Canada became involved in conflicts abroad in increasingly significant ways. Given the growing availability of photographic technology, its increasing capacities and the decreasing costs of photographs themselves, the increasingly global presence of the Canadian military went hand in hand with a growth in the depiction of its uniformed personnel.

This chapter uses the Colonial Copyright Collection to provide a lens on the two main conflicts in which Canadian soldiers were involved between 1895 and 1924: the South African and the First World Wars. While these conflicts involved significantly different numbers of Canadians and produced different kinds of material records (indeed, the amount of material produced by and for Canadian troops in the First World War was prodigious), they are both uniquely recorded in this collection. Particularly notable is that the collection depicts Canadians both at home and abroad, thus giving a nuanced sense of the impact of conflict on Canada in the late nineteenth and early twentieth centuries. It also shows how the home front reacted to, and was changed by, Canada's involvement in foreign wars.

After discussing Canada's involvement in the South African War, the chapter moves on to look at Canada's role in the First World War, a conflict many have argued was a formative moment in Canadian history. Historians have suggested this war created circumstances within which Canada could assert itself as a nation, independent of the influence of the British Empire. The Colonial Copyright Collection certainly shows the great efforts and sacrifices which, it has been argued, underpinned this shift. However, it is suggested in this chapter that the breadth and depth of the Colonial Copyright Collection, as well as the workings of the image world in which these photographs circulated, show something more profound: Canada's increasing interconnection with the world as an independent agent.

The South African War

In Canada, as well as in other former Dominion nations, there is a popular sense that contemporary national identities were forged in the fire of the First World War; that the blood shed on foreign battlefields acted as a uniting strand for a common national identity. While there are elements of truth in this, the argument is also historically and socially problematic, overlooking previous events that bound elements of the nation together and neglecting the severe damage often done to a broad sense of nationhood as a result of these conflicts.

The South African War illustrates both of these problems. In the shadow of the First World War it is often forgotten, and the profound social effect of a war that was, to Canadians, impossibly remote is today little appreciated beyond the sphere of Canada's historians. However, as Carman Miller notes, prior to the First World War the conflict in South Africa was one of the most discussed and defining sociopolitical issues for Canadians.[3] The contingent sent to South Africa may seem small, at 7,368 individuals, in the light of what was to come, but this is not the way to read history. To contemporaries it was a huge and contentious number of people to send on a dangerous mission in support of colonial ties not all Canadians felt enthusiastic about.

This is why photographs of then Prime Minister Wilfrid Laurier and Lieutenant-Colonel Sam Steele open this section (see Figs 6.1–6.2). These men represent two sides of the same coin, both patriotic Canadians, both bearing some form of relationship to Britain. Yet each man felt

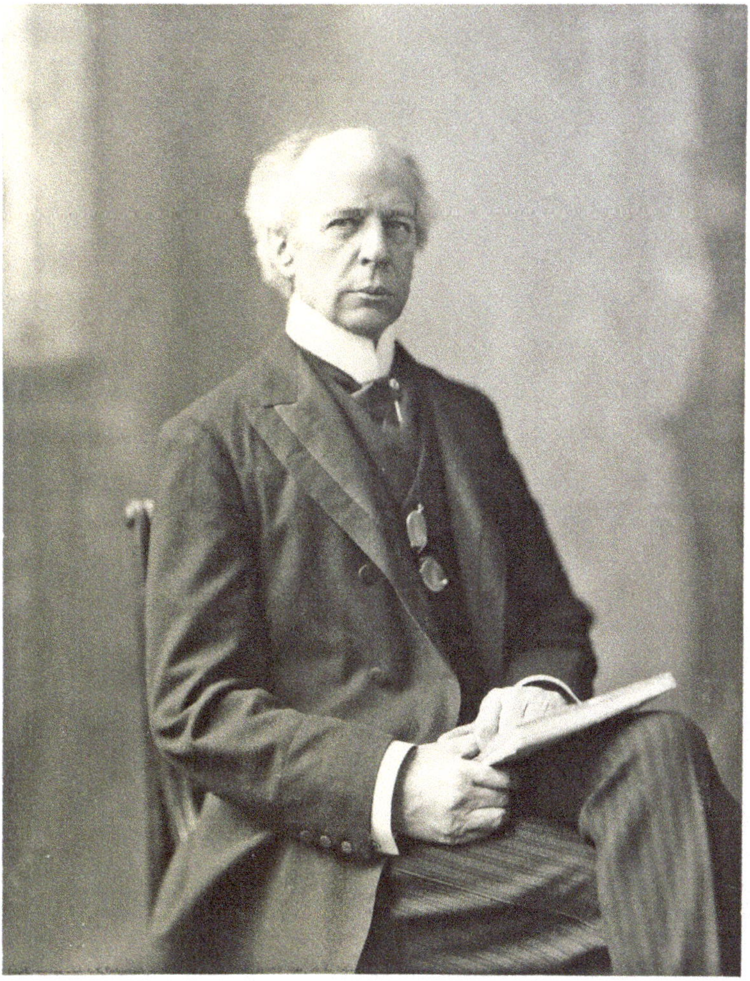

Fig. 6.1 'The Hon Sir Wilfrid Laurier'. Copyright W. J. Topley, 1906 (copyright number 16871).

very differently about the potential for Canadians to fight in South Africa. Laurier resisted attempts to thrust Canada into the conflict until the full weight of government peers, the press and public opinion was brought to bear on him. Men such as Steele, on the other hand, enthusiastically took up the call to show loyalty to the empire and to express Canada's prowess in defending Queen and country.

However, the internal conflict that characterised Canada's involvement in the South African War is not intimately borne out by the contents of the collection. As Carman Miller also notes, nationalism

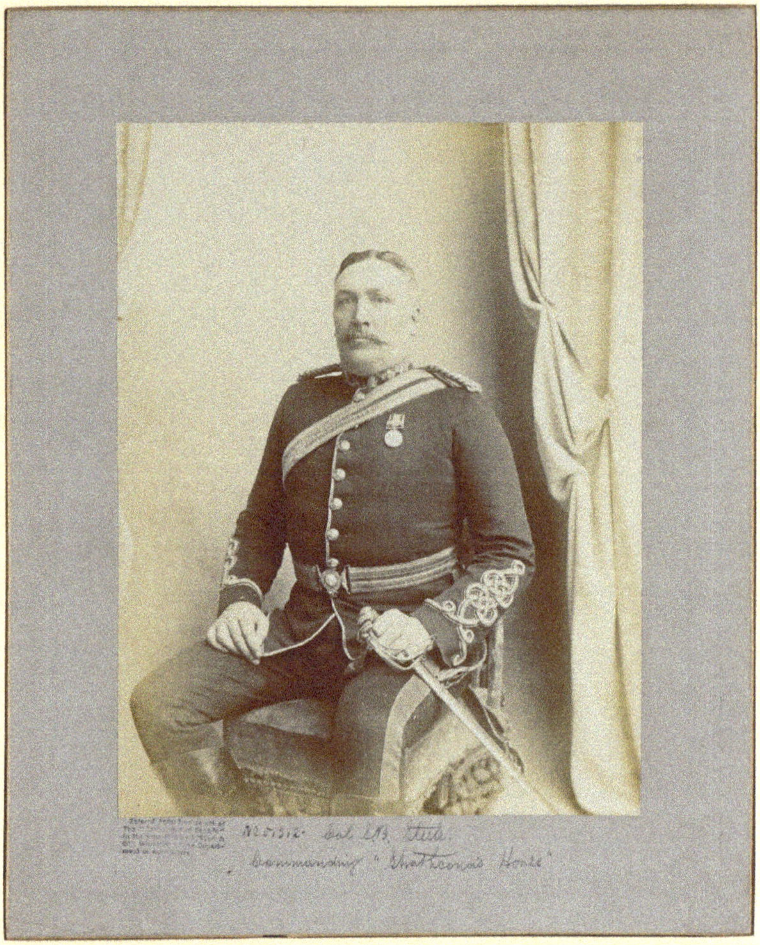

Fig. 6.2 'Col. S. B. Steele Commanding Strathcona's Horse'. Copyright Steele and Co., 1900 (copyright number 11352).

and imperialism were popular themes in late nineteenth- and earlier twentieth-century Canada, promoted by the school system, churches and some of the most influential writers of the time.[4] Indeed, nationalism was big business, and photographers should be included in any list of individuals trying to profit from catering to these prevailing sentiments. As a result, it is not a surprise that such a financially profitable theme, mixed with the South African War, should find its way into the Colonial Copyright Collection.

The departure of Canadian troops for South Africa comprises the main body of collection material relating to the South African War. In particular, Lord Strathcona's Horse – named after Lord Strathcona and

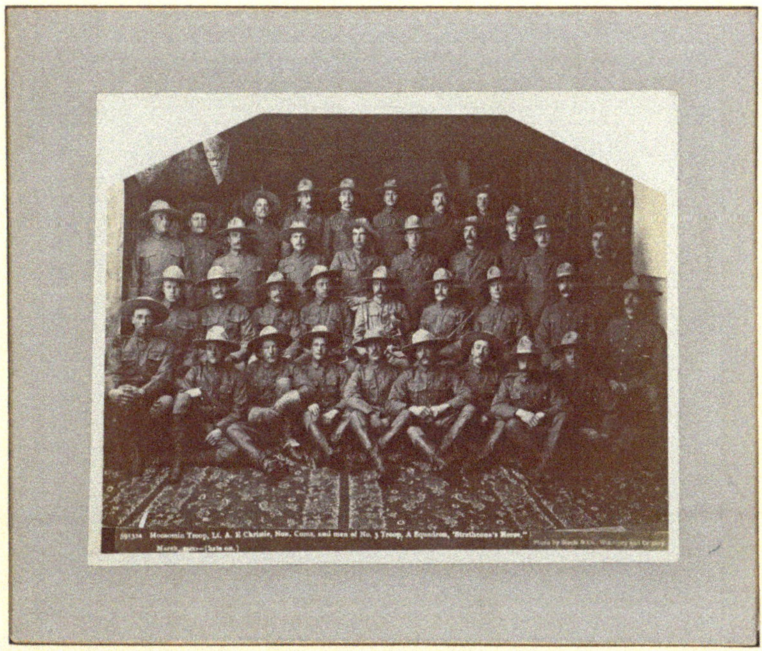

Fig. 6.3 'Moosomin Troop'. Copyright Steele and Co., 1900 (copyright number 11353).

Mount Royal who funded, created and raised the regiment – is well documented. As suggested at the opening of this section, Lieutenant-Colonel Sam Steele looms large with a number of portraits produced of him by Steele and Co. of Winnipeg in 1900. Steele and Co. seem to have taken a keen interest in the Strathcona's Horse and their departure for the war (see for example Fig.6.3); photographs taken in Halifax of the unit's ship *The Monterey* departing for South Africa are also registered in the company's name (see Fig.6.4). Such determination to record an event is not necessarily surprising, especially given the mobile nature of many other photographers in the collection. Steele travelled far and wide as part of his photographic work, to the extent that some of the Glenbow Museum's labels describe him as 'a professional itinerant photographer'.[5]

However, that Frederick Steele should photograph Lieutenant-Colonel Steele, the Strathcona's Horse and even journey to Halifax to capture their departure is suggestive of the significance of these troops being sent to South Africa.[6] The Strathcona's Horse was set up and funded by Lord Strathcona, High Commissioner for Canada in London at the time. While formally a British unit, it was within itself and Canada at large seen

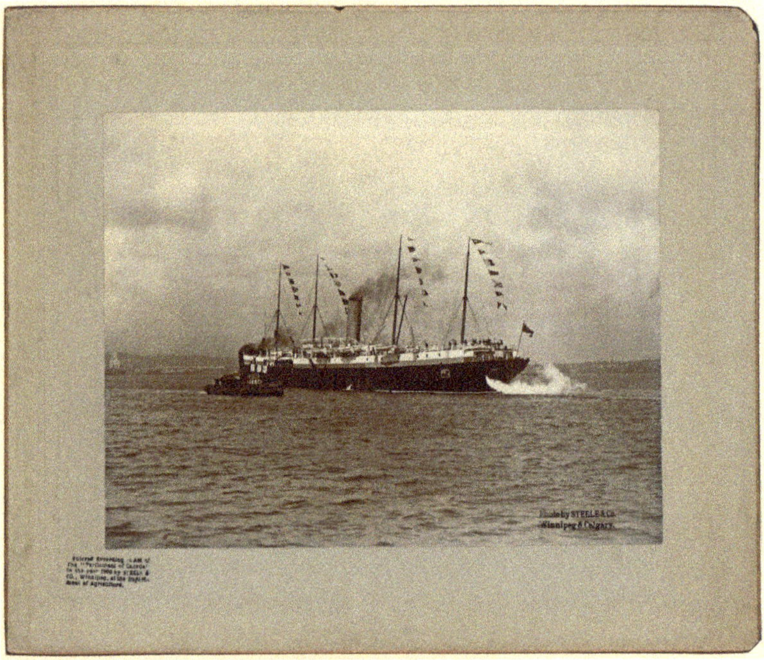

Fig. 6.4 'The Monterey Leaving Halifax'. Copyright Steele and Co., 1900 (copyright number 11272).

very much as a Canadian force. Indeed, being recruited from the west of Canada, uniformed in Canadian livery and led by men like Steele, a former militia man during the Fenian Raids and member of the North-West Mounted Police, it embodied the vigorous development of western Canada in the years since confederation. As a result, the regiment was tailor-made to perform the nationalist and imperialist sentiments that were apparent in Canada at the time.

While onboard *The Monterey*, photographs continued to be taken of Strathcona's Horse and deposited in the collection. A few photographs were copyrighted by H. H. Dunsford, a member of 'A' Company in Strathcona's Horse, showing the troops on deck after departure and practising rifle drills (see Figs 6.5–6.6). The photographs are technically accomplished in terms of their exposure and composure, and the shot of the rifle drill (Fig.6.6), is particularly impressive given the cramped confines and the fact that the work is obviously being done at sea. More importantly, the production of a formal, ordered and professional-looking rifle drill being conducted on the way to South Africa suggests the desire of the Strathcona's Horse to

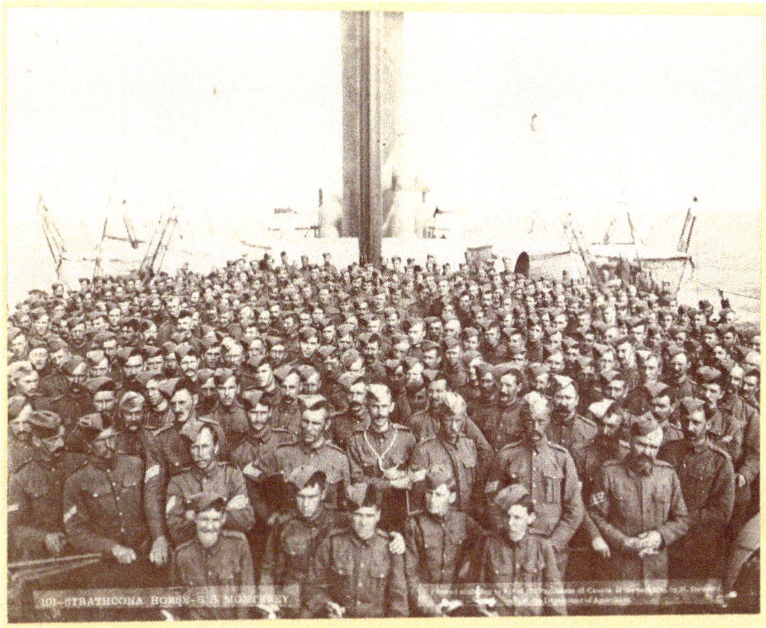

Fig. 6.5 'Strathcona Horse on SS Monterey'. Copyright H. H. Dunsford, 1900 (copyright number 11497).

present themselves, and be recognised, as an organised fighting force, even though the unit was formed and dispatched over a relatively short period of time.

Strathcona's Horse represented one of the more professional units sent to South Africa and was linked to a particular point of pride in the Canadian national psyche: horsemanship. It also symbolised a powerful connection of colonial aspiration and imperial power: a fighting force comprised of the best horsemen from Canada's newest territories, formed under the aegis of Canada's man at the heart of empire. However, other contingents of Canadians were also sent to the war, consisting of infantry men and artillery. Some of these, such as the Guelph Contingent photographed by W. Burgess and Son, are also present in the collection (see Fig.6.7). These images illustrate that it was not just the striking connection of westward expansionism and imperial connection that engendered pride in Canada's contribution to the war. Indeed, there was strong pride felt by some with regard to the more ordinary contributions of Canada's provinces and citizens.

In his published collection of letters *With the Guns in South Africa*, E. W. B. Morrison articulates many of these sentiments. During the early paragraphs a focus is placed on illustrating how the Canadian troops

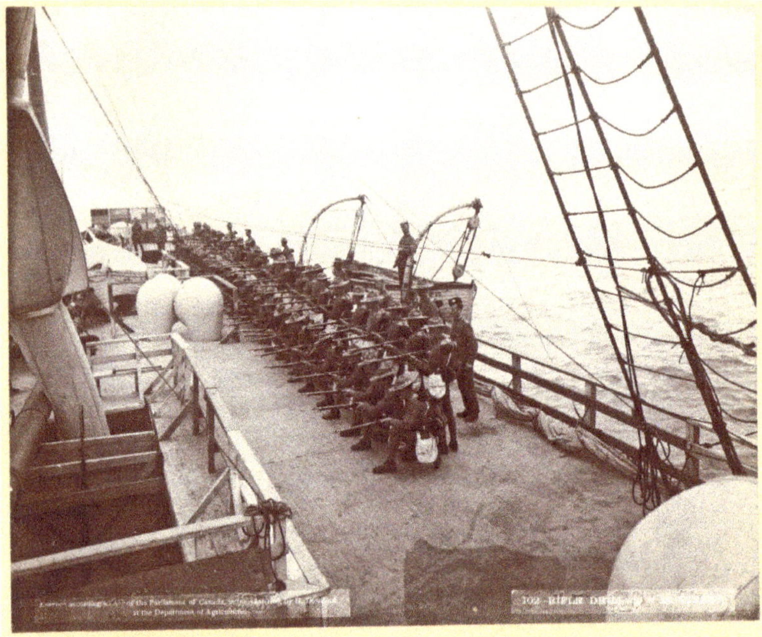

Fig. 6.6 'Rifle Drill onboard SS Monterey'. Copyright H. H. Dunsford, 1900 (copyright number 11498).

readied themselves for war; Morrison articulates a sense of Canada beginning to show what it can do on the world stage, stating at the end of one letter, 'But the world has yet to know that the Canadian soldier can go anywhere and do anything'.[7] These photographs, then, can be read as a provocative statement, an assertion of pride and belief that these men will go forth and change the world. As Miller puts it in the title of his later book, they would help to paint the map red.

Drawing this section on departures to a close, it is worth returning to the photograph of the Guelph Contingent mentioned earlier. At the front of the Guelph Contingent, about to lead them to South Africa, is John McCrae – the man who would, in a later conflict, write the poem 'In Flanders Fields'. McCrae is also mentioned in Morrison's *With the Guns*, in which he makes a few heroic interventions in the narrative and is therefore part of the broader story about Canada's developing role in the imperial and international sphere.[8] Given 'In Flanders Fields' enshrines the noble sacrifice of the soldier, it is suggestive that the sentiments held by a Canadian in the South African War translated across to a larger, bloodier conflict later in the century. The significance of this ideal to the First World War will be discussed later, but its role in memorialising the South African War is perhaps equally important.

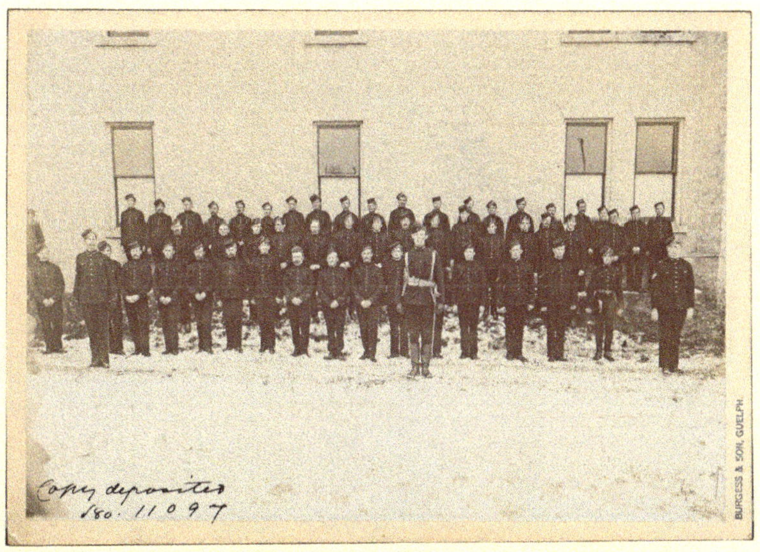

Fig. 6.7 'Guelph Contingent'. Copyright Burgess and Son, 1900 (copyright number 11097).

Upon their return from South Africa the majority of veterans returned to their original localities, assimilating back into civilian life while also occupying a revered place among Canadian nationalists. The significance of these individuals within their place of origin is best illustrated by a handful of photographs in the collection that have a distinctly formal air. In 1901 John Wallace Jones (whose work was previously discussed in Chapter 2) copyrighted a trio of photographs of the British Columbian Lieutenant Governor opening the parliament of Victoria, accompanied by an honour guard of South African War volunteers (Figs 6.8-6.10). It is interesting to return to a province, building and photographer previously discussed as being heavily involved in the performance of an (admittedly long delayed) political identity. Here we can see that three years later this political spectacle is still being played out, with the South African War volunteers bound up into it.

What we see on the soldiers' return, then, is that they were quickly assimilated into a particular part of Canadian society and politics – the performance of an imperialist, Anglo-Canadian, democratic identity. As the earlier case study on Jones's photographs of the first opening of the British Columbia parliament argued, the staging of these events – as well as the production and use of photography to frame the scene – were important to underscore a status and role that Victoria still felt

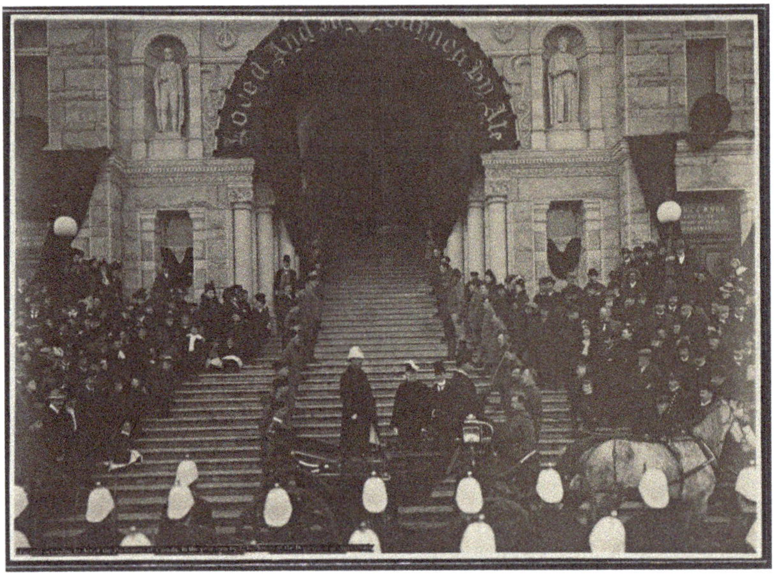

Fig. 6.8 'Lieut Gov of BC entering Parliament with Guard of SA Volunteers [1]'. Copyright J. W. Jones, 1901 (copyright number 12028).

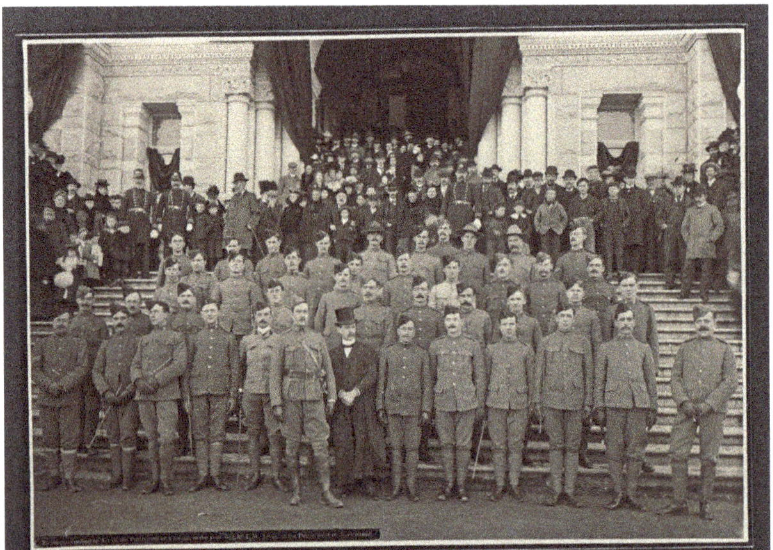

Fig. 6.9 'Lieut Gov of BC entering Parliament with Guard of SA Volunteers [2]'. Copyright J. W. Jones, 1901 (copyright number 12029).

uncertain about. In 1901 we can see this procedure was still in action, and the South African War volunteers became incorporated as exemplars of British Columbia's adherence to the imperial creed.

In his 1979 history *The Boer War*, Pakenham argues that Australia, Canada and New Zealand's 'enthusiastic' support for the conflict is a perfect illustration of the development of a functioning 'self-governing empire' with strong ties and loyalties to the metropole.[9] This historical view has been challenged and nuanced by subsequent research that shows Canada and Canadians, if taken as a whole, as having a much more ambiguous set of opinions towards the war. However, what we do see clearly from this collection is that there were elements of Canadian society who sought to inhabit this space, especially if they would benefit from this alignment, and that photographers were bound up in the performance of this 'self-governing empire' identity.

A further example here is the photographs of the Duke of York presenting medals to South African War veterans in Winnipeg during his visit of 1901 (see Figs 6.11-6.12). This royal tour was extensive and the distribution of medals was a key part of its itinerary; it is also clear that Winnipeg was a very important stop on the schedule.[10] Manitoba, and Winnipeg in particular, had undergone a meteoric process of change in the latter part of the nineteenth century, joining Canada in the wake of the Red River

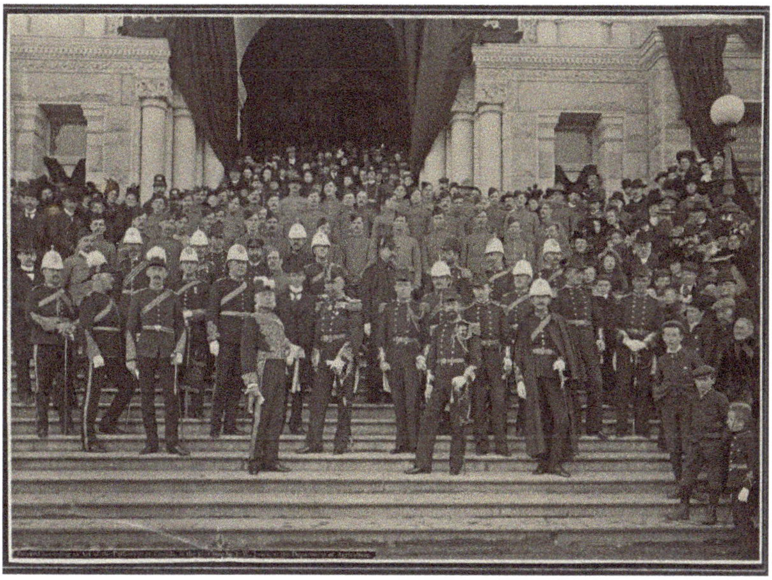

Fig. 6.10 'Lieut Gov of BC entering Parliament with Guard of SA Volunteers [3]'. Copyright J. W. Jones, 1901 (copyright number 12030).

Rebellion only to go through a prodigious railway boom in the 1890s. By 1901 Winnipeg had become a colonial jewel in Canada's west.

The royal tour covers all of Winnipeg's modernity. A photograph of the royal party by their train, found in Pope's account, illustrates Canada's comfortable modernity and the imperial family's understanding of the importance of the railway in binding this part of the empire together.[11] There was also an emphasis placed on performing Manitoba's identity as part of the British Empire, and the South African War was an important part of this. After all the Strathcona's Horse, which had performed well and would continue to do so (albeit in a different form) during the long Boer insurgency, were largely recruited from this part of Canada, as were many other Canadian troops.

The distribution of medals and the photographing of this event, then, underscore the achievement of the Canadian west and the British Empire's appreciation of its efforts. These records highlight that Winnipeg's officials, as well as a notable part of its population, understood themselves as being part of the same imperial, Anglo-Canadian, democratic nation to which the polity of British Columbia also claimed allegiance. Given that it was only 30 years previously that American

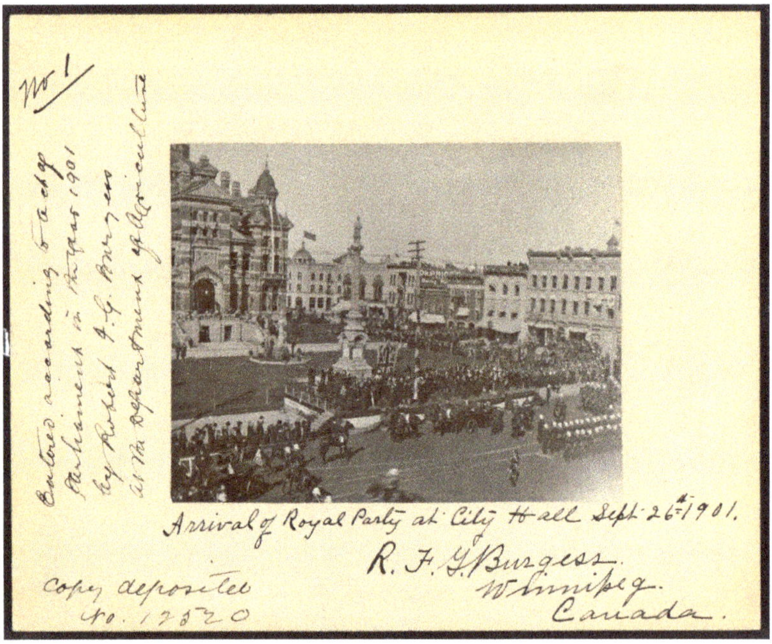

Fig. 6.11 'Duke of Cornwall and York Presenting South African Medals [1]'. Copyright R. J. Burgess, 1901 (copyright number 12522).

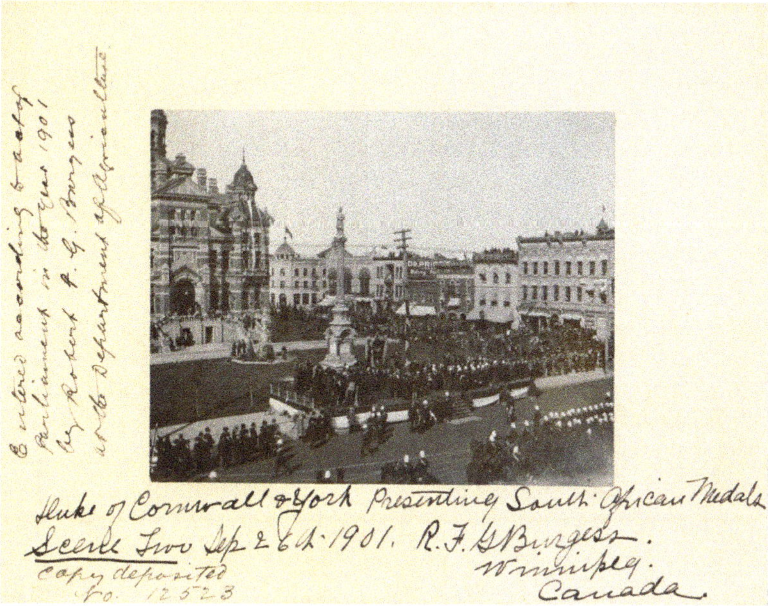

Fig. 6.12 'Duke of Cornwall and York Presenting South African Medals [2]'. Copyright R. J. Burgess, 1901 (copyright number 12523).

settlers and political aggressors were looking north to this part of Canada in anticipation, this must have seemed a significant achievement to those arranging and conducting the ceremony.

However, this was still not an identity with which all Canadians would claim a strong affiliation.[12] In the era of the 'Last Best West' Canada had become a nation of migrants from across Europe and the world. Not everyone here was keen to be part of an imperial democracy – nor, for that matter, of an Anglophile Canada. Indeed, in Winnipeg's case the original Métis settlement was there precisely because not everyone wanted to be part of this grand imperial structure of governance. This, then, is exactly why the performance of this identity, through the rewarding of the South African War's veterans, was so important in what had become a vastly profitable part of the empire.

Dissenting voices have not loomed large in this part of the collection. During the time of the South African War there were still relatively few photographs being deposited under Colonial Copyright Law. Among those photographers that used the legislation, there is a strong theme of civic pride, national development and imperial affiliation present in the contents of the photographs. As noted above, given the financial underpinning of the collection's creation, aligned with the popularity of nationalism and imperialism at the time, it is not surprising that this should be the case. Similarly, we can conclude that the overwhelmingly supportive view of the conflict provided by the photographs is in line with this prevailing trend; the photographs catered to a very particular part of the Canadian consumer market.

Taking this imbalance into account, the collection does still allow us to turn a critical gaze onto Canada's role in the South African War. The photographs from Victoria and Winnipeg suggest that the willing involvement of some Canadians in the conflict was not just driven by a one-sided and zealous belief in the British Empire, but because some individuals, groups and places had something to gain from the practice and performance of this affiliation. Indeed, for those groups who still wanted Canada to be a bastion of British values in the new world, involvement in the conflict was a useful tool to forge and perform this role. That this could then be written onto the landscape of Canada through the performance of civic ceremonies asserts the import of this dynamic relationship and suggests its significance in a community increasingly defined by migration and a complex sociology. Here values held by Anglo-Canadians could not be taken for granted.

When we come to consider the relationship Canada's diverse population had to the First World War, a more complex picture is certainly in evidence. This presents a more dynamic and multifaceted portrait of Canada and Canadians during the conflict, although the above themes carry through – especially in the photography of the Canadian War Records Office, but also in the work produced by photographers all but unknown to today's historians.

The First World War and photographic memory

The late twentieth-century conservation of the Colonial Copyright Collection was a complex affair. There was no standardised way of submitting copyright deposits and so photographers chose myriad ways of providing the requisite material copy; photographs of groups of photographs, books of photographs, backed photographs, postcards, panoramas and many more forms were used. As a result, when conserved, some of the collection was aggregated by form – in particular the large panoramas, some of which are over 3 feet long. During early work with the collection, due to the constraints of working with material of this size, I approached the panoramas as a set and was surprised to find a prevailing theme.

The panoramic photographs held at shelfmark HS85/10 in the British Library are overwhelmingly photographs of soldiers preparing to depart for the battlefields of the First World War. As a result, while working with the 28 folders of panoramic material I was presented with lines and lines of faces, male and female, either having battalion photographs taken or being photographed while leaving for war.

Being confronted with this was surprising and, initially, overwhelming; the amount of photography and the scale of the photographs forcefully communicates the number of Canadians who were involved in the conflict, either in support roles or on the front lines. Uniforms, ranks and faces can be seen clearly without the aid of any magnification, and the sheer amount of people captured in each frame makes it impossible not to think about the number of individuals who never saw Canada again.

For a long time these photographs dominated my thinking of how the Colonial Copyright Collection conveys Canadians' experiences of the First World War. Their overwhelming materiality, the scale of the conflict they conveyed without even leaving the shores of Canada and the diversity of life on display within the photographs draws you in, driving home that this was a very different conflict, both within Canada and without, from the one faced in South Africa. However, these photographs are not the only insights into the First World War in the collection, far from it, and the collection provides a range of views on how Canadians experienced the war. Despite photographic production dropping off markedly in Canada during the years of the war, many Canadians still turned to the camera as a way of depicting and communicating the scale and effect of the conflict.[13] Starting with the panoramas mentioned above, this section asks what they showed and explores why and how we read these a century after the Great War.

Printed on multiple sheets and then joined, the panoramic military photographs depict various parts of the armed forces on a prodigious scale: general infantry regiments, armoured regiments, sportsmen regiments, artillery, sappers, skilled engineers, medical staff and many others are photographed on this scale (see for example Figs 6.13–6.14). There are also a few war-related spectacle events recorded in panorama, most notably Premier Borden's review of the Highland Brigade at Aldershot Camp and the drama of the 26th Battalion leaving St. Johns, New Brunswick, in June 1915 (Figs 6.15–6.17).

The panoramic perspective performs two functions, allowing regimental photographs to operate as useful records for the group as a whole and the individuals within them, while also conveying the scale and drama of an event such as troops departing Canadian shores. This is well

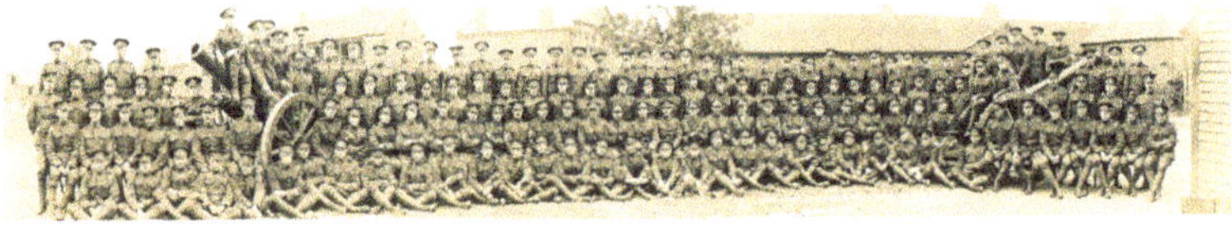

Fig. 6.13 'No 6 McGill Siege Artillery'. Copyright W. G. MacLaughlan, 1916 (copyright number 31991).

illustrated by the photographs of the 26th Battalion, as the photographs exist in both panoramic and regular formats. The difference the scale of reproduction provides is not sufficiently conveyed by Figs 6.15 and 6.16, but when the originals are seen together, or are digitally converted at a high resolution, the differences are striking.

The photographs discussed here also provide evidence of the wide range of people who became involved in the war, as illustrated by the large group of medical personnel shown in Fig.6.14. Medical personnel, in particular nurses, were crucial to the Canadian war effort, and the achievements in developing a functional medical infrastructure over such a great distance were a source of pride for Canadian officials.[14] The war also provided opportunities for the nursing personnel in these photographs, who not only saw themselves as contributing to the war effort as soldiers, but also achieved the status of rank during the conflict.[15]

Such variety and the dramatic scale of the conflict are important initial perceptions that can be gleaned from the collection. These are in line with earlier historical accounts, which have argued that for Canada the First World War was a formative, nation-building moment as a result of the scale of Canada's mobilisation. While this is true to some extent, today's historians paint a messier picture – one that shows Canada becoming more closely involved in an international story where its people had varied experiences of a conflict that reshaped the country in dramatic ways.[16]

The photographs of the Colonial Copyright Collection are an opportunity to view this messiness and also to question Canada's growing international role. The value of photographs as a particular kind of historical artefact is relevant here. In *Media, Memory, and the First World War*, Williams argues that photographs have an ability to circumvent time and pull us back into the past, as a result of the poignant details that are held in the frame.[17] Such an argument is similar to that put forth by Barthes in his *Camera Lucida*; here details of photographs act as *punctums* – that which punctures – to pull the viewer into highly

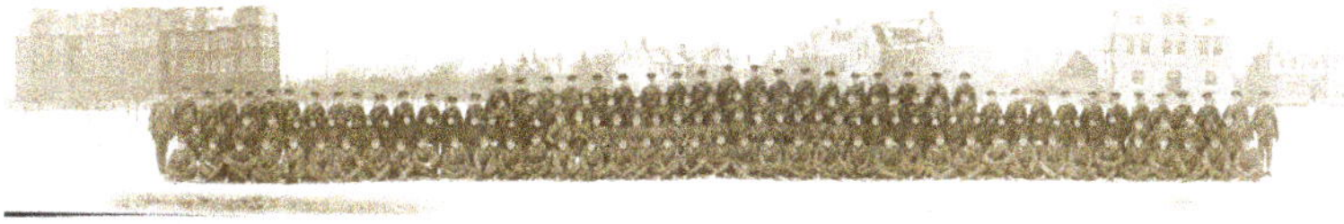

Fig. 6.14 'Officers, Nursing Sisters, NCOs and Men of No 7 Stationary Hospital'. Copyright W. G. MacLaughlan, 1916 (copyright number 31180).

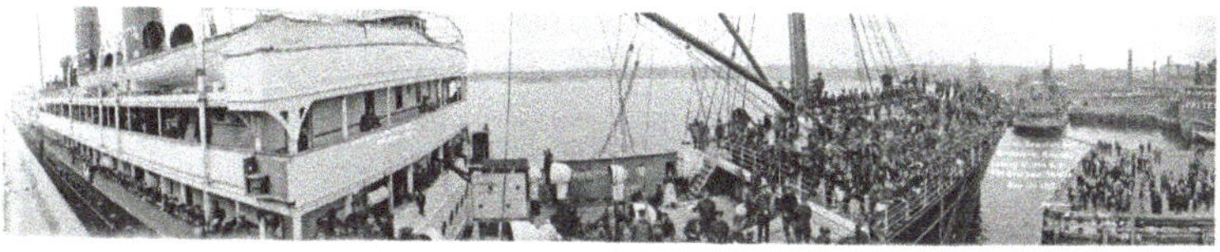

Fig. 6.15 'Embarkation of 26 Battalion, NB'. Copyright D. Smith Reid, 1916 (copyright number 30439).

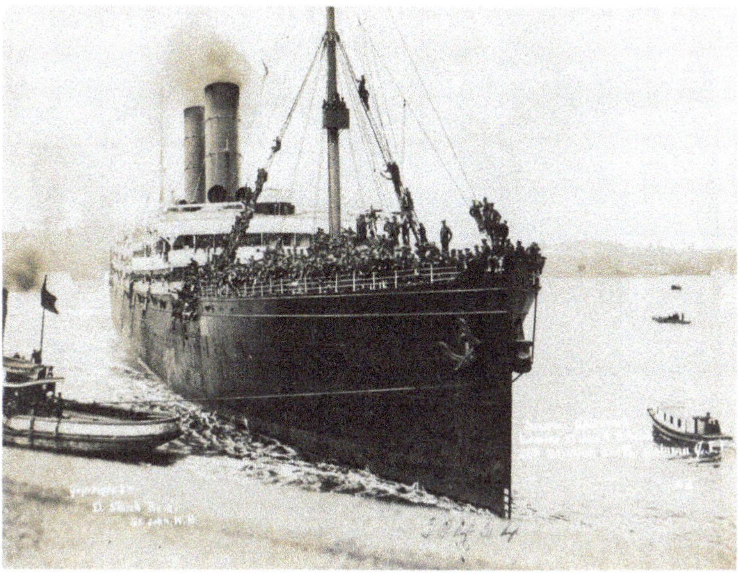

Fig. 6.16 '26 Battalion leaving'. Copyright D. Smith Reid, 1916 (copyright number 30434).

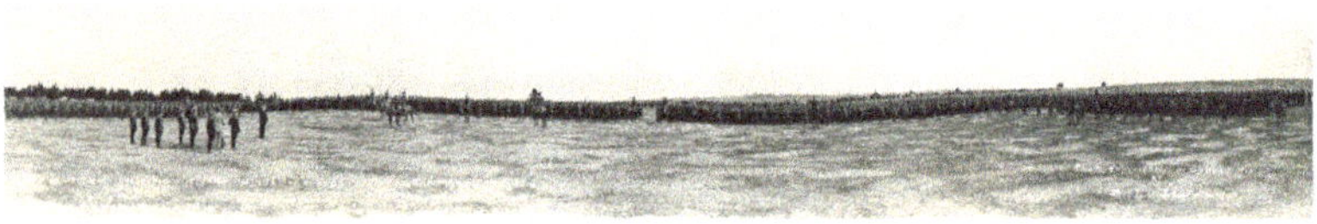

Fig. 6.17 'Premier Borden Inspecting Highland Brigade at Aldershot Camp'. Copyright MacLaughlan Picture Co., 1916 (copyright number 31911).

emotive and challenging pasts. Barthes's argument is one based on family photographs and lived experience, but that does not mean it is invalid for a historian's use. Instead the photograph and its details act as something that punctures any dispassion, connecting us to the past; perhaps most importantly, they can also puncture previous and prevailing assumptions, providing a more holistic view of well discussed conflicts. The photographs discussed above are reminders of such emotive power. However, there are others which move directly to challenge historians and previous historical arguments.

With regard to problematising the nation-building argument, two groups of photographs related to the war stand out in particular: those of Canada's First Peoples people and those of Canada's internment camps that sprung up during the war. Many from First Peoples groups saw service in the First World War, including Tom Longboat. The history here is long and complicated, as demonstrated by Winegard's *For King and Kanata*, which illustrates the connection many First Peoples people felt to the British Crown, as opposed to the Canadian state; the various roles First Peoples people performed, from fighting to financially supporting the war; and the attempts of the Canadian government to use the conflict to assimilate First Peoples soldiers into Canadian society.[18] The photographs shown here of the 'Patriotic Indian Chiefs' (Figs 6.18–6.21) were copyrighted by R. R. Mumford in 1915; they formed part of a broader effort to create positive propaganda for the war by showing the support for it even among Canada's First Peoples groups.

Here Mumford is photographing members of the Mosquito First Nation and the composition is striking; individuals are posed in a car, the epitome of modernity, with a Union Flag draped across the bonnet (see Fig.6.21). The photograph is a long way removed from the 'noble savage' depictions of someone like Edward Curtis, whose imagination of the American Indian often attempted to ignore the role of modernity in his sitters' lives. Instead Mumford's photograph situates his subjects in modernity, both

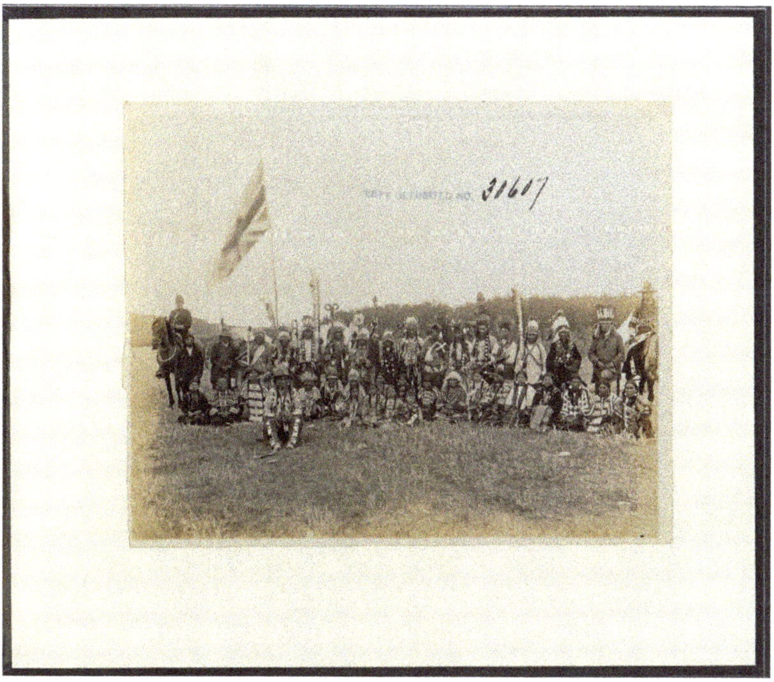

Fig. 6.18 'Patriotic Indian Chiefs [1]'. Copyright R. R. Mumford, 1916 (copyright number 30605).

in terms of their position in the car and in their affiliation to the British Crown in a modern war. Superficially this makes sense within the scope of relations between the First Peoples and the war's combatants at the time: in the South African War, many from First Peoples groups offered to serve the Crown (although these requests were blocked by Canadian administrators) and the First World War saw the same enthusiasm. However, the other photographs in the series complicate this picture.

The other three photographs show a larger group posing under a Union Flag at full mast (see Figs 6.18-6.20). The images are poor, suggesting that Mumford was not completely comfortable with the equipment. More importantly, however, they provide insight into who is organising the production of these images. Here we see Canadian Mounted Police and Canadian government officials, the field agents of the Department of Indian Affairs, in shot, acting as representatives of the Canadian state with whom many First Peoples groups had a poor relationship. These individuals and the groups they represent are, to First Peoples groups, very far removed from the British Crown with which they are aligned with. As a result the photographs can be read less as examples

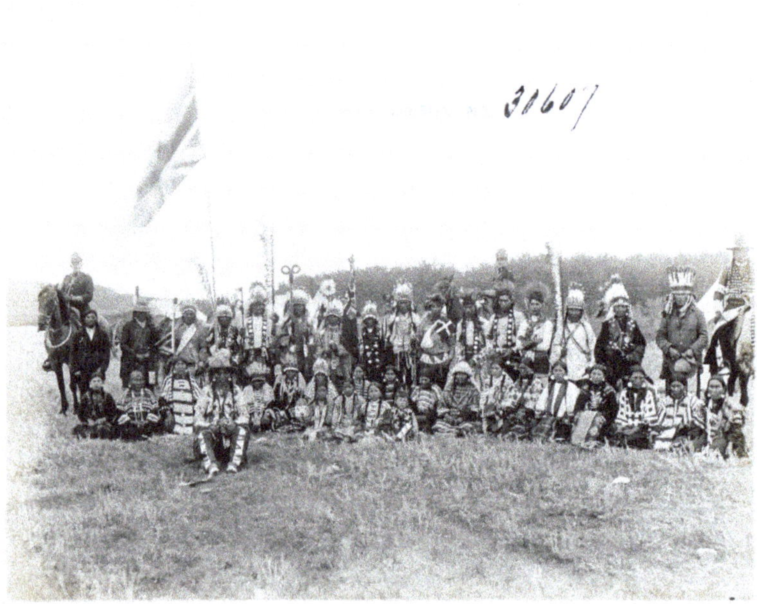

Fig. 6.19 'Patriotic Indian Chiefs [2]'. Copyright R. R. Mumford, 1916 (copyright number 30607).

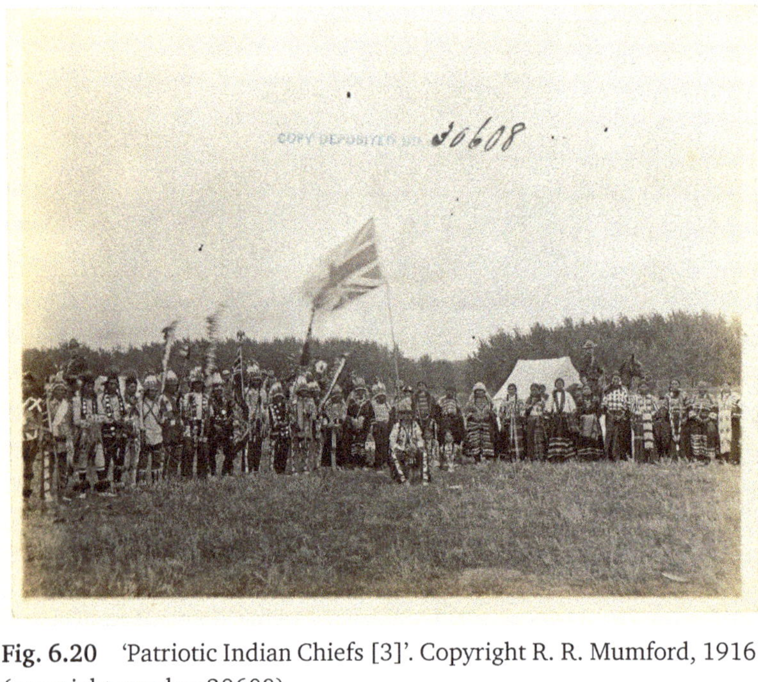

Fig. 6.20 'Patriotic Indian Chiefs [3]'. Copyright R. R. Mumford, 1916 (copyright number 30608).

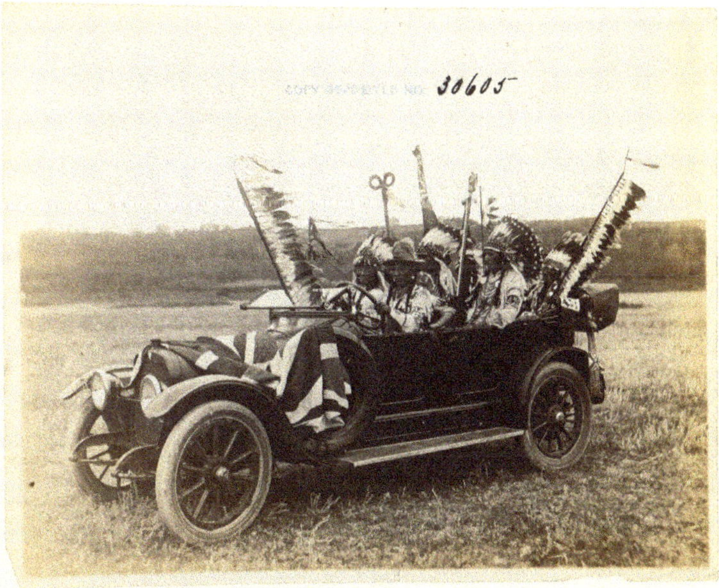

Fig. 6.21 'Patriotic Indian Chiefs [4]'. Copyright R. R. Mumford, 1916 (copyright number 30609).

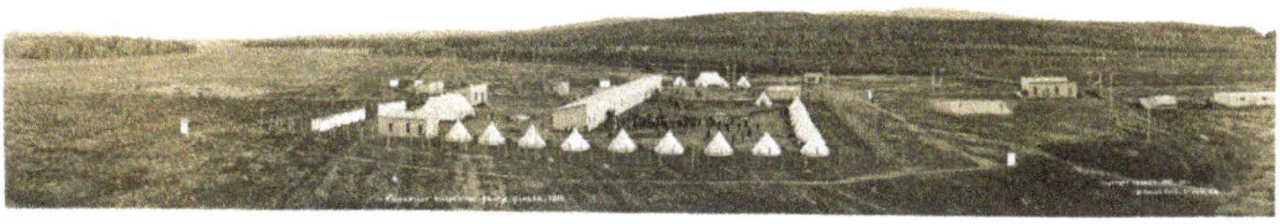

Fig. 6.22 'Valcartier Internment Camp'. Copyright D. Smith Reid, 1915 (copyright number 30874).

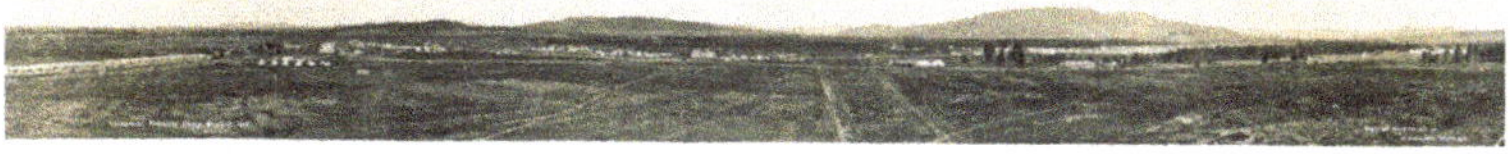

Fig. 6.23 'Valcartier Training Camp'. Copyright D. Smith Reid, 1915 (copyright number 30873).

of freely expressed patriotism and more as contrived, state-sponsored poses with the trappings of patriotism and imperial affiliation. The photograph thus illustrates the complex internal politics involved in Canada's war, as well as being a further instance of the complex colonial processes that were ongoing in Canada, and the photographic depiction of them discussed in Chapter 4.

There were many other groups in Canada that also had complex relationships with their home state and the war being waged overseas. French Canadians were often ambivalent to the conflict, and the many European immigrants who had arrived in the late nineteenth and early twentieth centuries were viewed with suspicion by the Canadian state. Again the collection reflects this: there are French language propaganda postcards imploring people to defend France, while a photograph of Laurier speaking at a Montreal recruitment rally is also copyrighted. More striking though are the photographs of Canada's internment camps.

Camps like the one at Valcartier were the result of Canada's fear of supposed 'enemy aliens' – recent migrants from Eastern Europe whose allegiance to Canada was questioned for little to no reason other than their country of birth (see Figs 6.22–6.23). As the South African War carved fissures into Canadian society that would last through the twentieth century,[19] so the First World War was exposing tensions and even writing them onto the landscape. Kordan's *Enemy Aliens, Prisoners of War* is an extensive account of the west coast internment camp experience; it focuses on how those interned were used as labour to construct infrastructure in the National Parks. Crucial to the argument of this book is the idea that this nation-building experience found in the Great War was an exclusive one, indeed '[a]s the country moved toward nationhood, the enemy alien – by reason of birthplace – was consciously left outside the national project'.[20] This illustrates another layer of the dynamics explored in Chapter 5, where migrants, on account of their actions, appearance or place of origin, could fall beyond the bounds of Anglo-Canadian identity and therefore be seen, in the case of the war, as a dangerous 'other'.

The photographs of these sites found in the collection are conspicuously devoid of detail. Depicting the camp from afar, they reveal their isolation to the viewer, but not the experiences of those within the camp. Nonetheless, the mere presence of the camp, the record of its having been there, acts as a *punctum*. Through it we are reminded of the divisive, wounding nature of the war, not just in Europe but in the homelands of soldiers who believed they were fighting to protect freedom and justice. In this context there is a striking contrast between the photograph of

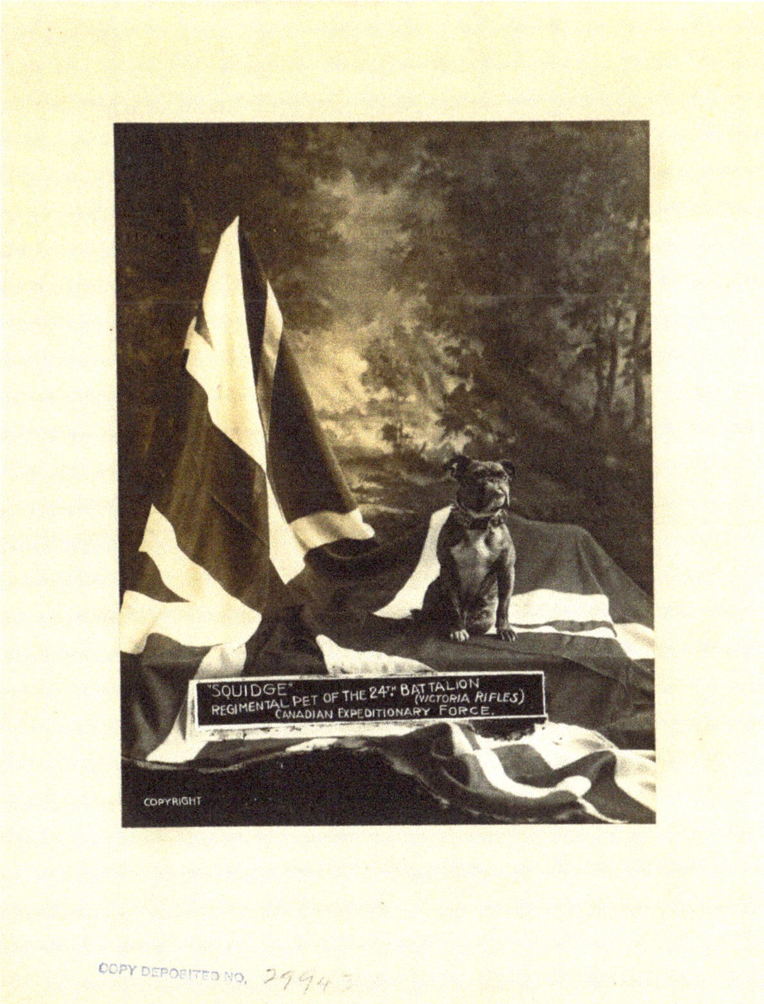

Fig. 6.24 'Squidge, 24 Battalion Mascot'. Copyright John A. Gunn, 1915 (copyright number 29943).

a young John McCrae (Fig.6.7), who was heading to South Africa to defend British values and would later write the heroic, moralising poetry of 'In Flanders Fields', and the injustice these sites represent. It is these random juxtapositions that lend the collection an historical weight and depth found in few other photographic records.

As Canadians were faced with massive military mobilisation, political strife, civic injustice and many other events, it is notable that the Colonial Copyright Collection also displays the allegiance Canadian

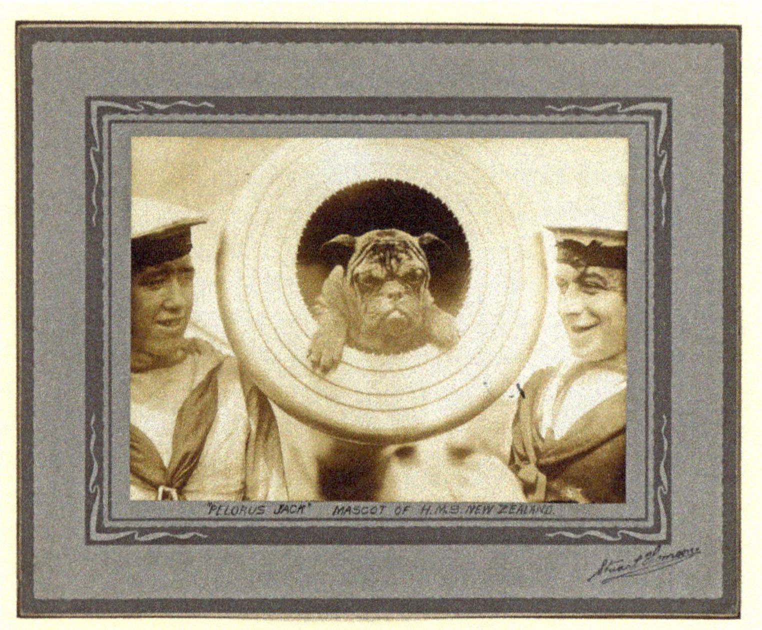

Fig. 6.25 'Pelorus Jack Mascot of HMS New Zealand'. Copyright Stuart Thompson, 1914 (copyright number 29327).

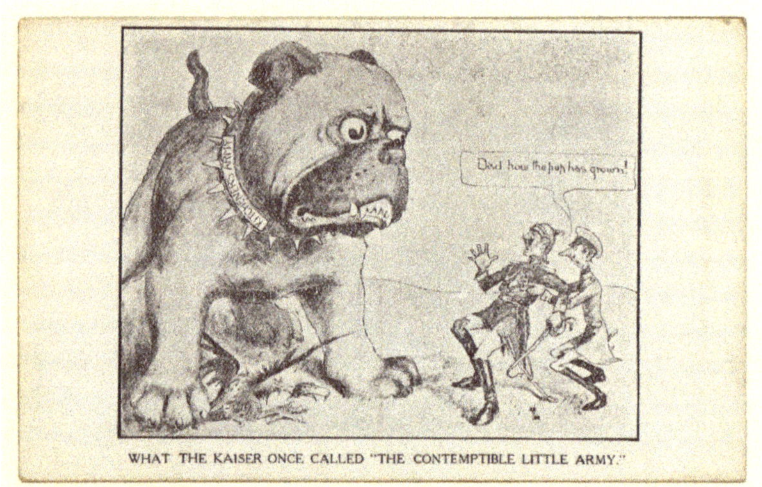

Fig. 6.26 'What the Kaiser Once Called a Contemptible Little Army'. Copyright William Springett, 1916 (copyright number 32614).

photographers and artists felt to Britain, the humorous side of propaganda and the lighter aspects of military life. A particularly noteworthy topic is the regimental or boat mascot, an especially popular photographic subject in the early years of the war. Pets with names such as 'Squidge', 'Joker' and 'Pelorus Jack' are placed in a variety of situations (Jack, in particular, looks rather miserable) to show Canadian animals' support for the cause (see Figs 6.24–6.25). Similarly, there are various cartoon postcards which address different aspects of the conflict; a significant majority of these are not only imperialist in tone, but also focus on the strength of the British Empire and its ability to win the war by drawing on its people from across the globe (Fig. 6.26).[21] Within this, then, is the same strand of faith in the support and ability of the 'self-governing empire' that was on display in the South African War.

Initially, what the Colonial Copyright Collection portrays to a contemporary viewer is something of Canada's continuing patriotism. However, unlike the images copyrighted for the South African War, it is a markedly more complex visual economy and shows some of the deep issues that challenged the idea, both at the time and subsequently, that the First World War represented a nation-building experience for Canada. That being said, positive propaganda is still a significant part of the collection's deposits, and the photographs show how varied in form and style photographic propaganda related to the war could be.

However, this is far from the most significant cache of war-related photographic material deposited to the collection. The largest body, the photographs of the Canadian War Records Office, adds depth not just to our understanding of the relationship between Canada, the war and photography, but to the appreciation of the changing relationship between Canada and Britain as a whole – and to the small part played by Colonial Copyright Law in all of this.

In Britain the War Office was notably reserved about the flow of information from the front. The actions of Lord Beaverbrook, the Ontario-born press baron and parliamentary minister, were a profound contrast to this as he and the Canadian War Records Office (CWRO) commissioned photographers, film makers and artists to record the work of the Canadian forces in various formats. Beaverbrook's aim was to record the efforts of Canadian soldiers so they would not be forgotten, while using the proceeds from the sale and display of these images to fund the construction of war memorials back in Canada. The result of Beaverbrook's aims was a prodigious amount of material that has had a profound impact on the understanding of Canada's involvement in the war. As Tim Cook has argued, '[t]he conscious moulding of memory

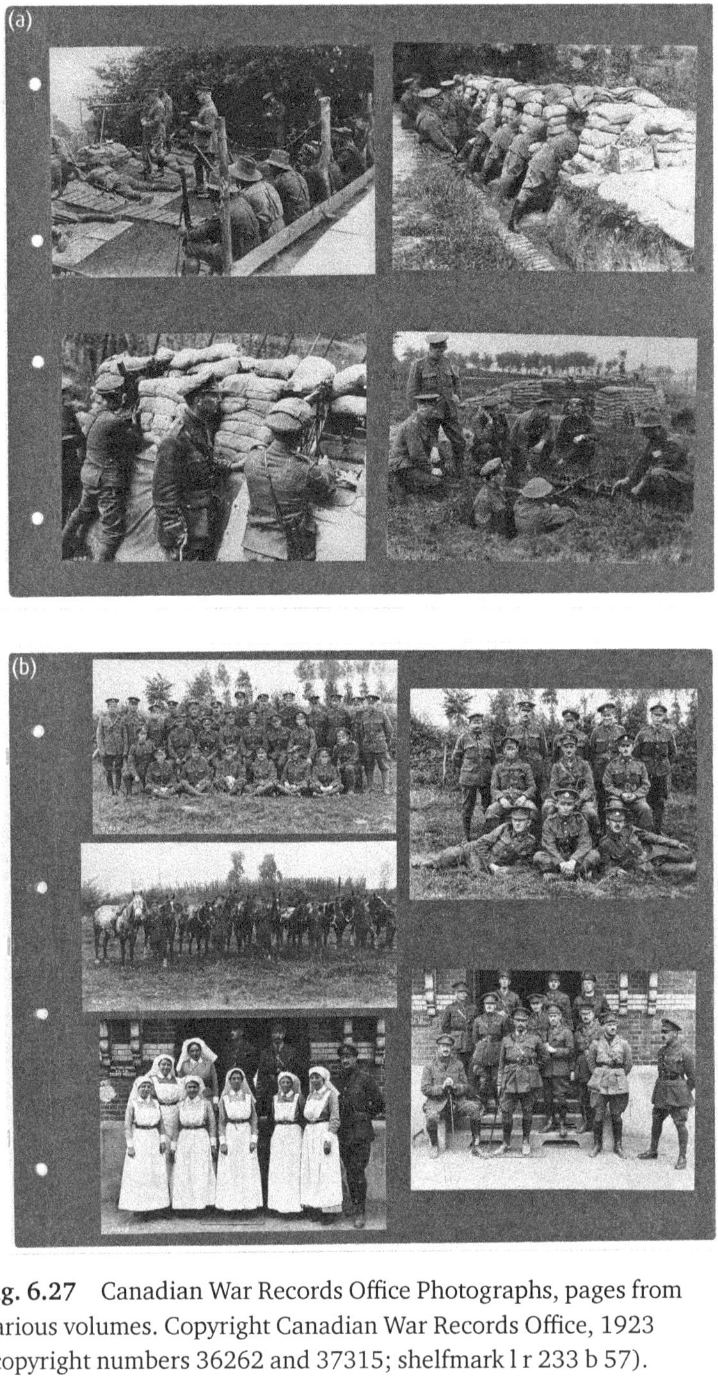

Fig. 6.27 Canadian War Records Office Photographs, pages from various volumes. Copyright Canadian War Records Office, 1923 (copyright numbers 36262 and 37315; shelfmark l r 233 b 57).

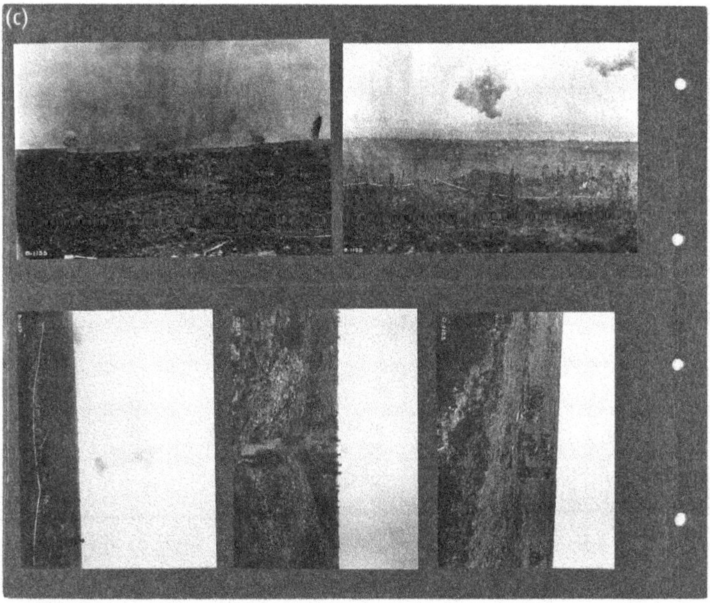

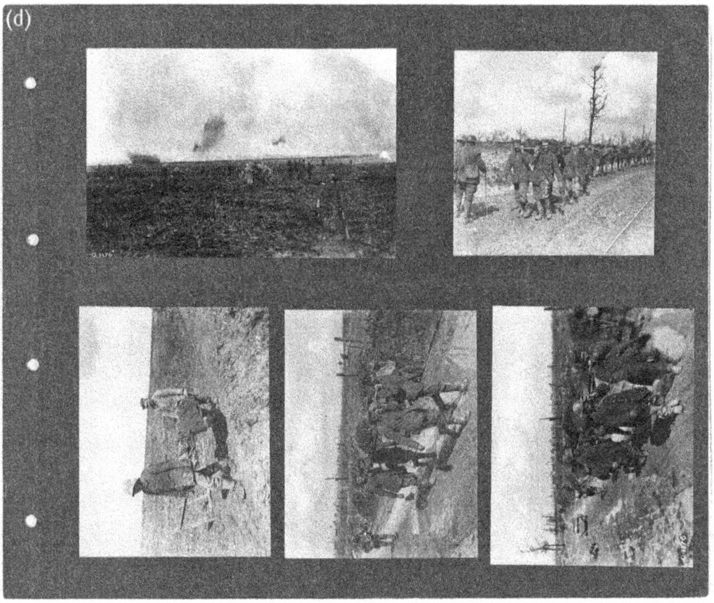

Fig. 6.27 (*Continued*)

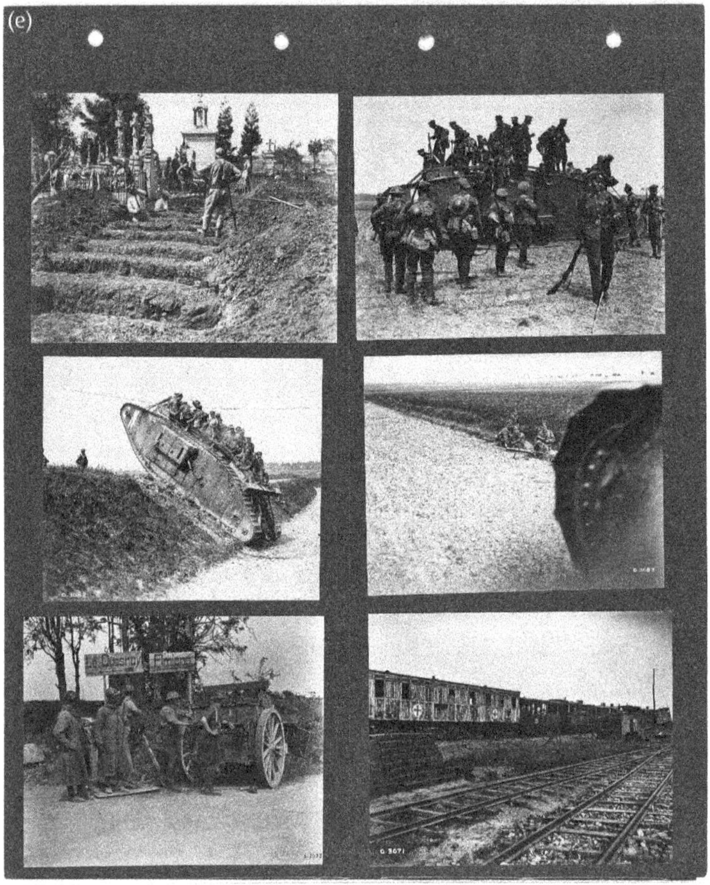

Fig. 6.27 (*Continued*)

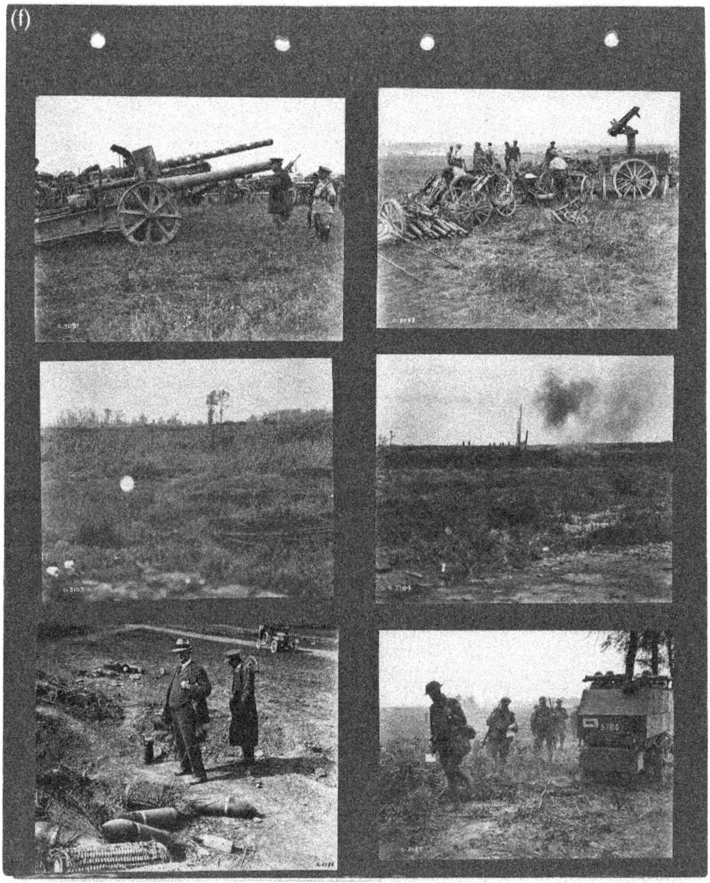

Fig. 6.27 (*Continued*)

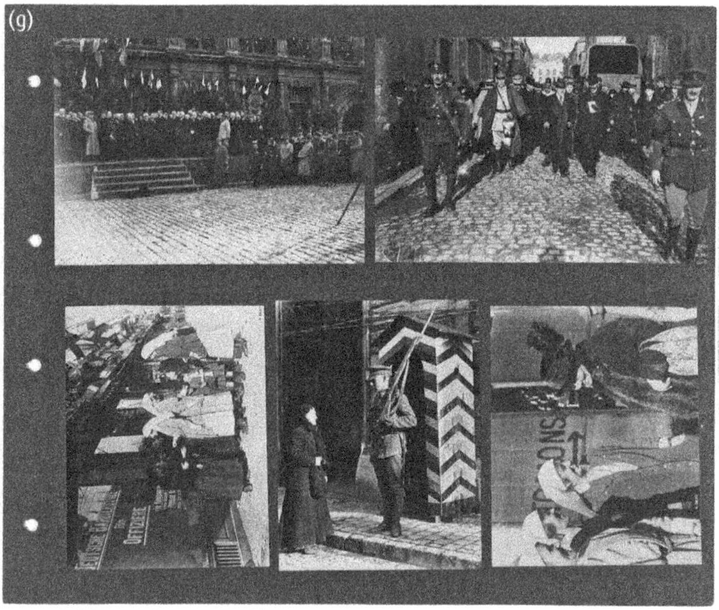

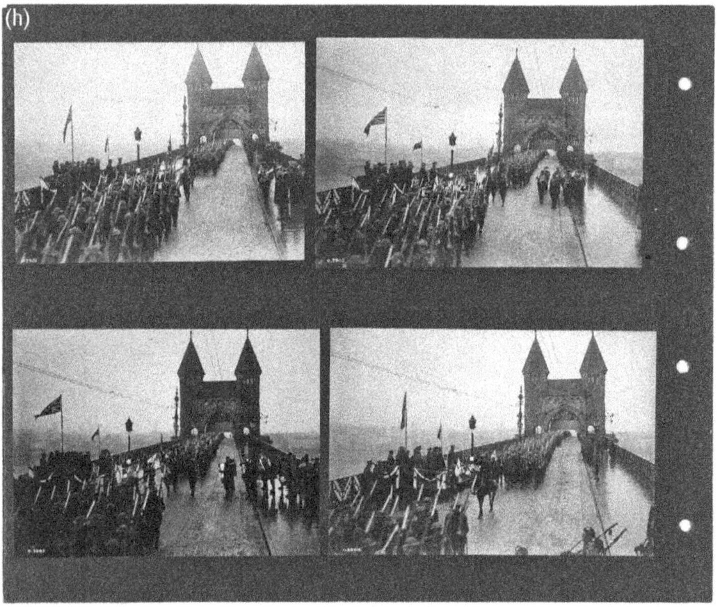

Fig. 6.27 (*Continued*)

and laying of an historical foundation by Lord Beaverbrook has had an enduring legacy on Canadian historiography since the guns fell silent on 11th November 1918'.[22]

A fraction of this material found its way into the Colonial Copyright Collection – a selection of 1,772 photographs from the total produced by Canada's official war photographers, which totalled just under 8,000 images (see for example Fig.6.27). Despite this, the album contains a cross-section of Canada's role in the conflict. Training camps, front line duty, grisly war trophies, memorial services, soldiers marching through a ruined Europe and many more scenes are depicted through the lenses trained on the Canadian armed forces. It is argued that the Canadian War Records Office was a gigantic and well executed propaganda campaign, albeit one that reflects rather than distorts the achievements of Canadians in the field.[23] What is notable from this collection of photographs is that great lengths have been gone to in order to achieve a suitably impressive record of Canadian efforts; shots are (on the whole) well composed and technically accomplished (especially in contrast to the work of copyrighters such as R. R. Mumford, above). The selection also presents a varied portrait of the war, conveying glory, tragedy, pathos and banality; it wears its multiple photographers and extended time frame overtly, as subjects, styles and foci differ and change.

For all of this, the photographs were poorly received at home. Maria Tippet highlights that this photographic work was criticised for providing few insights into the personal drama of the war. Most notably, it was felt that the photographs failed to communicate a sense of the humanity of the scenes they illustrated to viewers back in the relative safety of home.[24] Laura Brandon's later work takes up this thread. She suggests that Beaverbrook's endeavours in turn drove audiences to painting and other forms of art as a way of experiencing, connecting to and perhaps understanding the experience of war on the continent, with this in turn stimulating support for war art and the work of the Group of Seven.[25] As a result, the photographs probably act more effectively as an historical record than they did as a means of communication and spreading propaganda at the time of their production. Home consumption was not, however, the only function that these images were expected to perform.

Tim Cook has published a great deal of analysis of the photographs and other works of the Canadian War Records Office, illustrating the complex view of the war these materials present and how their message has evolved over time.[26] Within the context of this analysis the sub-collection deposited at the British Library is significant. It adds weight and nuance to the large amount of material discussed earlier in this section and illustrates the level of concern Canadians felt about the war. Perhaps most importantly, the Colonial Copyright Collection also contributes to the broader understanding of the CWRO's work, reminding us that, for all the volume of the CWRO work and the scale of its influence on foreign perceptions of Canadian involvement in the First World War, this is an incomplete story. It neglects to show the profound and divisive impact the war had on Canada at home – a significant omission given the importance of these photographs and other materials to the understanding of the war as a nation-building event.

There is a further nuance of note here: the CWRO's decision to copyright these photographs under Colonial Copyright Law. The series of photographs were deposited as two records, copyright numbers 36262 and 37315, and as a result constitute by far the largest single deposit made to the collection. This also illustrates the legal nous and economic sense of those administrating the CWRO as, unlike copyrighters such as Bishop and Barker, it was understood that a single deposit of all photographs was as valuable as an individual deposit for each photograph copyrighted under the law.[27]

More importantly, it shows that the CWRO used a British imperial law in order to support the aims of the CWRO, protect its financial investment and institutionally preserve a further record of the contribution made by Canadian soldiers to the First World War. Colonial Copyright Law, as the Introduction showed, was something of a failure from the perspective of the metropole. However, it was used and appreciated by photographers in Canada, and the CWRO's use of the law is perhaps the prime example of this reversal of fortunes. It shows an individual and group, with strong, nationalistic ties to the metropole and London, reusing an imperial law designed to facilitate oversight as a means to promote a favourable perspective on the efforts of Canadians fighting to protect the bonds of empire. The CWRO was viewed by some at the time of the war as propaganda for Canadians, and it has been interpreted as such since – a perspective perhaps compounded by evidence that the Colonial Copyright Law and its resulting collection have been reused and reinterpreted to the benefit of this media savvy and independently agent group of Canadians.

The collection therefore allows us to glimpse the evolving role of the collection and Colonial Copyright Law as Canada gained status and reputation in the twentieth century. In the CWRO photographs we perceive not just a visual economy of propaganda, but also a manipulation of that economy and the mechanisms of the empire to memorialise the achievements of Canadian soldiers. Such an insight is important to our understanding of this collection and the role of Colonial Copyright Law in the British Empire. It also provides more depth to how the CWRO photographs are understood, and to our historic impression of Lord Beaverbrook. The copyright deposit further confirms the belief in the financial value of these photographs, their significance as propaganda and the deep understanding Beaverbrook possessed of intercolonial connections and networks.

***

If we understand these photographs as depicting Canadians as actors in complex colonial networks, conducting themselves with a developing sense of independence from the empire and dealing with the consequences of this interaction and conflict at home as well as abroad, then we can glimpse a Canada becoming not simply a nation, but part of a transnational network of places and politics that would come to define the twentieth century. Increasing numbers of historians argue that Canada's involvement in the First World War should be understood in transnational rather than nationalistic terms. This collection, even as far back as the photographs of the South African War, supports such an argument.[28]

This chapter has shown the many impacts of conflict on Canada and the way in which Canadian photographers became bound up in these conflicts. Often patriotic in tone, these photographs nonetheless serve to remind us of the complex terrain of Canada's involvement in the war, as with the distant images of internment camps, and act as memorials to its costs at home as well as abroad. Furthermore, complex readings of photographs from both conflicts illustrate how much some in Canadian society stood to gain from bolstering Canada's reputation abroad and developing a particular Anglo-centric idea of cohesive nationhood. Photographs of South African war veterans at civic events and the use of Colonial Copyright Law by an expatriate Canadian press baron are but two examples of who strove to gain what, while others around them lost their lives or were marginalised from these nationalistic and imperial projects. In short, then, these photographs illustrate how deep and meaningful the visual economy that drove the Colonial Copyright Collection was.

Photographs are frozen instances in time that endure, evolve in meaning and continue to make new connections well beyond the instant when the camera's shutter is released. Events of great national – indeed, international – significance and emotional weight tend to force a greater depth of evolution and span of connection due to the accrued emotional weight placed behind them. This is what drives the *punctums* that Barthes encountered in family photographs and raises questions for us in viewing this collection, bound together by nothing other than copyright.

Conclusion: Canada in the photographer's century

This book has explored the significance of the Colonial Copyright Collection of Canadian photographs and the view they provide of the history of Canada. Through the interpretation of individual images and sets of images deposited by a variety of photographers across Canada between 1895 and 1924, the collection adds rich understanding to the development of Canada as a nation. In places it adds detail to – and challenges the acceptance of – established grand narratives; in others it allows a glimpse of rarely considered fragments of the Canadian story.

The origins of the collection, and the particular mechanisms of its growth, provide an eclectic and unusual slideshow of Canada at this time. The context and nature of the collection's development through formal legislation and institutionalised practice have a significant bearing on the analysis presented in this book. It has also meant that the collection has spent much of its life in the British Museum Library, and latterly in the British Library, in something of a twilight zone, with successive curators unsure what to make of it and researchers unable to access it. In this conclusion I provide a synthesis of the argument presented in this book, highlighting themes which cut across the specific chapters. I also address the contemporary possibilities opened up by new digital technologies for the management of such photographic collections in the twenty-first century.

Canada in the frame

The account of Colonial Copyright Law presented in the Introduction initially situated the Colonial Copyright Collection within the context of wider projects of knowledge accumulation associated with the British Empire in the nineteenth century. As such, the collection examined in this book may be considered part of a geography of knowledge which centred on the imperial metropole and institutions such as the British Museum Library in particular. However, consideration of the nature of copyright also illustrates the role of the individual, the market and the commercial value of photography in the formation of the collection. As its development was ultimately dependent on the decisions of individual photographers seeking to protect the commercial value of their photography, this collection reflects the logic of the market for photography as understood by producers at this time. This being the case, the view of Canada and its history presented by the collection is unique. It bears a more chaotic quality and multiplicity of views than a collection such as the stills division of the National Film Board, which Payne characterised as displaying a 'benign nationalism'.[1] However, this sense of chaos recedes once the collection is viewed geographically, historically or thematically, as the previous chapters have illustrated.

To this end, the Colonial Copyright Collection required a different methodological approach. The concept of a 'visual economy', explored throughout this book, explicitly acknowledges the materiality of the photographic image and its status as a commodity, as well as its location within specific local and regional contexts of production and consumption. That is to say notions of the market, of consumption and of the value of the photograph were neither abstract nor homogenous across Canada or across different periods of time. Each chapter in this book has illustrated the way in which local photographers catered to somewhat different markets, responded to different popular tropes and articulated different photographic values. These differences are inherent to a collection founded on local initiative and the logic of the market. They also invite us to appreciate the multiplicity of views sought by ever greater numbers of consumers.

The substantive studies making up the body of this book were selected on the basis of the content and format of the collection. They explore the significance of particular themes (the overarching importance of modernity and Canada's peoples considered via the city, the railway, the postcard, the portrait, migration and war) for the Canadian image world as a whole during the period between 1895 and 1924. Chapter 2, for example, illustrates how the urban landscape provided opportunities for photographers to respond to various kinds of place-making projects. Here the camera is not just a witness to urban change, but also was actively involved in the process of change. The relationship was also reciprocal: the city provided the subject and the camera articulated ways of seeing, with the city and its administrative networks then providing the visual economy through which these images circulated. Chapter 1, meanwhile, highlighted the importance of a particularly significant photographic medium – the postcard – in creating a market for the increasing number of photographers operating across Canada in the period. In these and other chapters of the book, photographic imagery is also used as a means to address wider questions about the visualisation of both landscape and people in an era of significant change.

In undertaking this research, I have therefore sought to broaden the understanding of the Colonial Copyright Collection, its place within the British Library and its relationship to the Canadian image world. In the process, the work has highlighted the historical and material depth of a significant component of the library's collections as a whole, contributing to an established body of research on the library's history.[2] This has been done by intensive scrutiny of the materials within the Colonial Copyright Collection itself, and also by linking them to other materials within the library. These include, for example, newspapers, government papers, journal articles and books, as well as collections elsewhere – notably at The National Archives (Kew), The British Museum and Library and Archives Canada. The research also paid close attention to the colonial origins and significance of the collection, as these factors have important consequences for its future uses, particularly in the context of the British Library's commitment to public engagement. (This is considered in a digital context below.)

The book has also sought to show how work on the collection can provide insight into both Canadian history and visual culture in the late nineteenth and early twentieth centuries, contributing to a growing body of research on the history of Canadian photography in particular. Chapter 2, for example, illustrated how important the photograph was to developing contrasting visions of the urban environment in Canada, while also highlighting the complexity of the photographic networks of production, exchange and meaning making. Chapter 3 used images in the collection to reconsider Canada's relationship with the railway, starting from Charland's call to problematise Canada's 'technological nationalism'.[3] Chapter 1, meanwhile, makes a significant contribution to the history of the postcard by locating it more firmly in the context of Canadian visual culture and economy.[4] As suggested in that chapter, the material form, as well as the content, of many of the photographs contained in the Colonial Copyright Collection provides further clues as to their intended function, in this case as postcard images. Chapters 4 and 5 illustrate how the depictions of different people in Canada varied significantly across Canada, reflecting differences in the regional context of settler–indigenous relations in the case of First Peoples subjects, and revealing the intended photographic market and the nature of the relationship between photographer and subject. As in the other chapters, the research in this chapter is intended to contribute to a substantial body of existing research, much of it non-Canadian, on portraiture in colonial contexts. Finally, Chapter 6 shows the complex national and international roles of Canadian photography, with the images themselves and the legislation underpinning this collection being used for personal, nationalistic and interimperial aims. In this respect, it contributes to a large body of academic work on how the visual arts are manipulated by particular groups and individuals to achieve personal or national gains, while also considering the less discussed and flexible role of legislation and copyright in facilitating the impact of the visual arts.

The book has also highlighted the relevance of the collection to contemporary concerns within Canada, as illustrated in particular by the study of portraits of First Peoples in Chapter 4. Rafton-Canning's images provide some of the few records we have of nineteenth-century Blackfoot material culture, partial though his perspective undoubtedly was.[5] Similarly, Geraldine Moodie's images have been used in the late twentieth century to reinvigorate the Inuit oral history tradition; they provide important material links with a past at risk of being lost if histories are not passed on.[6] Many of the other First Peoples images in the Colonial Copyright Collection could be put to similar use, and the research presented in Chapter 4, while contextualising and problematising the images, also opens the door to different kinds of work with these images.

This book also seeks to contribute to the history of photography in more general terms, working at both the level of individual images and at the level of the collection as a whole. By extending the notion of 'visual economy' beyond the specific context in which it was initially developed by Deborah Poole, I have sought to demonstrate the value of focusing specifically on the market value and materiality of photographs.[7] While the approach departs from Poole's concerns (for example, I have not dwelt at any length on the connections between photography and the worlds of literature, painting and the creative arts), the idea of visual economy and the 'image world' has particular resonance in the case of the Colonial Copyright Collection. It has also helped to illustrate the ways in which photographs and photographers themselves circulated in national and international networks.

In the search for new contexts for the interpretation of photographs in the collection, a number of general themes have recurred throughout the book. The first thematic context is that of colonialism and colonial networks. As noted in the Introduction, there is an increasing body of work which emphasises the spatial differentiation of colonial networks, whether they be political, legislative or economic.[8] Through this book we have seen Canada's photographers and their work being drawn into a colonial network which sought to regulate the intellectual property of empire and aggregate a vast span of knowledge about the places of the globe under imperial rule. We have also seen the colonial landscape and colonised peoples visualised through the lenses of individuals and firms operating across Canada.

In this respect, the images of civic ceremonies discussed in Chapter 2 and of the railway in Chapter 3 can be seen as attempts to re-imagine Canada's spaces in the light of the various colonial projects which spread out across a nation that had only relatively recently spanned the continent. Similarly, Chapter 4 considers photographs of First Peoples produced directly or indirectly as part of Canada's colonial projects. Born of colonial legislation, the collection as a whole must be viewed in the context of the effects of British colonialism in Canada between 1895 and 1924.

A second thematic context running in parallel, and sometimes in contradiction, to this colonial history concerns the lure of modernity within Canada during this period. This is frequently expressed through images of technological modernity and its impact on the Canadian landscape and society. The culture of technology is an inescapable aspect of Chapters 1 and 3, in which the aeroplane and the railway are depicted as having significant effects upon the landscape imaginary. Similarly, in Chapter 5 the significance of the railway in not just facilitating the colonisation of Canada's prairies, but also directly affecting its geography and demography is apparent.

Wider landscapes of technological modernity are also evident in Chapter 6, where modern transportation took Canadians around the world into a mechanised battlefield. The evolution of the camera itself, along with changes to printing and postal technology, was just as significant as other elements of this technological modernity.[9] The significance of modernity as a theme is also reflected in the history of the Toronto Industrial Exhibition (and its later guise, the Canadian National Exhibition) as discussed in several chapters. The images contained in the Colonial Copyright Collection both depict and were most probably sold at this significant site of Canadian modernity.

Alongside colonialism and modernity, the emergence of a market for photographic imagery has provided a third thematic context for the substantive analyses undertaken in this book. The visual materials forming the basis of the Colonial Copyright Collection were assembled through a piece of legislation designed to protect the market value of photographs for their producers. The development of this market provided opportunities for photographers across Canada to depict new subjects and to disseminate their work in myriad ways. This is perhaps most clearly evident in Chapter 4, where the market for particular views of First Peoples encouraged the production of portraits showing Canada's indigenous people as either unchangeably exotic or increasingly white. In Chapters 2 and 3 we also saw how larger-scale business interests (in the form of Eaton's consumer empire and the Canadian railway companies) grasped the opportunity to use photography to present particular views of the modern Canadian landscape.

A final thematic context is provided by geography itself, both material and imaginative. At the level of the collection as a whole, geography mattered to the very definition of Colonial Copyright. A colonial geography of knowledge pulled information about the colonies back to the imperial hub, creating an archival, museum and library system which is still of worldwide significance and shaped by its imperial past, often in surprising and shifting ways.

Furthermore, a geographical perspective on the contents of the collection provides a lens on how the Canadian landscape and nation was persistently rearticulated and reinterpreted in light of the progress of technological modernity, producing insights into successive 'drafts' of the Canadian landscape as discussed by Cole Harris.[10] It is clear from the various chapters that the Canadian image world itself had a distinctive geography which both reflected and shaped the modern history of Canada. Taken as a whole, the collection illustrates the complexity of the Canadian landscape and its constantly changing nature, perceived from the perspective of many photographers and communities.

The Colonial Copyright Collection in a digital age

If the late nineteenth century was a time of paper empires, today's world is one of digital domains. This presents challenges and opportunities for research on the Colonial Copyright Collection, which was born of the material mobilities and collecting impulses of the nineteenth century. Given its origins in a systematic process of information relocation across the Atlantic, it is ironic that the collection then languished for so long in the back rooms of the British Museum Library, until the cataloguing work of curators and academics in the 1980s prepared the path that led eventually to the undertaking of this book. However, *Canada in the Frame* does not represent an end point in the academic engagement with this collection, nor in the social life of these photographic objects. Research for this book has suggested many ways in which work on the collection could be taken further, notably highlighting the potential of digital technology in shaping the twenty-first-century life of the collection. This relationship between the material, the institution and new technology will form the main avenue for future work with the Colonial Copyright Collection.

Canada in the Frame has highlighted that the Colonial Copyright Collection is a mobile, internationally significant collection of potential interest to many different public audiences in both the UK and Canada. Given the emphasis throughout the book on the plurality of these images, their ability to be produced in particular contexts and subsequently to speak to broader themes, this should come as no surprise. Such a perspective on the continuing life of collections is very much in tune with the argument of Elizabeth Edwards in *Raw Histories*, which suggests that the rawness and infinite re-codability of the image invests it with significant potential for re-engagement and rearticulation, particularly within the context of the museum, archive and library collection. Indeed Edwards argues that it is the responsibility of the institution to provide opportunities within which the image can be 'articulated, digested and made active' in a variety of contexts.[11] Such a call resonates with a wider body of work on the role of museums and other public institutions involved in the promotion of access to culturally significant artefacts, which asserts the inherent role of these sites in recontextualising the meaning of objects. Charles Saumarez-Smith made this argument in his chapter in *The New Museology*, pointing out that from their inception museums (and by extension other public institutions of this ilk) were conceived as spaces which would change the meaning of objects, by virtue of moving them from the private sphere to the public.[12] Similar arguments have been taken up in geography by Hilary Geoghegan, Jude Hill and others.[13] The digital landscape of the twenty-first century offers yet a further context for engagement with the Colonial Copyright Collection, with the possibility of its virtual mobility bringing access to a global audience.

The account of the shape and development of the collection has illustrated its sheer size, diverse contents and varied forms. As a result of its obdurate and sometimes awkward materiality the collection is relatively stationary, and its audience is therefore somewhat limited. By this I do not simply refer to the absolute geographical distance between, say,

London and the rest of the UK, let alone Canada, but also the relative distances between the Colonial Copyright Collection and the various specialist and non-specialist publics who may potentially be interested in its holdings. As many of the case studies have suggested, a large number of the images in the collection could potentially speak to these sorts of publics. To re-mobilise the collection digitally provides opportunities for engagement of these photographs with these publics, and for the sorts of rearticulation of these 'raw histories' envisaged by Edwards and others.

Mapping out the next phase in the life of the collection presents some serious challenges, as highlighted by wider discussions regarding the digitisation of various types of material object, image and text. Here I take my cue from Joanna Sassoon's work in *Photographs, Objects, Histories*, where she suggests that the digitisation of material objects is more than just a translation of the object from physical to digital form, but also represents the creation of a new object, which speaks to different audiences and has different cultural effects.[14] This perspective needs to be nuanced as the 'raw histories' of the digital images themselves are liable to undergo change and yield multiple interpretations, just as the original images themselves are. In both forms, paper and digital, the object would be open to being read in specific ways, mediated by the setting of engagement and the audience doing the reading. Digitisation, in this respect, does not bypass the need to consider the forms and channels of engagement, nor does it diminish the importance of the material object. Rather it opens up opportunities for further and more varied kinds of engagement.

The potential of the digital era can be exemplified with reference to the images discussed in Chapter 4. The photographs of Albert Rafton-Canning and Geraldine Moodie have recently been used to re-establish links with the lived and imagined histories of the 'Plains Indian' and Inuit groups, whose cultures and memories had been eroded by the colonial projects discussed in this chapter. Dorothy Eber, for example, used the photographs of Geraldine Moodie to prompt discussions about the history of the Inuit of Fullerton Bay with individuals who were the elders of the area in the 1980s.[15] Similarly, Dempsey used Rafton-Canning's images from the Galt Museum Archives to construct a book about the material culture of his ancestors. In both these contexts the colonial gaze of these images is redirected in order to reconnect with, and redefine, the culture and identity of these indigenous groups. However, in both these cases, and others like them, regret is frequently expressed that the collections are not more extensive and, most importantly, more publicly accessible. An opportunity therefore exists to exploit the full potential of the Colonial Copyright Collection, using readily available digital technology.

The digitisation of images in this collection has benefits beyond the immediate context of First Peoples and indigenous history. The scale and depth of the collection is such that it would provide a useful resource for studying and teaching a variety of subjects, such as the growth of Canadian cities during the early twentieth century, the study of immigrants, the history of transportation – including the railway, the automobile and the aeroplane – and the history of Canada's involvement in the South African and First World Wars. While these have been the themes of this book, much material remains only thinly considered here, begging for more eyes and further historic and cultural interpretations to be built around them. Furthermore, the photographic views of landscape will be particularly valuable, especially to those wishing to research the expansion of agriculture, industry and the railways across Canada.

In this respect, the collection also constitutes a notable resource for artists and scientists interested in the possibility of re-photography. Photographers such as Byron Harmon (discussed in Chapter 3 for his railway photographs) depicted much of Canada's natural heritage. Harmon in particular extensively photographed the eastern side of the Rockies and its many glaciers; his work provides opportunities for considering how the landscape around these features has changed through re-photography and other techniques.

A further opportunity presented by the digitisation of the images of the Colonial Copyright Collection would be the possibility of undertaking a full reappraisal of the contents of the original collection by comparing photographs held in London with those in Canada. Neither the British Library nor Library and Archives Canada hold a complete collection as a result of historical damage or other forms of loss. On the basis of a 2008 research visit to Ottawa and Gatineau, the sites of Library and Archives Canada, I was able to confirm that the two collections are nearer completion than previously assumed, suggesting that obtaining an accurate overview of the original collection would be feasible. A digital 'bridge', highlighting duplicates and displaying each collection's unique images, would in principle provide the possibility of access to the complete collection on either side of the Atlantic.

It is with this context and thinking as background that the British Library recently undertook a small project to digitise part of the Colonial Copyright Collection of photographs.[16] In partnership with Wikimedia Commons and the Eccles Centre for American Studies, I and

Andrew Gray, the Library's 'Wikipedian in Residence', used a small grant to digitise the main bulk of the collection.[17] These digital objects, released into the public domain, are now available on the British Library's digital delivery service as well as Wikimedia Commons, allowing them to be referenced and dynamically reused by a globalised community of researchers and people with a general interest in the content of the collection. This work, known as 'Picturing Canada', is still ongoing and evolving, but it should be mentioned here as it grounds some of the theory above.

From the beginning of the digitisation work it was clear that, as Edwards and Sassoon have argued,[18] this work was not creating a replica or a supplement; it was rather producing an object with a new, independent and dynamic agency of its own. The physical and digital objects are not separate, divorced entirely from one another; instead they are already operating a complex dialogue of interaction. Photographs from the 'Picturing Canada' series currently illustrate over 100 Wikipedia pages in upwards of 20 languages, including an image by G. E. Fleming entitled, 'Young Cree Man' which illustrated the site's 'Cree' entry in multiple languages. More dynamically, the images have also been used by the Canadian and American press to illustrate articles on Canada's history or landscape. The *Huffington Post* for example published an article using photographs from the collection, which it placed against twenty-first-century photographs from a similar spot.[19] Meanwhile the *National Post* ran a week-long series using the collection to talk about lesser known elements of Canadian history and culture.[20]

The use of archival photography within the news media is unremarkable, but it has served to illustrate two things. Firstly, it has shown the new dynamism and agency of these imaginations of Canada generated by the creation of new digital objects. In both of these articles the photographs have also been heavily commented on, generating debate on local figures such as Joe Fortes or reflections on tragedies such as the Enterprise train disaster (discussed in Chapter 3). The latter of these is notable, especially as commenters drew direct links between these photographs and similar recent tragedies; the photograph indeed caused one commenter to note the enduring relationship between transport and accidents.[21]

This raises a second significant issue, the connection and re-connection of these images with personal and local histories. In the above these images are becoming bound into people's understanding not just of the history of Canada, but also of the world around them. They provide a way of making sense of the world, as they did for the Canadians who produced and consumed the images during their period of physical circulation. As a curator I also inhabit a privileged space where I hear other stories the collection stimulates, such as the presence of a photograph from the collection in a family album or its reminding of a significant local event, with these instances often generating new questions or routes of research. Furthermore, there is evidence that the circulation of these new digital objects is also driving interest and traffic back to their physical counterparts – an interesting development that may begin to undermine some of the assumptions about the relationship between digitisation and physical collections.

While concluding *Canada in the Frame* I am not going to try and make meaning of all the above; it is far too early to do so and the points noted here are observational rather than quantified. However, it is appropriate to note that the use observed fits the frameworks for understanding digitised collection objects proposed by Edwards and Sassoon.[22] These observations also begin to suggest some of the ways in which the peculiarities of this collection, and the complex local–international relations it maintains, may develop the understandings suggested by these frameworks. Most importantly these few examples show that the images contained in the Colonial Copyright Collection are not done forging new connections and developing new meanings. Indeed the visual economy of the twenty-first century, where the images can be in more than one place at once, is just as dynamic as that of the previous centuries this collection has encountered.

As a result the Colonial Copyright Collection, born of a 'paper empire' and composed of myriad individual deposits, will take on a new life in a digital age. Despite, or rather because of, its colonial origins, the histories and geographies it depicts remain relevant to Canada in the twenty-first century. I have sought in this book to make a case for the significance of the collection, and to provide examples of the sort of stories that can be told about and through it. Transforming the material form of the collection through digitisation has enabled these stories to be engaged with by a much larger and diverse public audience. It also allows new stories to be added. Given the origins of the collection in the experience of mobility and the possibilities presented by the communications technology of the twenty-first century, the only thing we should truly fear for this collection in the future is immobility.

Sources

List of archive, library and museum collections consulted (primary sources)

British Library (St. Pancras, London)
British Library Newspaper Collections (Colindale, London)
British Museum (Bloomsbury, London)
National Archives (Kew, London)
Scott Polar Research Institute (Cambridge)
Library and Archives, Canada (Ottawa, Ontario and Gatineau, Quebec)
Galt Museum & Archives (Lethbridge, Alberta)
Royal British Columbia Archives (Victoria, British Columbia)
Archives of the Times-Colonist Newspaper (Victoria, British Columbia)

Digital only resources (primary sources)

Camera Workers website (http://www.members.shaw.ca/bchistorian/cw1858-1950.html. (last accessed, 1 December 2010).

Delcampe website http://postcards.delcampe.net/page/main/language,E.html (last accessed 20 April 2009).

Discover Your Legislature (History of B. C. Legislature website) http://www.leg.bc.ca/_media/flash/history-swf.html. Last accessed 21 October 2010.

Primary sources

Acts and Official Documents

Public and General Acts, 15 & 16 Vict., c.12, British Library Holdings.

Public and General Acts, 49 & 50 Vict., c.33, British Library Holdings.

'Correspondence on the subject of the Law of Copyright in Canada', *Parliamentary Papers; Accounts and Papers*, 1895, no.10, c.7783, British Library Holdings.

'House of Commons Parliamentary Paper, c.7785, presented 27th June, 1895', British Library Holdings.

Moodie, J. D. (1905), 'Report of Superintendent J. D. Moodie', in *Sessional Papers No.2 (Session 1903–1904)*, Scott Polar Research Institute holdings.

Moodie, J. D. (1907), 'The Hudson Bay Expedition', in *Sessional Papers No.9, Third Session of the Tenth Parliament of the Dominion of Canada (Session 1906–1907)*, Scott Polar Research Institute holdings.

Correspondence between J. D. McLean to British and Colonial Photo. Co., 23 January 1914 (from NAC, RG10, vol.3826, file 60,5 11–3), Galt Museum and Archives, Lethbridge, Alberta.

Newspaper materials (physical holdings and online)

'Canadian Won Big Race', *Toronto Daily Star*, 19 April 1907, p.1, British Library Newspaper Collections.

'Longboat Married', *Toronto Daily Star*, 29 December 1908, p.8, British Library Newspaper Collections.

'Death Claims John W. Jones: Well Known Naval Photographer Dies', *The Times*, Victoria, 9 March, 1938, provided by Times-Colonist Archive.

'John, W. Jones Passes Away: Former Naval Photographer Dies; here since 1888', *Victoria Colonist*, 8 March 1938, provided by Times-Colonist Archive.

'Every G20 Nation Wants to be Canada, Insists PM', Reuters, 25 September 2009. Available at http://www.reuters.com/article/idUSTRE58P05Z20090926. Last accessed 12 November 2010.

The Times (of Victoria); report in *The Colonist*, 23 February 1901, archived in Leona Taylor and Dorothy Mindenhall, *Index of Historical Victoria Newspapers*, host, Victoria's Victoria (http://web.uvic.ca/vv/newspaper/about.php), 2007. Last accessed 5 August 2008.

Photographic sources

Colonial Copyright Collection, British Library. Main Shelfmark: HS85/10.

Toronto, Album of Views for the T. Eaton Co., British Library. Shelfmark: 20.c.25.

Geraldine Moodie holdings, British Museum, Department for Africa, Oceania and the Americas. Reference: Am-A42-1-69.

Photographs of Newfoundland, National Archives, Kew. Can be found as part of series CO 1069.

Photographs of Canada (British copyrighters), National Archives, Kew. Can be found as part of series COPY 1.

Copyright deposit photographs held by Library and Archives Canada, 1895–1924, Library and Archives Canada, Ottawa and Gatineau (Ontario and Quebec). Embedded in wider photographic collection.

Arthur Rafton-Canning holdings, Galt Museum & Archives, Lethbridge (Alberta). Holdings searchable by photographer name.

J. W. Jones holdings, Royal British Columbia Archives, Victoria (British Columbia). Holdings searchable by photographer name.

Notes

Introduction

1. Note that the images discussed are produced up until 1923. The 1924 of the title reflects the completion date of the collection as deposit receipts suggest material was received at the British Museum Library during 1924.
2. The British Museum Library and much of its collections became a significant part of the founding of the British Library. In 1973 the British Library Act came into operation, beginning the history of the institution that now operates predominantly out of 96 Euston Road, London. Over subsequent years various libraries and collections would coalesce to create the varied collection known today.
3. Overviews of the significance of these collections can be found in works such as Batchen, G. (2008), *William Henry Fox Talbot*, London: Phaidon; Dodds, G., Hall, R. and Triggs, S. (1994), *The World of William Notman: The Nineteenth Century Through a Master Lens*, Toronto: McClelland & Stewart; Hawton-Booth, M. (1997), *Photography: An Independent Art – Photographs from the V & A Museum, 1839–1996*, London: V & A Publications; and Helibrun, F. and Bocard, H. (2009), *A History of Photography: the Musée d'Orsay Collection 1839–1925*, London: Flammarion.
4. This led to the creation of a vast library collection, drawn from many sources and consisting of various material forms. For more on the Library's printed collections see Mandelbrote, G. and Taylor, D. (eds) (2009), *Libraries Within the Library: the Origins of the British Library's Printed Collections*, London: British Library.
5. Sloane's collection was an underpinning element of the collections of the British Museum and, later, the British Library. Works such as Sloane, H. (1707–25), A *Voyage to the Islands of Madera, Barbados, Nieves, St. Christopher's and Jamaica*, London, illustrate the scale of Sloane's collation of information and the lengths to which he went in order to codify it into a logic useful to his medicinal and entrepreneurial interests. On the reinvention of this collecting ethos in the case of Henry Wellcome see; Hill, J. (2004), *Cultures and Networks of Collecting: Henry Wellcome's Collection*, unpublished PhD thesis, London: Royal Holloway, University of London; Larson, F. (2009), *An Infinity of Things: How Sir Henry Wellcome Collected the World*, Oxford: Oxford University Press.
6. The 1980s saw a concerted effort to reappraise the Library's Canadian collections as it was in the process of becoming a separate entity from the British Museum. The Colonial Copyright Collection of Canadian photographs was reviewed as part of this work, resulting in the following papers and texts: O'Neill, P. B. (1984), 'Canadiana Deposited in the British Museum Library between 1895 and 1924', in *British Library Occasional Papers: Canadian Studies* (1: 83–90); O'Neill, P. B. (1989), *A Checklist of Canadian Copyright Deposits in the British Museum, 1895–1923: Vol.V Photographs*, Halifax, N. S.: Dalhousie University School of Library and Information Studies.
7. This work covers a period from publications such as Koltun, L. (ed.) (1985), *Private Realms of Light*, Markham, Ont.: Fitzhenry and Whiteside to the recent Payne, C. and Junard, A. (eds) (2011), *The Cultural Work of Photography in Canada*, Montreal, Que.: McGill-Queen's University Press.
8. Richards, T. (1993), *The Imperial Archive: Knowledge and the Fantasy of Empire*, London: Verso; Poole, D. (1997), *Vision, Race and Modernity: a Visual Economy of the Andean Image World*, Chichester: Princeton University Press.
9. Richards, T. (1993), *The Imperial Archive: Knowledge and the Fantasy of Empire*, London: Verso (p.4).

10. Ogborn, M. (2007), *Indian Ink: Script and Print in the Making of the English East India Company*, Chicago: University of Chicago Press, p.xvii.
11. Public and General Acts, 49 & 50 Vict., c.33, section 1–2.
12. Harris, *A History of the British Museum Library.*
13. The *Royal Colonial Institute Yearbook, 1913*, in a passage about its own library, discusses at length the significance and importance of repositories of colonial knowledge and asserts them as being a key to the understanding and control of the Empire. Evans-Lewin, P. (1913), 'IX. – The Library', in *Royal Colonial Institute Yearbook, 1913*, London: Royal Colonial Institute (pp. 30–2). The role of the Institute as an imperial archive is discussed in detail by Craggs, R. (2008), 'Situating the Imperial Archive: The Royal Empire Society Library, 1868 – 1945', in *Journal of Historical Geography* (34: 48 – 67).
14. Harris, *A History of the British Museum Library*; Sternberg, *Acquisitions of Printed Books at the British Library, 1837–1960.*
15. An abbreviated list would include members of the Colonial Office, the Board of Trade and the Law Office.
16. House of Commons Parliamentary Paper, *c*.7785, presented 27 June, 1895.
17. Harris, *A History of the British Museum Library*; O'Neill, 'Canadiana Deposited in the British Museum Library between 1895 and 1924'.
18. Sternberg, 'The British Museum Library and Colonial Copyright Deposit', in *The British Library Journal* (17: 61–82).
19. Correspondence on the Law of Copyright in Canada, 1895, No.44, p.77; Sternberg, 'The British Museum Library and Colonial Copyright Deposit'.
20. Esdaile, A. (1946), *The British Museum Library: a Short History and Survey*, London: George Allen and Unwin Ltd.; Harris, *A History of the British Museum Library.*
21. O'Neill, 'Canadiana Deposited in the British Museum Library between 1895 and 1924'.
22. O'Neill, 'Canadiana Deposited in the British Museum Library between 1895 and 1924', p.87.
23. Illustrated in 'Correspondence on the subject of the Law of Copyright in Canada', *Parliamentary Papers; Accounts and Papers*, 1895, no.10, c.7783; and Harris, *A History of the British Museum Library.*
24. Payne, C. (2013), *The Official Picture: The National Film Board of Canada's Still Photography Division and the Image of Canada, 1941–1971*, Montreal, Que.: McGill-Queen's University Press.
25. As such, the use of the term excludes other forms of Canadiana (such as literature and music) collected under Colonial Copyright Law or photographic materials from other colonial territories (such as Australia and India); Harris, *A History of the British Museum Library*; O'Neill, 'Canadiana Deposited in the British Museum Library between 1895 and 1924'.
26. Harris, *A History of the British Museum Library*; O'Neill, P. B. (1984), 'Canadiana Deposited in the British Museum Library between 1895 and 1924'; Public and General Acts, 49 & 50 Vict., c. 33, section 1–2.
27. This is borne out by Joan Schwartz's discussion of the materiality of the daguerreotype, in which she asserts the characteristics of the daguerreotype meant that it acted in a unique and significant way as a souvenir and 'photographic' object; Schwartz, J. M. (2004), '*Un Beau Souvenir du Canada*: Object, Image, Symbolic Space', in Edwards and Hart (eds), *Photographs, Objects, Histories: On the Materiality of Images*, London: Routledge, pp.16–31.
28. It is worth noting here that a comparative analysis between the British Library and Library and Archives Canada collections would provide a fascinating case study of how institutional histories and frameworks affect collections, as both these bodies of photography have been curated and conserved differently as well as placed in proximity to completely different collection items.
29. The item, once copyrighted, had to be acquired by the library under the terms of the law. It could be subsequently de-accessioned, but this was rare for material from significant colonial territories and Dominions. As a result, the Colonial Copyright Collection photographs were deposited in the Woolwich Arsenal storage area.
30. Poole, D. (1997), *Vision, Race and Modernity: a Visual Economy of the Andean Image World*, Chichester: Princeton University Press.
31. Richards, *The Imperial Archive*, pp.3–4 and 11–18 in particular.
32. Within his own context Richards considers the impossibility of logically ordering the imperial archive into knowledge in the chapter *Archive and Entropy*. Richards, *The Imperial Archive*, pp.73–109.

33. As a result, the collection mostly languished in the Woolwich Arsenal Depository between 1924 and 1980, when it was attended to as part of the division of materials between the British Museum and the British Library.
34. Butlin, R. (2009), *Geographies of Empire: European Empires and Colonies c.1880*–1960, Cambridge: Cambridge University Press.
35. Driver, F. and Gilbert, D. (1999), 'Imperial Cities: Overlapping Territories, Intertwined Histories', in Driver and Gilbert (eds), *Imperial Cities: Landscape, Display and Identity*, Manchester: Manchester University Press, pp.1–20; Jacobs, J. (1996), *Edge of Empire: Postcolonialism and the City*, London: Routledge.
36. Processes which bear a similarity to those outlined in Lambert, D. and Lester, A. (2006), 'Introduction: Imperial Spaces, Imperial Subjects', in Lambert and Lester (eds), *Colonial Lives Across the British Empire: Imperial Careering in the Long Nineteenth Century*, Cambridge: Cambridge University Press, pp.1–31.
37. Barringer, T. (1998), 'The South Kensington Museum and the colonial project', in Barringer, T. and Flynn, T. (eds), *Colonialism and the Object: Empire, Material Culture and the Museum*, London: Routledge, pp.11–27; Edwards, E. (2001), *Raw Histories: Photographs, Anthropology and Museums*, Oxford: Berg; Walden, K. (1997), *Becoming Modern in Toronto: The Industrial Exhibition and the Shaping of a Late Victorian Culture*, London: University of Toronto Press.
38. The Toronto Industrial Exhibition and its later iteration, the Canadian National Exhibition, are considered in Chapter 1.
39. For example, in a Canadian context events such as the Great Exhibition of 1851 were hugely important in stimulating economic development and maintaining colonial interest. These events allowed individuals such as William Logan (head of the Canadian Geological Survey, 1842–69) a global stage on which to assert the potential of, in this case, Canadian geology for economic benefit. See Zeller, S. (2009, 2nd ed.), *Inventing Canada: Early Victorian Science and the Idea of a Transcontinental Nation*, London: McGill-Queen's University Press, Carleton Library Series.
40. This material was in the form of exchange agreements that existed between Britain and the more significant Dominion territories. Here we can see another facet of this colonial geography of knowledge where colonies were engaged with in different ways dependent upon their relationship with, and geopolitical closeness to, the metropole.
41. Harris, *A History of the British Museum Library.*
42. The lack of detailed cataloguing, the assignment of the material to the Woolwich repository and the fact that it was largely unavailable to the public are all important signifiers here. Similar conclusions are drawn in O'Neill, 'Canadiana Deposited in the British Museum Library between 1895 and 1924'.
43. Indeed even those who were known in Canada, such as Notman and Sons, Byron Harmon and J. W. Jones, were often unknown in Britain outside of practising photographers and photographic societies.
44. Even by the late nineteenth century the photograph still inhabited an ambivalent position between document and art. See Falconer, J. and Hide, L. (2009), *Points of View: Capturing the Nineteenth Century in Photographs*, London: British Library.
45. Hannavy, J. (2008), 'Markets, Photographic', in Hannavay, J. (ed.), *Encyclopaedia of Nineteenth-Century Photography*, London: Routledge, pp.896–8; Heinsch, H. K. and Heinsch, B. A. (1994), *The Photographic Experience, 1839–1914*, University Park: Pennsylvania State University Press; Kõdar, T. (1996), 'The Canadian Photographic Periodical Press', in *History of Photography: Special Issue on Canadian Photography* (20: 138–45). The special issue as a whole illustrates how dynamic the Canadian photographic economy was by the period of 1895–1924, as shown by Schwartz, J. M. (1996), 'Guest Editorial', in *History of Photography: Special Issue on Canadian Photography* (20: ii).
46. Hannavy, 'Markets, Photographic'.
47. Hannavay, J. (2008), 'Printing-Out Paper', in Hannavay, J. (ed.), *Encyclopaedia of Nineteenth-Century Photography*, London: Routledge, pp.1174–5; Harding, C. (2008), 'Camera Design: General', in Hannavay, J. (ed.), *Encyclopaedia of Nineteenth-Century Photography*, London: Routledge, pp.254–5; Ward, J. (2008), 'Dry Plate Negatives: Gelatine', in Hannavay, J. (ed.), *Encyclopaedia of Nineteenth-Century Photography*, London: Routledge, pp.438–9.
48. Zeller gives a detailed indication of the increasing respect afforded to Canada by Britain as the nineteenth century progressed. Zeller, *Inventing Canada.*

49. Harris, *A History of the British Museum Library*; Sternberg, 'The British Museum Library and Colonial Copyright Deposit' and Sternberg, *Acquisitions of Printed Books at the British Library, 1837–1960.*
50. The conservation of the collection was undertaken during the 1990s, with the support of the Canadian High Commission. Where possible and practical the photographs were bound into the black albums, which provide a secure way of making the images publicly available while protecting them from wear. Materials which were too numerous to be placed in these volumes sensibly (for example, with postcards a photographer's collection could fill many of these expensive volumes on its own) or too large to fit practically were boxed in separate small storage boxes or oversize folios. Here the photographs have been individually laminated to increase their durability when used by the public.
51. Edwards, E. and Hart, J. (2004), 'Mixed Box: the Cultural Biography of a Box of "Ethnographic" Photographs', in Edwards and Hart (eds), *Photographs, Objects, Histories: On the Materiality of Images*, London: Routledge, pp.47–61.
52. Much has been written on the subject of display, narrative and meaning, including the work of Bal, M. (1996), 'The discourse of the museum', in Greenberg, R. et al. (eds), *Thinking About Exhibitions*, London: Routledge, pp.201–18; Crang, M. (1993), 'On Display', in Blunt, A. et al. (eds), *Cultural Geography in Practice*, London: Hodder Arnold, pp.255–68; McMaster, G. (1996), 'Creating spaces', in Greenberg, R. et al. (eds), *Thinking About Exhibitions*, London: Routledge, pp.191–200; and, Saumarez-Smith, C. (1989), 'Museums, artefacts and meanings', in Vergo, P. (ed.), *The New Museology*, London: Reaktion, pp.6–21.
53. Craig, D. (1997), *Royal Geographical Society Illustrated: A Unique Record of Exploration and Photography*, London: Scriptum Editions. This work was reviewed by James Ryan, who noted at length how the work embodied the colonial perspective of the Royal Geographical Society photographic collections, as opposed to critiquing the images from the post-colonial perspectives of the late twentieth century; Ryan, J. (2000), 'Photos and Frames: Towards an Historical Geography of Photography', in *Journal of Historical Geography* (26: 119–24).
54. Pierce, P. (1985), *Canada: The Missing Years*, London: Hamlyn.
55. See Fig.0.3 as an example.
56. Edwards, E. and Hart, J. (2004), 'Introduction: Photographs as Objects', in Edwards and Hart (eds), *Photographs, Objects Histories: On the Materiality of Images*, London: Routledge, pp.1–15.
57. Sassoon, J. (2004), 'Photographic Materiality in an Age of Digital Reproduction', in Edwards and Hart (eds), *Photographs, Objects Histories: On the Materiality of Images*, London: Routledge, pp.186–202.
58. The complexity of the images of the Colonial Copyright Collection and the availability of multiple opportunities to reinterpret their meanings and significance, as a result of the interaction of image and institution, means they are often discussed in ways similar to the approach taken by Elizabeth Edwards in *Raw Histories*. As noted in this paragraph, this has particular significance for the twenty-first-century life of the collection. Edwards, E. (2001), *Raw Histories: Photographs, Anthropology and Museums*, Oxford: Berg.
59. Barthes, R. (2009, revised edition), *Camera Lucida: Reflections on Photography*, London: Vintage Classics.
60. Langford, M. (2008), *Suspended Conversations: The Afterlife of Memory in Photographic Albums*, Montreal, Que.: McGill-Queen's University Press.
61. *Studium* means the overall and accepted reading which can be applied to an image.
62. Previous work illustrating these significances includes Hamlett, J. (2006), '"Nicely Feminine Yet Learned": Student Rooms at Royal Holloway and the Oxford and Cambridge Colleges in Late Nineteenth Century Britain', in *Women's History Review* (15: 137–61); Langford, M. (2008), *Suspended Conversations: The Afterlife of Memory in Photographs*, London: McGill-Queen's University Press.
63. This tendency was not unique to British colonialism, but instead is a pervasive trait of Western colonialism underpinned by technological modernity, as illustrated in Butlin, R. (2009), *Geographies of Empire*.
64. Sontag, S. (1973), *On Photography*, London: Farrar, Straus and Giroux.
65. Ryan, J. R. (1997), *Picturing Empire: Photography and the Visualisation of the British Empire*, London: Reaktion Books.

66. Schwartz, J. M. and Ryan, J. R. (2003), 'Introduction: Photography and the Geographical Imagination', in Schwartz, J. M. and Ryan, J. R. (eds), *Picturing Place: Photography and the Geographical Imagination*, London: I. B. Tauris, pp.1–18.
67. MacQuire, S. (1998), *Visions of Modernity: Representations, Memory, Time and Space in the Age of the Camera*, London: Sage.
68. This is summed up well by John Thomson's statement, 'We are now making history, and the sun picture supplies the means of passing down a record of what we are and what we have achieved in this nineteenth century'; Falconer, J. and Hide, L. (2009), *Points of View: Capturing the Nineteenth Century in Photographs*, London: British Library, p.2. Works such as Ryan, *Picturing Empire* and Sontag, *On Photography* consider this point of view at length from a critical perspective. See also Berger, J. (1972), *Ways of Seeing*, London: BBC and Penguin Books; Lutz, C. A. and Collins, J. L. (1993), *Reading National Geographic*, London: The University of Chicago Press; MacQuire, S. *Visions of Modernity* and Price, D. and Wells, L. (2009, 4th ed.), 'Thinking About Photography: Debates, Historically and now', in Wells, L. (ed.), *Photography: A Critical Introduction*, London: Routledge, pp.9–64.
69. An example of the use of photography to understand societies and individuals within them is the anthropological documentation of aboriginal groups across various empires using the camera and the photographic image. The combination of the camera and what was considered to be scientific practice aspired to document and illustrate racial and therefore cultural characteristics of groups and establish them within a racialised global hierarchy. See Edwards, E. (2001), *Raw Histories: Photographs, Anthropology and Museums*, Oxford: Berg; Lutz and Collins, *Reading National Geographic*; Thomas, N. (1994), *Colonialism's Culture: Anthropology, Travel and Government*, London: The Polity Press.
70. Edwards, *Raw Histories*; Pinney, C. (1994), 'The Parallel Histories of Anthropology and Photography', in, Edwards, E. (ed.), *Anthropology and Photography: 1860–1920*, London: Yale University Press, pp.74 – 93.
71. For example, individuals such as Dali and Moholy-Nagy were avid in their assertions that photography was not an all-seeing eye but a creative media. See Dali, S. (1927), 'Photography, pure creation of the mind', in *L'Amic de les Arts* (no.18, 30 September 1927), reprinted in *Oui 12*; Dali, S. (1929), 'Photographic Data', in *La Gaceta Literaria* (no.6, February 1929), reprinted in *Oui 70–71*. Moholy-Nagy warned about the potential effects of a world 'compelled to see' through the camera's gaze; Moholy-Nagy, L. (1967), *Painting, Photography, Film*, London: Lund Humphries, esp. p.28.
72. In those exceptional cases where the photographer is invisible, other factors in the biography of the image come into play. This topic is considered further in Chapter 1.
73. The image world that we live in today is much richer and more diverse. See, Lister, M. (2009, 4th ed.), 'Photography in the Age of Electronic Imaging', in Wells, L. (ed.), *Photography: A Critical Introduction*, London: Routledge, pp.311–44; Poole, D. (1997), *Vision, Race and Modernity*; Sassoon, J. (2004), 'Photographic Materiality in the Age of Digital Reproduction', in Edwards and Hart (eds), *Photographs, Objects, Histories: On the Materiality of Images*, London: Routledge, pp.186–202.
74. Staff, F. (1979, 2nd ed..), *The Picture Postcard and its Origins*, London: Lutterworth Press; Woody, H. (1998), 'International Postcards: Their History, Production and Distribution (circa 1895– 1915)', in Geary and Webb (eds), *Delivering Views: Distant Cultures in Early Postcards,* London: Smithsonian Institution Press, pp.13–45.

Chapter 1

1. Briggs, A. (2003, 4th ed.), *Victorian Things*, London: Sutton Publishing.
2. Staff, F. (1979, 2nd ed.), *The Picture Postcard and its Origins*, London: Lutterworth Press, p.8.
3. Coe, B. and Gates, P. (1977), *The Snapshot Photograph: The Rise of Popular Photography, 1888–1939*, London: Ash and Grant Ltd.
4. Geary, C. M. and Webb, V. L. (1998) (eds), *Delivering Views: Distant Cultures in Early Postcards*, London: Smithsonian Institution Press.
5. Edwards, E. (1994), 'Introduction', in Edwards, E. (ed.), *Anthropology and Photography 1860–1920*, London: Yale University Press, pp.3–17; Edwards, E. and Hart, J. (2004), 'Introduction: Photographs as Objects', in Edwards and Hart (eds), *Photographs, Objects Histories: On the Materiality of Images*, London: Routledge, pp.1–15.

6. Anderson, A. and Tomlinson, B. (1978), *'Greetings From Canada': An Album of Unique Canadian Postcards from the Edwardian Era, 1900–1916*, Toronto: Macmillan.
7. Amyot, C., Gendreau, B. and Willis, J. (2000), *Special Delivery: Canada's Postal Heritage*, Fredricton, N. B.: Goose Lane (pp.57–8).
8. Anderson and Tomlinson, *'Greetings From Canada'*, p.xiii. The number is derived from the amount of penny stamps sold in Canada in that year. Penny stamps could only be used for posting items of postcard size and dimensions.
9. Le Corbusier (1988, first published 1935), *Aircraft*, New York: Universe, p.5.
10. For more on Canadians using photography to understand the consequences of the war and what it meant for Canada, see Chapter 6.
11. Cronin, M. (2007), 'Northern Visions: Aerial Surveying and the Canadian Mining Industry, 1919–1928', in *Technology and Culture* (48: 303–30); Shaw, S. B. (2001), *Photographing Canada from Flying Canoes*, Brunstown, Ont.: General Store Publishing House. More global contexts can be found in Cosgrove, D. and Fox, W. L. (2010), *Photography and Flight*, London: Reaktion Books.
12. Shaw, *Photographing Canada from Flying Canoes*, p.8.
13. A detailed discussion of the life of William Barker and his acquaintance with Billy Bishop is given in Ralph, *William Barker, V. C.*
14. Cowan, P. (1982), *The Kid Who Couldn't Miss* (film), Ontario: National Film Board of Canada. Available at: http://www.nfb.ca/film/the-kid-who-couldnt-miss (last accessed 7 December 2010).
15. Ralph, *William Barker, V. C*, p.167; Shaw, *Photographing Canada from Flying Canoes*, p.8.
16. Avery, T. E. (1977, 3rd ed.), *Interpretation of Aerial Photographs*, Minneapolis, Minn.: Burgess Publishing Co.; McKinley, A. C. (1929), *Applied Aerial Photography*, London: Chapman & Hall, Ltd., p.330. Also, in *Photography and Flight*, Cosgrove and Fox provide a detailed account of the effects of different types of vehicle and mounting on aerial photography in chapter two, 'The Camera in the Sky'; Cosgrove and Fox, *Photography and Flight*, pp.26–51.
17. Cosgrove and Fox, *Photography and Flight*; Hauser, *Shadow Sites.*
18. Hauser, *Shadow Sites*, p.187.
19. Cosgrove, D. (1997), 'The Measures of America', in Corner, J. and MacLean, A. S. (1997), *Taking Measures Across the American Landscape*, London: New Haven, pp.3–13.
20. Cosgrove, 'The Measures of America', p.3.
21. Shaw, *Photographing Canada from Flying Canoes*, p.8.
22. Shaw, *Photographing Canada from Flying Canoes.*
23. Harris, R. C. (2008), *The Reluctant Land: Society, Space and Environment in Canada before Confederation*, Vancouver: University of British Columbia Press.
24. See chapter 5 of McCannon, J. (2012), *A History of the Arctic: nature, exploration and exploitation*, London: Reaktion.
25. Generally see Bennett, 'The Exhibitionary Complex'; Greenhalgh, P. (1988), *Ephemeral Vistas: The Expositions Universelles, Great Exhibitions and World's Fairs, 1851–1939*, Manchester: Manchester University Press; Mitchell, T. (1992), 'Orientalism and the Exhibitionary Order', in Dirks, N. B. (ed.), *Colonialism and Culture*, Michigan: University of Michigan Press, pp.289–316 and Rydell, R. W. (2006), 'World Fairs and Museums', in Macdonald, S. (ed.), *A Companion to Museum Studies*, London: Blackwell, pp. 135–51.
26. Bennett, 'The Exhibitionary Complex'; Greenhalgh, *Ephemeral Vistas.*
27. Mitchell, 'Orientalism and the Exhibitionary Order'.
28. Bennett, 'The Exhibitionary Complex'; Rydell, 'World Fairs and Museums'.
29. Walden, K. (1997), *Becoming Modern in Toronto.*
30. Walden, *Becoming Modern in Toronto.*
31. Rydell, R. W. (1998), 'Souvenirs of Imperialism: World's Fair Postcards', in Geary and Webb (eds), *Delivering Views: Distant Cultures in Early Postcards*, London: Smithsonian Institution Press, pp.47–63.
32. Ralph, *William Barker, V. C*, p.165.
33. Many of these aerial materials were used to scout Canada's interior areas to locate lumber, hydro-electric and mineral resources. As a result, they opened up much of the country's landmass to development in the twentieth century. Ralph, *William Barker, V. C* and Shaw, *Photographing Canada from Flying Canoes* provide more details on the postwar use of Imperial Gift materials to develop Canadian natural resources.
34. Ralph, *William Barker, V. C*, p.165.

Chapter 2

1. Trachtenberg, A. (1989), *Reading American Photographs: Images as History, Mathew Brady to Walker Evans*, New York: Hill and Wang.
2. Hales, P. B. (2005), *Silver Cities: Photographic American Urbanization, 1839–1939*, Albuquerque: University of New Mexico Press.
3. In this year J. W. Jones moved from Winnipeg where he had operated as part of the studio 'Jones Bros.' with his brother, T. M. Jones; Mattison, D. (1985), *Camera Workers: the British Columbia Photographer's Directory, 1858–1900*, Vancouver, B.C.: Camera Workers Press.
4. Jones died still living in Victoria, commemorated in the town for his work on photographing Victoria's naval heritage; 'J. W. Jones, Well Known Naval Photographer, Dies', *Victoria Colonist*, 8 March 1938.
5. Gregson, H. (1970), *A History of Victoria, 1842–1970*, Victoria: Victoria Observer Publishing Co. Ltd., p.72.
6. Between 1883 and 1890 Victoria saw a huge boom in public and per capita wealth (with the latter increasing fourfold in the period), largely due to the city's status as a free port with easy links to the mainland. See Gregson, *A History of Victoria*, p.73.
7. Schwartz, J. M. (1981), 'The Past in Focus: Photography and British Columbia, 1858–1914', in *B. C. Studies* (52: 5–15).
8. The Royal British Columbia Archives of Victoria hold many images produced by Jones that did not make it into the copyright collection in Canada or London, suggesting selectivity in the deposition of images.
9. Charland discusses the importance of the camera and other technologies in developing images of identity that fit with the nation-building projects of governments and companies active in Canada in the nineteenth century. See Charland, M. (1986), 'Technological nationalism', *Canadian Journal of Political and Social Theory* (10: 196–221) A similar discussion (though in this case the photographs discussed fail to elicit the desired response) is also advanced in an imperial context in Richard Huyda's work on the location of Canada's capital. See Huyda, R. J. (1996), 'Photography and the Choice of Canada's Capital', in *History of Photography: Special Issue on Canadian Photography* (20: 104–7).
10. Druick, Z. (2007), *Projecting Canada: Government Policy and Documentary Film at the National Film Board*, London: McGill-Queen's University Press. For the imagination of the Canadian landscape by government agencies in the later twentieth century see Payne, C. (2013), *The Official Picture: The National Film Board of Canada's Still Photography Division and the Image of Canada, 1941–1971*, Montreal, Que.: McGill-Queen's University Press.
11. Fort Victoria was founded in order to strengthen British claims over Vancouver Island; Gregson, *A History of Victoria*.
12. Nye, D. E. (1994), *The American Technological Sublime*, London: The MIT Press. As Nye argues that the Golden Gate Bridge represents 'an ideal America' in the mode of the technological sublime, so the images Jones produced of the naval yards and ships seem to represent an ideal British Columbia. In this sense the ideal is rational and mechanical, as opposed to wild and biological.
13. This early colonial history is discussed at length in Clayton, D. (2000), *Islands of Truth: the Imperial Fashioning of Vancouver Island*, London: University of British Columbia Press.
14. It is worth noting that Jones did make use of this sort of protection for his images, as evidenced by his taking a rival local photographer to court for copyright infringement on one of his images of the Victoria legislature. In 1901 he filed against his rival, 'Mr. Maynard' for publication of a copyrighted image (copyright number 12030 in appendix 1) in *The Times* (of Victoria). See report in *The Colonist*, 23 February 1901, archived in Taylor, L. and Mindenhall, D., *Index of Historical Victoria Newspapers*, host 'Victoria's Victoria' (http://web.uvic.ca/vv/newspaper/about.php), 2007, last accessed 7 December 2010.
15. It has been noted in work on photography and copyright that one of the factors motivating photographers who copyrighted their work was a desire to protect and assert the artistic originality of their work, and to protect this from financial and creative impingement by others. See Padfield, T. (2008), 'Copyright', in Hannavay, J. (ed.), *Encyclopaedia of Nineteenth-Century Photography*, London: Routledge, pp.337–8. This protection is still an important part of photographic copyright today and is represented by the aspects of copyright law that cover 'originality' (this concept is fairly universal among nations using copyright laws similar to those of Britain, Canada and the United States). See Gendreau, Y., Nordemann, A. and Oesch,

R. (eds) (1999), *Copyright and Photographs: An International Survey*, London: Kluwer Law International.

16. See Price, D. and Wells, L. (2000), 'Thinking About Photography: Debates, Historically and Now', in Wells, L. (2000, 2nd ed.), *Photography: A Critical Introduction*, London: Routledge, pp.9–64; Price, D. (2000), 'Surveyors and the Surveyed: Photography Out and About', in Wells, L. (2000, 2nd ed.), *Photography: A Critical Introduction*, London: Routledge, pp.65–116.
17. Viceroy Li Huang Cheng arrived in 1896 with the intent of conducting talks that would strengthen links between China and British Columbia.
18. The development, construction and opening of these buildings was a significant event that finalised Victoria's position as the capital of British Columbia and announced the city and the province's arrival as significant entities in the nation of Canada. See Gregson, *A History of Victoria*. It also marked another stage in the development and re-situation of British Columbia as a modern, colonial hub, as noted in, Clayton, *Islands of Truth*.
19. See http://www.leg.bc.ca/_media/flash/history-swf.html. Last accessed 21 October 2010.
20. See Rattray, A. (1862), *Vancouver Island and British Columbia: Where They Are; What They Are; and What They May Become*, London: Smith, Elder & Co. Rattray pays a significant amount of attention to the resource and trade potential of the area, as well asserting its importance to the British Empire. However, in this can be seen the seeds of competition between Vancouver Island and the mainland, areas with the potential to grow and succeed at different rates at different times. Also see Gregson, *A History of Victoria*.
21. Gregson, *A History of Victoria*, p.16.
22. For example, after confederation British Columbia was added onto the Canadian rail network in 1886. However, this terminated in Gastown (now Vancouver) rather than Victoria, and acted as a major contributor to Vancouver's economic predominance in the area from that point.
23. *Victoria Colonist*, 16 March 1883.
24. As discussed in Clayton, D. (2000), *Islands of Truth*.
25. Roy, P. (1976), 'The Illumination of Victoria: Late Nineteenth Century Technology and Municipal Enterprise', in *B. C. Studies* (32: 79–92), p.85.
26. The use of the guard of honour would continue to be an important part of provincial performance by the legislature, as discussed in Chapter 6, 'A Global Presence'.
27. Driver, F. and Gilbert, D. (eds) (1999), *Imperial Cities: Landscape, Space and Identity*, Manchester: Manchester University Press; Hobsbawn, E. and Ranger, T. (eds) (1983), *The Invention of Tradition*, Cambridge: Cambridge University Press; Jacobs, J. (1996), *Edge of Empire: Postcolonialism and the City*, London: Routledge; Keene, D. (2005), 'Cities and Empire', in *Journal of Urban History* (32: 8–21).
28. For more on the maritime history of Vancouver Island see Clayton, *Islands of Truth*.
29. Gregson, *A History of Victoria*, p.72.
30. T. Eaton Co., *Toronto: Album of Views*, Toronto: Dominion Publishing Co. It is worth noting that this book is not formally part of the Colonial Copyright Collection; it resides at a different shelfmark due to its deposition as a printed book. This reflects the organisational and cataloguing structures of the British Museum Library (and suggests contexts where photographic material was less problematic for receipt), but for the purposes of this analysis a printed book that consists solely of photographs and very minimal captioning text is being treated as part of the Colonial Copyright Collection. A similar logic has been used in O'Neill, P. B. (1989), *A Checklist of Canadian Copyright Deposits in the British Museum, 1895–1923: Vol.V Photographs*, Halifax, N. S.: Dalhousie University School of Library and Information Studies.
31. Eaton's impact on the geography, employment patterns and consumer habits of the city are drawn out in Dennis, R. (2008), *Cities in Modernity: Representations and Productions of Metropolitan Space, 1840–1930*, Cambridge: Cambridge University Press, pp.296–321 (esp. pp.304–5).
32. Dennis, *Cities in Modernity*, p.21.
33. Domosh, M. (1996), *Invented Cities: The Creation of Landscape in Nineteenth-Century New York and Boston*, London: Yale University Press; Schein, R. H. (1993), 'Representing Urban America: 19th Century Views of Landscape, Space and Power', in *Environment and Planning D: Society and Space* (11: 7–21).
34. McQueen, R. (1998), *The Eatons: The Rise and Fall of Canada's Royal Family*, Toronto: Stoddart; Nasmith, G. G. (1923), *'Timothy Eaton'*, Toronto: McClelland & Stewart; Santink, J. L. (1990), *Timothy Eaton and the Rise of his Department Store*, Toronto: University of Toronto Press.

35. Eaton and his family negotiated access to high society in Toronto in a way similar to that in Boston; see Domosh, *Invented Cities*. This social structure and its origin is described at more length in Story, R. (1980), *The Forging of an Aristocracy: Harvard & the Boston Upper Class, 1800–1870*, Middletown, Con.: Wesleyan University Press.
36. McQueen sums this up well with the following quote: 'In Ireland generations were reared on potatoes and the shorter catechism. In Canada it was Cornflakes and the Eaton's catalogue.' McQueen, *The Eatons*, p.2. It is also notable in the significant presence given to Eaton's and its catalogue in Canadian fiction, for instance Margaret Atwood's *Cat's Eye*; Atwood, M. (1988), *Cat's Eye*, Toronto: McClelland-Stewart.
37. This is the focus of McQueen, *The Eatons*.
38. In this sense the media world was changing due to an exponential growth of the newspaper industry across the world, a growing level of interconnectedness (facilitated by the train, steam ship, telegraph and so on) and new forums of public engagement (such as the exposition and the fair).
39. Indeed the term 'Empire' was of great significance to the T. Eaton Co., as it asserted the significance of the company to the British Empire at large and testified to the stature of the company itself. The term was even used in the *Illustrated London News* (18 February 1911), cited in McQueen, *The Eatons*; and Santink, *Timothy Eaton and the Rise of his Department Store*. The dynamic here is similar to the rhetoric of empire used by department stores in London, as described in Driver, F. and Gilbert, D. (1999), 'Introduction: Overlapping Territories, Intertwined Histories', in Driver and Gilbert (eds), *Imperial Cities: Landscape, Display and Identity*, Manchester: Manchester University Press, pp.1–20.
40. Eaton's Window displays were so iconic that they are reproduced to this day. The Canadian Museum of Civilizations recreates an Eaton's window scene to commemorate a man whom it considers to be one of the most significant individuals in the country's history (*Face to Face: the Canadian Personalities Hall*, Ottawa: Canadian Museum of Civilizations).
41. Edwards, E. and Hart, J. (2004), 'Introduction: Photographs as Objects', in Edwards and Hart (eds), *Photographs, Objects Histories: On the Materiality of Images*, London: Routledge, pp.1–15, referencing McCauley, E. A. (1985), *A. E. A. Disdéri and the Carte de Visite Portrait Photograph*, New Haven, CT: Yale University Press.
42. With regard to city hall in particular (see Fig.2.9), the building has clear similarities (in its clock tower, roof composition and facade decoration) to the national parliament of Ottawa.
43. Schein ('Representing Urban America') discusses the virtues of the bird's-eye view technique, stating that it afforded an empowering gaze to both the producer and the viewer.
44. Again, largely due to Eaton's use of advertising, which asserted Eaton's to be a store of high quality that could be afforded, to some measure, by everyone in the city. This played upon the store's position in the city and was summed up by the advertising catch phrase of the 1870s, 'Eaton's for the masses, Simpson's for the classes'. This was printed in Industrial Exhibition promotional literature and other advertisements, see Walden, K. (1997), *Becoming Modern in Toronto: The Industrial Exhibition and the Shaping of a Late Victorian Culture*, London: University of Toronto Press.
45. The prominent archway and large windows seen in the image were viewed as a huge risk by many commentators when Timothy Eaton upgraded and expanded the store in the 1880s. However, the exterior architecture and interior design were so loved by the public that it became one of the major reasons for Eaton's success in the market. McQueen, *The Eatons*; Santink, *Timothy Eaton and the Rise of his Department Store*.
46. Indeed it could be argued that it did this very successfully, as Jack Eaton was influential in the development of Eaton's in Canada before Timothy Eaton passed away. Jack Eaton lobbied his father for, and then took the lead in developing, the T. Eaton Co.'s Winnipeg store, its first major branch outside of Toronto. McQueen, *The Eatons*; Nasmith, *Timothy Eaton*.
47. Both Nasmith, *Timothy Eaton* and Santink, *Timothy Eaton and the Rise of his Department Store* discuss the significance of the church to Eaton at length.
48. For more on Harrods and the empire see Driver and Gilbert, 'Heart of Empire?'.
49. Walden, *Becoming Modern in Toronto*.
50. Nasmith, *Timothy Eaton*; Walden, *Becoming Modern in Toronto*.
51. Santink, *Timothy Eaton and the Rise of his Department Store*, p.153.
52. McQueen, *The Eatons*; Santink, *Timothy Eaton and the Rise of his Department Store*.
53. Schwartz, J. M. (1981), 'The Past in Focus'; Schwartz, J. M. (1996), 'Guest Editorial', in *History of Photography: Special Issue on Canadian Photography* (20: 2, ii).

54. The Colonial Copyright Collection contains examples of this from across Canada, as companies such as the Winnipeg Photographic Co. and the Panoramic Photo. Co. deposited large amounts of photographs for copyright. Further, the individual photographer is particularly well represented, with the railway providing a lucrative market and the promise of steady trade. See Chapter 3.

Chapter 3

1. Berton, P. (1974), *The National Dream and the Last Spike* (abridged by author), Toronto: McClelland & Stewart; Stevens, G. R. (1960), *Canadian National Railways: Volume 2, Towards the Inevitable (1896–1922)*, Toronto: Clarke, Irwin and Co. Ltd., p.3.
2. This can be seen in works such as Birrell, A. (1981), 'Survey Photography in British Columbia, 1858 – 1900', in *B. C. Studies* (52: 39–60); Foster, J. (2003), 'Capturing and Losing the "Lie of the Land": Railway Photography and Colonial Nationalism in Early Twentieth-Century South Africa', in Schwartz and Ryan (eds), *Picturing Place: Photography and the Geographical Imagination*, London: I. B. Tauris, pp.141–61 and McDougall, M. H. (1981), 'R. H. Trueman, Artist and Documentarian', in *B. C. Studies* (52: 129–41).
3. Berton, P. (1974), *The National Dream and The Last Spike*; Stevens, G. R. (1960), *Canadian National Railways: Volume 1, Sixty Years of Trial and Error (1836–1896)*, Toronto: Clarke, Irwin and Co. Ltd.
4. This view is expressed in the writings of Berton, who attributes to the railway the role of lifting Canada out of its national hibernation (p.16) and thrusting it towards its destiny as a truly unified and productive nation (pp.492–3).
5. See Charland, M. (1986), 'Technological Nationalism', in *Canadian Journal of Political and Social Theory*, (10: 196–221); Daniels, S. (1993), *Fields of Vision: Landscape Imagery and National Identity in England and the United States*, Cambridge: The Polity Press, pp.174–99; Foster, 'Capturing and Losing the "Lie of the Land"' and Freeman, M. (1999), *Railways and the Victorian Imagination*, London: Yale University Press.
6. The reprinting of Charland's work in Daniel Robinson's *Communication History in Canada* is illustrative of this, as the work situates Charland's piece with other works on nineteenth- and twentieth-century communication technologies and their uneven effects on the spaces of Canada. Charland, M. (2009), 'Technological Nationalism', in Robinson, D. (ed), *Communication History in Canada*, Don Mills, Ontario: Oxford University Press, pp.50–72.
7. Osborne, B. S. (2003), 'Constructing the State, Managing the Corporation, Transforming the Individual: Photography, immigration and the Canadian national railways, 1925–30', in Schwartz, J. M. and Ryan, J. R. (eds), *Picturing Place: Photography and the Geographical Imagination*, London: I. B. Tauris, pp.162–92.
8. This positivist narrative is exemplified by Berton, *The National Dream and The Last Spike*.
9. Historical geographers have highlighted the contested, complex landscape of Canada in various social and political settings. Among them are Clayton, D. (2000), *Islands of Truth*; Dennis, R. (2008), *Cities in Modernity* and Harris, C. (2008), *The Reluctant Land: Society, Space and Environment in Canada before Confederation*, Vancouver: University of British Columbia Press.
10. Berton, *The National Dream and The Last Spike*.
11. Harris, *The Reluctant Land*.
12. For illustration of the extent of this literature see: Glazebrook, G. P. de T. (1964), *A History of Transportation in Canada: Volume II, National Economy (1864–1936)*, Toronto: Carleton Library and McClelland & Stewart Ltd.; Innis, H. (1923), *A History of the Canadian Pacific Railway*, Toronto: McClelland & Stewart Ltd.; Kroker, A. (1984), *Technology and the Canadian Mind: Innis/McLuhan/Grant*, New York: St. Martin's Press; Robinson, D. (ed.) (2009), *Communication History in Canada*, Don Mills, Ontario: Oxford University Press.
13. See, Charland, 'Technological Nationalism'.
14. As examples see Osborne, 'Constructing the State, Managing the Corporation, Transforming the Individual'; Osborne, B. S. (1988), 'The Iconography of Nationhood in Canadian Art', in Cosgrove, D. and Daniels, S. (eds), *The Iconography of Landscape*, Cambridge: Cambridge University Press (pp.162–78); Schwartz, J. M. (1981), 'The Past in Focus: Photography and

British Columbia, 1858–1914', in *B. C. Studies* (52: 5–15); Zeller, S. (2009, 2nd ed.), *Inventing Canada: Early Victorian Science and the Idea of a Transcontinental Nation*, London: McGill-Queen's University Press.

15. Even the exemplars of this are too extensive to mention in full, but a good example can be found in the illustrations of Frances Palmer in New York. These are discussed at length in Daniels, *Fields of Vision*, pp.174–99.
16. Stevens, *Canadian National Railways:* Vol.1 and Vol.2.
17. This can be seen both in the writings for *The Reluctant Land* and in the assembly and juxtaposition of maps from various historical periods in the historical atlas of Canada. Harris, ed., R. C. (1987), *Historical Atlas of Canada: Vol.1 From the Beginning to 1800*, London: University of Toronto Press; Harris, *The Reluctant Land.*
18. Harris, *The Reluctant Land*, p.264.
19. Harris, *The Reluctant Land*, pp.356–7.
20. Innis, H. (1950), *Empire and Communications*, Oxford: The Clarendon Press.
21. Harris asserts, for example, that the regional economic and demographic primacy of Quebec was undermined and eventually replaced by Montreal as the city's rail links with the ice free ports of the United States made it a more efficient and profitable entry point to the global economy: Harris, *The Reluctant Land*, p.265.
22. The figures provided in Chapter 3 give an illustration of the proportion of photographs depicting the railway contained within the Colonial Copyright Collection, though the total (155) is an estimate due to the blurring of subject boundaries as explained in Chapter 3.
23. It had fallen victim to a substantial amount of over-enthusiasm of investment and many prospectors had built railways on the assumption that markets could be developed without leaving the time or the finance to allow this to occur. In short, many line investments were fundamentally short-sighted. Stevens, *Canadian National Railways: Vol.1.*
24. Significant social and geographical impacts included increased migration, settlement of the North West territories, the expansion of agricultural production and the increased exploitation of mineral resources. See Cobb, M. and Duffy, D. (1981), '"A Picture of Prosperity": The British Columbia Interior in Promotional Photography, 1890–1914' in *B. C. Studies* (52: 142–56); Harris, *The Reluctant Land* (especially pp. 356–7), Osborne, 'Constructing the State, Managing the Corporation, Transforming the Individual'; and, Stevens, *Canadian National Railways: Vol.1* and *Vol.2.*
25. Byron Harmon was primarily a 'druggist' (pharmacist) and photographer who ran his photography business from his pharmacy in the town of Banff, Alberta. Details from Phillips, G. C. (1997), *The Western Canada Photographers List (1860–1925)*, London, Ont.: Iron Gate Publishing Co.
26. After the completion of the transcontinental railways in the United States and Canada, the time it took to cross from one ocean to the other was reduced from months to around a week.
27. Berton, *The National Dream and The Last Spike*; Harris, *The Reluctant Land.*
28. See Berton, *The National Dream* and *The Last Spike*; Harris, R. C. (1991), *Canada Before Confederation: a Study in Historical Geography*, Ottawa: Carleton University Press; Harris, *The Reluctant Land*; Osborne, 'The Iconography of Nationhood in Canadian Art'.
29. Berton, *The National Dream* and *The Last Spike*, pp.16–18.
30. Foster, 'Capturing and Losing the "Lie of the Land"'; Kennedy, D. (1996), *The Magic Mountains: Hill Stations and the British Raj*, Berkeley: University of California Press; Osborne, 'The Iconography of Nationhood in Canadian Art'.
31. Brown, J. K. (2000), 'The Baltimore & Ohio and Pennsylvania Railway Displays: Chicago World's Columbian Exposition, 1893', in *History of Photography* (24: 155–62).
32. The image itself is actually 950 mm long, a staggering reproduction for the time (especially to submit for copyright).
33. Freeman discusses at length how the 'straightening' of the landscape was seen as a challenge to the agrarian ideal in Victorian England, and how the work of the artist was deployed to render the effect more palatable within the new order of things. Freeman, *Railways and the Victorian Imagination*, p.221.
34. At least, structurally uninhabited by Europeans. Fig.2.5 has different meanings in the context of Native American habitation, as will be discussed in Chapter 4. For more on the reordering of the landscape by settler societies, in the broader North American context, see Daniels, *Fields of Vision*, p.174.
35. Harris, *The Reluctant Land.*

36. In the early days of the railway it was primarily used for the transport of bulky goods such as grain and lumber. While these materials provided a constant amount of custom, it was the transit of the public that was required to turn a large profit. Stevens, *Canadian National Railways: Vol.1* and *Vol.2*.
37. In this context the camera was important to the construction of the railway (specifically in surveying the proposed path of a potential railway). As a result, the rigours of using the camera in such a field stimulated the technical development and reliability of the camera and image production considerably. As Schwartz points out, 'By the time the last spike was driven, advances in photographic technology had reduced the cumbrousness of equipment and the length of exposure'. Schwartz, J. M. (1981), 'The Past in Focus: Photography and British Columbia, 1858–1914', in *B. C. Studies* (52: p.12). This is drawn out further in Birrell, A. (1981), 'Survey Photography in British Columbia, 1858–1900', in *B. C. Studies* (52: 39–60).
38. Lyall's were active in Winnipeg between 1910 and 1925 and represented one of Winnipeg's main professional photographic companies. They photographed a variety of Winnipeg events and businesses during this time and employed various stock photographers. From Phillips, *The Western Canada Photographers List (1860–1925)*.
39. Mackenzie and Mann (the founders of the Canadian Northern Rail System) originally founded the line after becoming aware of the agricultural possibilities of the prairie and realising there was profit to be made in providing a means of transport for this material to the rest of Canada. Regehr, T. H. (1976), *The Canadian Northern Railway: Pioneer Road of the Northern Prairies, 1895–1918*, Toronto: Macmillan of Canada.
40. Dorin, P. C. (1975), *The Canadian National Railways' Story*, Seattle: Superior Publishing Co.
41. Nationalisation began in 1918 and the system expanded until 1925, when it reached a stable state and ceased taking over bankrupt lines. See Dorin, *The Canadian National Railways' Story*; Stevens, *Canadian National Railways: Vol.2*; Regehr, *The Canadian Northern Railway*.
42. Virilio, P. (2007, trans. Rose, J.), *The Original Accident*, London: Polity Press, p.10.
43. Aldrich, M. (2006), *Death Rode the Rails: American Railway Accidents and Safety, 1828–1965*, Baltimore: Johns Hopkins University Press; Featherstone, M. et al. (eds) (2004), *Automobilities*, London: Sage; Schnapp, J. T. (1999), 'Crash (Speed as Engine of Individuation)', in *Modernism/Modernity* (6: 1–49); Virilio, *The Original Accident* provide a selection of examples.
44. Featherstone (2004), 'An Introduction', in Featherstone et al. (eds), *Automobilities*, London: Sage, p.3.
45. Featherstone et al., *Automobilities*.
46. Freeman gives a good account of how the image and text were mobilised in Victorian England to promote the railway and calm safety concerns. The imageries developed by artists during these campaigns form the basis of much subsequent railway imagery. Freeman, *Railways and the Victorian Imagination*.
47. Berman, M. (1988, orig. 1982), 'Penguin Preface: *The Broad and Open Way*', in *All That is Solid Melts Into Air*, London: Penguin, p.1.
48. The settlement is still known for its train accident even today, and it is recorded extensively in online local histories.
49. See Littau, K (2003), 'Eye Hunger: Physical Pleasure and Non-Narrative Camera', in Arthurs, J. and Grant, I. (eds), *Crash Cultures*, Bristol: Intellect, pp.35–51.
50. This is with regard to the waning predominance of Victoria in British Columbia, as the coming of the railway to Vancouver created new economic geographies; see Chapter 2. The politics of this is discussed in Gregson, H. (1970), *A History of Victoria, 1842–1970*, Victoria: Victoria Observer Publishing Co. Ltd.
51. See, as an example, the work of Richard Steinheimer on the North American railway; Steinheimer, R. and Brouws, J. (2004), *A Passion for Trains: The Railway Photography of Richard Steinheimer*, London: W. W. Norton and Co.
52. Virilio, *The Original Accident*, p.5.
53. Virilio, *The Original Accident*, p.70.
54. See Virilio, *The Original Accident* and Beckmann, J. (2004), 'Mobility and Safety', in Featherstone et al. (eds), *Automobilites*, London: Sage, pp.81–100.
55. Virilio, *The Original Accident*, p.70.
56. Taking the definition given in Berman, *All That is Solid Melts Into Air*, p.1.
57. The economic networks set up by individuals such as Timothy Eaton and the impact this had on the Canada's perception of itself, as discussed in Chapter 2, are illustration of the significance of these networks. See also Charland, 'Technological Nationalism'.

58. Harris, *The Reluctant Land.*
59. See Fig.2.3, for example.
60. This is in contrast to accounts such as Berton, *The National Dream and the Last Spike* and Charland, 'Technological Nationalism'. Both these accounts focus on the highest level of the formation of railway policy and culture (businesses, governments and national broadcast networks).

Chapter 4

1. In previous versions of this work the term 'Native American' was used instead of 'First Peoples'. Given the prevailing acceptance of 'First Peoples' as a term within Canada at present, this is used as the broadest terminology to describe the many indigenous peoples from across Canada, sometimes even including the Inuit. However, at every point where specificity is required and appropriate the name of particular groups will be used.
2. Francis, D. (1992), *The Imaginary Indian: The Image of the Indian in Culture*, Vancouver, B. C.: Arsenal Pulp Press.
3. Schwartz, J. M. (2007), 'Photographic Reflections: Nature, Landscape, and Environment', in *Environmental History* (12: 966–93); Skidmore, C. (2008), *Notman, William and Sons (1856–1935)*, in Hannavay, J. (ed.), *Encyclopaedia of Nineteenth-Century Photography*, London: Routledge, pp.1011–12; Skidmore, C (2002), 'Photography in the Convent: *Grey Nuns*, Québec, 1861', in *Histoire Sociale/Social History* (70: 279–310); Triggs, S. (1994), *The World of William Notman: The Nineteenth Century Through a Master Lens*, Toronto: McClelland & Stewart.
4. Schwartz, J. M. (1996), 'Guest Editorial', in *History of Photography: Special Issue on Canadian Photography* (20, 2: ii).
5. West (2004), *Portraiture.*
6. Ljunggren, D. (2009), 'Every G20 Nation Wants to be Canada, Insists PM', for *Reuters*, available at http://www.reuters.com/article/idUSTRE58P05Z20090926. Last accessed 12 November 2010.
7. Harris, R. C. (1987), *Historical Atlas of Canada*; Harris, R. C. (2008), *The Reluctant Land*.
8. Zeman, B. (1988), *To Run With Longboat: Twelve Stories of Indian Athletes in Canada*, Edmonton, Alberta: GMS Ventures Inc.
9. James, C. L. R. (2005, orig. 1963), *Beyond a Boundary*, London: Yellow Jersey Press.
10. The agency of sport in the development and questioning of national and colonial identities is taken further in Bairner, A. (1996), 'Ireland, Sport and Empire', in Jeffery, K. (ed.), *'An Irish Empire'? Aspects of Ireland and the British Empire*, Manchester: Manchester University Press, pp.57–76; Gemmell, J. (2004), *The Politics of South African Cricket*, London: Routledge; Hutchinson, R. (1996), *Empire Games: The British Invention of Twentieth-Century Sport*, London: Mainstream Publishing; Mangan, J. A. (1992), 'Prologue: Britain's Chief Cultural Export: Imperial Sport as Moral Metaphor, Political Symbol and Cultural Bond', in Mangan, J. A. (ed.), *The Cultural Bond: Sport, Empire and Society*, London: Frank Cass, pp.1–10.
11. Carrington, B. (2010), *Race, Sport and Politics: The Sporting Black Diaspora*, London: Sage; Gems, G. R. (2005), 'Negotiating a First Peoples Identity Through Sport: Assimilation, Adaptation and the Role of the Trickster', in King, C. R. (ed.), *Native Athletes in Sport and Society: A Reader*, London: University of Nebraska Press, pp.1–21; Simpson, K. (2005), 'Sporting Dreams Die on the "Rez"', in Eitzen, D. S. (ed.), *Sport in Contemporary Society: An Anthology*, London: Paradigm, pp.259–65; Springwood, C. F. (2005), 'Playing Football, Playing Indian: A History of the First Peoples Who Were the NFL's Oorang Indians', in King, C. R. (ed.), *Native Athletes in Sport and Society: A Reader*, London: University of Nebraska Press, pp.123–42.
12. Kidd, B. (1980), *Tom Longboat*, Don Mills, Ont.: Fitzhenry and Whiteside; Nabokov, P. (1981), *Indian Running*, Santa Barbara: Capra Press.
13. Kidd, *Tom Longboat*, pp.2–10.
14. *Toronto Daily Star*, 19 April 1907, p.1.
15. Berkhofer, R. F. (1979), *The White Man's Indian: Images of the American Indian from Columbus to Present*, New York: Vintage.
16. *Toronto Daily Star*, 19 April 1907, p.1, British Library Newspaper Collections.

17. *Toronto Daily Star*, 29 December 1908, p.8, British Library Newspaper Collections.
18. These misconceptions are still common today, as articulated in Gems, 'Negotiating a First Peoples Identity Through Sport'; Nabokov, *Indian Running*; Springwood, 'Playing Football, Playing Indian'.
19. Kidd, *Tom Longboat*. This was – and is – a common perception of aboriginal athletes that is often proven erroneous, as highlighted in King, C. R. (2005) 'Identities, Opportunities, Inequities: An Introduction', in King, C. R. (ed.), *Native Athletes in Sport and Society: A Reader*, London: University of Nebraska Press, pp.xi–xxxiii.
20. Zeman, *To Run With Longboat*.
21. Batten, J. (2002), *The Man Who Ran Faster Than Everyone: The Story of Tom Longboat*, Toronto: Tundra. Publications such as this children's book illustrate too how the achievements and legacy of Longboat continue to be rearticulated and redefined, even in the twenty-first century.
22. See, Jackson, 'Constructions of Culture, Representations of Race'.
23. Rafton-Canning's significance to the visual record of Lethbridge and Alberta is borne out by the reliance of recent research work upon his images for illustrative purposes. See Brownstone, A. (2002), 'Ancestors: The Deane-Freeman Collections from the Bloods', in *American Indian Art Magazine* (Summer 2002: 38–77); Dempsey, *Blackfoot War Art*.
24. Dempsey, *Blackfoot War Art*; Tobias, 'Canada's Subjugation of the Plains Cree, 1879–1885' are specific Plains examples. Wider similarities can be seen in the representations discussed in Dippie, B. W. (1994), 'Representing the Other: The North American Indian', in, Edwards, E. (ed.), *Anthropology and Photography: 1860–1920*, London: Yale University Press (pp.132–6); Francis (1992), *The Imaginary Indian*; Street, B. (1994), 'British Popular Anthropology: Exhibiting and Photographing the Other', in, Edwards, E. (ed.), *Anthropology and Photography: 1860–1920*, London: Yale University Press, pp.122–31.
25. The exemplar here is the work of Edward Curtis, as discussed by Faris, 'Navajo and Photography' and Jackson, 'Constructions of Culture, Representations of Race'. The importance of the postcard industry in driving photographic markets was discussed in Chapter 1.
26. See White, D. (1998), *In Search of Geraldine Moodie*, Saskatchewan: Canadian Plains Research Centre; Eber, D. (1994), 'A Feminine Focus on the Last Frontier', in Arctic Circle (Spring: 16–21).
27. Moodie, J. D. (1905), 'Report of Superintendent J. D. Moodie', in *Sessional Papers No.2 (Session 1903–1904)*, Scott Polar Research Institute holdings, pp.3–12; Moodie, J. D. (1907), 'The Hudson Bay Expedition', in *Sessional Papers No.9, Third Session of the Tenth Parliament of the Dominion of Canada (Session 1906–1907)*, Scott Polar Research Institute holdings, pp.179–81; Burant, J. (1998), 'Using Photography to Assert Canadian Sovereignty in the Arctic: The A. P. Low Expedition of 1903–04 aboard the CGS *Neptune*', in King, J. C. H. and Lidchi, H., *Imaging the Arctic*, London: British Museum Press, pp.77–87.
28. Burant, 'Using Photography to Assert Canadian Sovereignty in the Arctic'; Ross, W. G. (1984), *An Arctic Whaling Diary: The Journal of Captain George Comer in Hudson Bay 1903–05*, London: University of Toronto Press.
29. See Burant, 'Using Photography to Assert Canadian Sovereignty in the Arctic'.

Chapter 5

1. It is notable that the photographs deposited in this collection were not those of urban slums or migrants living in impoverished conditions as considered in works such as Bassnett's 'Shooting Immigrants'. However, the photographs do share a theme with those considered by Bassnett, in that they provide a group perspective on these migrants as their press counterparts did in Canada's larger urban areas. Bassnett, S. (2011), 'Shooting Immigrants: Ethic Diversity in Early Twentieth-Century Press Photography', in Payne and Kunard (eds), *The Cultural Work of Photography in Canada*, Montreal: McGill-Queen's University Press (pp.107–19).
2. Knowles, V. (2007, rev. ed.), *Strangers at Our Gates: Canadian Immigration and Immigration Policy, 1540–2006*, Toronto: Dundurn.
3. Kelley, N. and Trebilcock, M., *The Making of the Mosaic: a History of Canadian Immigration Policy*, London: University of Toronto Press, 114.
4. Eagle, J. A. (1989), *The Canadian Pacific Railway and the Development of Western Canada, 1896–1914*, Kingston: McGill-Queen's University Press (pp.173–212).
5. Knowles, *Strangers at Our Gates* (pp.56–7).

6. A significant number of successful farmers still made the journey across borders due to the possibilities presented by farm and transport technology aligned with the wider availability of land in Canada. Troper, H. M. (1972), *Only Farmers Need Apply: Official Canadian Government Encouragement of Immigration from the United States, 1896–1911*, Toronto: Griffin House.
7. Burnet, J. R. and Palmer, H. (1988), *Coming Canadians: an introduction to a history of Canada's peoples*, Toronto: McClelland & Stewart.
8. See Kelley and Trebilcock, *Making of the Mosaic*; Burnet and Palmer, *Coming Canadians*; Widdis, R. W. (1998), *With Scarcely a Ripple: Anglo-Canadian migration into the United States and Western Canada, 1880–1920*, London: McGill-Queen's University Press.
9. Kaye, V. J. (1964), *Early Ukrainian Settlements in Canada 1895–1900*, University of Toronto Press (p.56).
10. Fujiwara, A. (ed.) (2012), *Ethnic Elites and Canadian Identity: Japanese, Ukrainian and Scots, 1919–1971*, Winnipeg: University of Manitoba Press; Lubomyr, L. and Hryniuk, S. (1991), *Canada's Ukrainians: Negotiating an Identity*, Toronto: University of Toronto Press; Subtelny, O. (1991), *Ukrainians in North America: An Illustrated History*, Toronto: University of Toronto Press.
11. See Fujiwara, *Ethnic Elites and Canadian Identity.*
12. Knowles, *Strangers at Our Gates* (p.67).
13. See Clarke, G. E. (2005), 'This is no hearsay: Reading the Canadian Slave Narratives', in *Papers of the Bibliographical Society of Canada* (43:1, pp.7–32) and Nelson, C. A. (2010), 'Introduction', in Nelson, C. A. (ed.), *Ebony Roots, Northern Soil: Perspectives on Blackness in Canada*, Newcastle: Cambridge Scholars Publishing (pp.1–35).
14. For more on the black Empire Loyalists see Schama, S. (2009), *Rough Crossings: Britain, the slaves and the American Revolution*, London: Vintage Books. More on the response of white Canadians to the black Empire Loyalists can be found in the manuscripts of John Clarkson (who encouraged Loyalists settled in Halifax, Nova Scotia to emigrate to the Sierra Leone colony) held at the British Library; see 'Remarks, Halifax', at Add MS 41262 B.
15. Troper, *Only Farmers Need Apply.*
16. Schama, S. (2009), *Rough Crossings*; Jasanoff, M. (2011), *Liberty's Exiles: the loss of America and the Remaking of the British Empire*, London: Harper Press.
17. Troper, *Only Farmers Need Apply.*
18. Schama, *Rough Crossings.*
19. Atkinson Bros. (1904), *Souvenir of the Canadian Northwest: Containing 50 views of the principle [sic] places from Winnipeg to the Pacific Coast*, Toronto and New York: Atkinson Bros.
20. Knowles, *Strangers at Our Gates* (pp.66–7).
21. Thus placing him as another of the collection's many photographers who were professionals working in the sciences and/or with chemicals while practising photography as a hobby. It is worth noting that Simpson deposited little of his work for copyright – only these photographs of the Doukhobors, an image of lightning in Yorkton and another of a local First Peoples man named Fighting Cloud. A larger collection of Simpson's materials can be found at the Glenbow Archives, Alberta.
22. Bothwell, R. et al. (1987), *Canada 1900–1945*, Toronto: University of Toronto Press; Knowles, *Strangers at Our Gates.*
23. See *Los Angeles Herald*, 5 May 1903 (p.3) and 17 July 1908 (p.12).
24. Osborne, B. S. (2003), 'Constructing the State, Managing the Corporation, Transforming the Individual: Photography, immigration and the Canadian national railways, 1925 – 30', in Schwartz, J. M. and Ryan, J. R. (eds), *Picturing Place: Photography and the Geographical Imagination*, London: I. B. Tauris, pp.162–92.
25. This is also seen in the way in which images of railway disasters were circulated as postcards.
26. Fujiwara, *Ethnic Elites and Canadian Identity.*

Chapter 6

1. James, P. (2012), *Canada and Conflict*, Don Mills, Ont.: Oxford University Press.
2. This means the First and Second South African War, a period covering 1880–1902. It was Canada's involvement in the 1900–02 conflict that was to have a significant impact on Canadian politics and identity.
3. Miller, C. (1993), *Painting the Map Red: Canada and the South African War, 1899–1902*, London: McGill-Queen' s University Press and the Canadian War Museum, p.4.

4. Miller, *Painting the Map Red*, pp.5–10.
5. See p. 8 of this learning resource from the Museum: http://www.glenbow.org/media/Archival%20Photos_NWMP.pdf. Last accessed 15 December 2013. For more information on the Museum see the Appendices.
6. It is worth noting here that, despite sharing a name, I have found nothing to link Frederick Steele and Sam Steele as family members. However, whether or not there is such a link, Frederick's photographs still suggest pride in, and enthusiasm for, the endeavour about to be undertaken by Sam Steele and his unit.
7. Morrison, E. W. B. (1901), *With the Guns in South Africa,* Hamilton: Spectator Printing Co., p.17.
8. See Morrison, *With the Guns in South Africa*, pp.15, 29 et al.
9. Pakenham, T. (1993, orig. 1979), *The Boer War*, London: Weidenfeld & Nicolson, p.249.
10. For information on the schedule and more see the official publication of the tour, especially Chapter 4 of Pope, J. (1903), *The Tour of their Royal Highnesses the Duke and Duchess of Cornwall and York through the Dominion of Canada in the Year 1901*, Ottawa: S. E. Dawson. It is worth noting too that a number of photographs from the Colonial Copyright Collection appear in this work, for example the group portrait at Government House in Toronto.
11. See Pope, *The Tour of their Royal Highnesses the Duke and Duchess of Cornwall and York through the Dominion of Canada in the Year 1901*, facing p.66.
12. Again Miller's *Painting the Map Red* gives a strong account of the divisions in Canada's collective identity and how the war exacerbated these, particularly in Quebec. Chapter 28 (pp.424–44) deals with this and other home front issues at length.
13. Andrew Rodger has noted the effect of the war on Canadian photographic production. The conflict had a negative impact on both the amount of people doing photography and the limitations placed on available material for photographic practice. Rodger, A. (1984), 'So Few Earnest Workers: 1914–1930', in Koltun, L. (ed.), *Private Realms of Light*, Markham, Ont.: Fitzhenry and Whiteside, pp.72–87.
14. This is illustrated by the tone and content of Canadian War Records Office publications such as Adami, J. G. (1918), *The War Story of the Canadian Army Medical Corps*, London: Canadian War Records Office.
15. In the introduction to Toman's *An Officer and a Lady* this First World War context is drawn out to set the scene for the main discussion of the book. Toman, C. (2007), *An Officer and a Lady: Canadian nursing and the Second World War*, Vancouver: UBC Press.
16. Neiberg, M. S. (2008), 'Toward a Transnational History of World War I', in *Canadian Military History* (17:1, article 4); Keshen, J. (2003), 'The Great War Soldier as Nation Builder in Canada and Australia', in Busch, B. C. (ed.), *Canada and the Great War: Western Front Association Papers*, Montreal: McGill-Queen's University Press (pp.3–26).
17. Williams, D. (2009), *Media, Memory, and the First World War*, Montreal: McGill-Queen's University Press (pp.178–81).
18. Winegard, T. C. (2012), *For King and Kanata: Canadian Indians and the First World War*, Winnipeg: University of Manitoba Press.
19. Miller, *Painting the Map Red*, pp.443–4.
20. Kordan, B. S. (2002), *Enemy Aliens, Prisoners of War: Internment in Canada during the Great War*, Montreal: McGill-Queen's University Press, p.xxv.
21. As noted earlier in the book, these hand-illustrated postcards have been photographically reproduced for copyright registration, but added to the Colonial Copyright Collection by virtue of the organisational decisions taken at the British Museum Library.
22. Cook, T. (2006), *Clio's Warriors: Canadian Historians and the writing of the world wars*, Vancouver: UBC Press, p.40.
23. Cook, T. (2003), 'Immortalising the Canadian Soldier: Lord Beaverbrook and the Canadian War Records Office in the First World War', in Busch, B. C. (ed.), *Canada and the Great War: Western Front Association Papers*, Montreal: McGill-Queen's University Press, pp.46–65.
24. Tippett, M. (1984), *Art at the Service of War: Canada, Art and the Great War*, Toronto: University of Toronto Press.
25. Brandon, L. (2000), *Canvas of War: Painting the Canadian Experience, 1914 to 1945*, Ottawa: Canadian War Museum.

26. In this respect, the account of the film *Lest We Forget* illustrates how the use and interpretation of materials changed in the years following the war. Cook, T. (2005), 'Canada's Great War on Film: *Lest We Forget* (1935)', in *Canadian Military History* (14: 3, article 2).
27. For more on Bishop and Barker, see Chapter 1. To illustrate the difference in cost, Bishop and Barker's deposits, each of which has a unique number and therefore suggests a unique copyright for each photograph, would have cost the aviators over £15.00. By contrast the Canadian War Records Office paid 10 pence to copyright all of their photographs; acquiring an individual copyright for each, in the manner of Bishop and Barker, would have cost the Office £88.10.
28. For an early intervention in this discussion see Keshen, 'The Great War Soldier as Nation Builder in Canada and Australia', pp.3–26.

Conclusion

1. Payne, C. (2013), *The Official Picture: The National Film Board of Canada's Still Photography Division and the Image of Canada, 1941–1971*, London: McGill-Queen's University Press.
2. See Harris, P. R. (1998), *A History of the British Museum Library, 1753–1973*, London: The British Library.
3. Charland, M. (1986), 'Technological Nationalism', in *Canadian Journal of Political and Social Theory* (10: 196–221).
4. Anderson and Tomlinson, *'Greetings From Canada'*; Poole, D. (1997), *Vision, Race and Modernity: a Visual Economy of the Andean Image World*, Chichester: Princeton University Press.
5. Dempsey, L. J. (2007), *Blackfoot War Art: Pictographs of the Reservation Period, 1880–2000*, Norman: University of Oklahoma Press.
6. Writing about this work can be found in Eber, D. (1989), *When the Whalers were up North: Inuit Memories from the Eastern Arctic*, Montreal: McGill-Queen's University Press.
7. Poole, D., *Vision, Race and Modernity.*
8. Benton, L. (2002), *Law and Colonial Cultures: Legal Regimes in World History; 1400–1900*, Cambridge: Cambridge University Press; Butlin, R. (2009), *Geographies of Empire: European Empires and Colonies, c.1880–1960*, Cambridge: Cambridge University Press; Lambert, D. and Lester, A. (2006), 'Introduction: Imperial Spaces, Imperial Subjects', in Lambert and Lester (eds), *Colonial Lives Across the British Empire: Imperial Careering in the Long Nineteenth Century*, Cambridge: Cambridge University Press, pp.1–31.
9. The significance of the development of increasingly efficient and easy to carry camera equipment is illustrated in Schwartz, J. M. (1981), 'The Past in Focus: Photography and British Columbia, 1858–1914', in *B. C. Studies* (52: 5– 15); Birrell, A. (1981), 'Survey Photography in British Columbia, 1858–1900', in *B. C. Studies* (52: 39–60).
10. Harris, C. (2008), *The Reluctant Land: Society, Space and Environment in Canada before Confederation*, Vancouver: University of British Columbia Press.
11. Edwards (2001), *Raw Histories: Photographs, Anthropology and Museums*, Oxford: Berg, p.237.
12. Saumarez-Smith, C. (1989), 'Museums, artefacts and meanings', in Vergo, P. (ed.) (1989), *The New Museology*, London: Reaktion Books, p.6.
13. Geoghegan, H. (2010), 'Museum Geography: Exploring Museums, Collections and Museum Practice in the U. K.', *Geography Compass* (4: 1462–76); Hill, J. (2006), 'Travelling Objects: the Wellcome Collection in Los Angeles, London and Beyond', *Cultural Geographies* (13: 340–66).
14. Sassoon, J. (2004), 'Photographic Materiality in the Age of Digital Reproduction', in Edwards and Hart (eds), *Photographs, Objects, Histories: On the Materiality of Images*, London: Routledge, pp.186–202.
15. Dempsey, *Blackfoot War Art*; Eber, *When the Whalers were up North.*
16. The reason I say 'part' of the collection has been digitised is based on practicality. While the majority of the collection (over 90 per cent of images) has been digitised as part of this project, there were some items that it was not possible, practically or financially, to digitise. While most of the collection now exists in preserved volumes put together in the 1980s and 90s, there are some materials that were not conserved as part of this project. This was down to their materiality, as they had either been submitted in large, bound volumes by photographers (such as William Notman and Sons) or as panoramas too large to be conserved under the remit and finance of this project. As such, much of this material was

too fragile to be digitised in the BL-Wikimedia project (which had only a small amount of conservation / preservation funding).

17. I also have to note the supplementary funding that arose from Europeana as part of the Europeana Collection 1914–1918 project. This was used to digitise content related to the First World War, including the Canadian War Records Office photographs.
18. Edwards (2001), *Raw Histories*; Sassoon, J. (2004), 'Photographic Materiality in the Age of Digital Reproduction'.
19. '10 Vintage Photos Of Canada That Prove The Country Looks Good Young Or Old', *Huffington Post* (unattributed), 4 February 2014: http://www.huffingtonpost.ca/2014/02/04/old-canada-photos_n_4718117.html?ncid=edlinkusaolp00000003. Last accessed 8 February 2014.
20. 'Forgotten Canada', *National Post* (Tristin Hopper), series running 1 February–7 February 2014: http://news.nationalpost.com/tag/forgotten-canada/. Last accessed 8 February 2014.
21. Comment placed on 'Forgotten Canada No. 5', *National Post* (Tristin Hopper), 6 February 2014: http://news.nationalpost.com/2014/02/06/forgotten-canada-cities-and-parliament-burned-to-the-ground-deadly-train-wrecks-and-horrific-mine-explosions/.
22. Edwards (2001), *Raw Histories;* Sassoon, J. (2004), 'Photographic Materiality in the Age of Digital Reproduction'.

Bibliography

Adami, J. G. (1918), *The War Story of the Canadian Army Medical Corps*, London: Canadian War Records Office.

Albers, P. C. (1998), 'Symbols, Souvenirs and Sentiments: Postcard Imagery of Plains Indians, 1898–1918', in Geary, C. M. and Webb V. L. (eds), *Delivering Views: Distant Cultures in Early Postcards*, London: Smithsonian Institution Press, pp.64–89.

Aldrich, M. (2006), *Death Rode the Rails: American Railway Accidents and Safety, 1828–1965*, Baltimore: Johns Hopkins University Press.

Amyot, C., Gendreau, B. and Willis, J. (2000), *Special Delivery: Canada's Postal Heritage*, Fredricton, N. B.: Goose Lane (pp.57–8).

Anderson, A. and Tomlinson, B. (1978), *'Greetings From Canada': An Album of Unique Canadian Postcards from the Edwardian Era, 1900–1916*, Toronto: Macmillan.

Atwood, M. (1988), *Cat's Eye*, Toronto: McClelland-Stewart.

Atwood, M. (2007), *The Tent*, London: Bloomsbury.

Avery, T. E. (1977, 3rd ed.), *Interpretation of Aerial Photographs*, Minneapolis, Minn.: Burgess Publishing Co.

Bairner, A. (1996), 'Ireland, Sport and Empire', in Jeffery, K. (ed.), *'An Irish Empire'? Aspects of Ireland and the British Empire*, Manchester: Manchester University Press, pp.59–76.

Bal, M. (1996), 'The discourse of the museum', in Greenberg, R. et al. (eds), *Thinking About Exhibitions*, London: Routledge, pp.201–18.

Barnes, J. J. (1974), *Authors, Publishers and Politicians: The Quest for an Anglo-American Copyright Agreement, 1815–1854*, Ohio: Ohio State University Press.

Barringer, T. (1998), 'The South Kensington Museum and the colonial project', in Barringer, T. and Flynn, T. (eds), *Colonialism and the Object: Empire, Material Culture and the Museum*, London: Routledge, pp.11–27.

Barthes, R. (2009, rev. ed.), *Camera Lucida: Reflections on Photography*, London: Vintage Classics.

Bassnett, S. (2011), 'Shooting Immigrants: Ethic Diversity in Early Twentieth-Century Press Photography', in Payne and Kunard (eds), *The Cultural Work of Photography in Canada*, Montreal: McGill-Queen's University Press (pp.107–19).

Batchen, G. (2008), *William Henry Fox Talbot*, London: Phaidon.

Batten, J. (2002), *The Man Who Ran Faster Than Everyone: The Story of Tom Longboat*, Toronto: Tundra.

Beckmann, J. (2004), 'Mobility and Safety', in Featherstone et al. (eds), *Automobilites*, London: Sage, pp.81–100.

Bennett, T. (1994), 'The Exhibitionary Complex', in Dirks, N. B., Eley, G. and Ortner, S. B. (eds), *Culture/Power/History*, Chichester: Princeton University Press, pp.123–54.

Benton, L. (2002), *Law and Colonial Cultures: Legal Regimes in World History; 1400–1900*, Cambridge: Cambridge University Press.

Berger, J. (1972), *Ways of Seeing*, London: B.B.C and Penguin Books.

Berkhofer, R. F. (1979), *The White Man's Indian: Images of the American Indian from Columbus to Present*, New York: Vintage.

Berman, M. (1988), *All That is Solid Melts Into Air*, London: Penguin.

Berton, P. (1974), *The National Dream and The Last Spike* (abridged by author), Toronto: McClelland & Stewart.

Birrell, A. (1981), 'Survey Photography in British Columbia, 1858–1900', in *B. C. Studies* (52: 39–60).

Blunt, A. (1994), *Travel, Gender and Imperialism: Mary Kingsley and West Africa*, London: The Guildford Press.
Booth, A. (1996), *Postcards From the Trenches: Negotiating the Space Between Modernism and the First World War*, Oxford: Oxford University Press.
Bothwell, R. et al. (1987), *Canada 1900–1945*, Toronto: University of Toronto Press.
Brandon, L. (2000), *Canvas of War: Painting the Canadian Experience, 1914 to 1945*, Ottawa: Canadian War Museum.
Briggs, A. (2003, 4th edition), *Victorian Things,* London: Sutton Publishing.
Brown, J. K. (2000), 'The Baltimore & Ohio and Pennsylvania Railway Displays: Chicago World's Columbian Exposition, 1893', in *History of Photography* (24: 155–62).
Brownstone, A. (2002), 'Ancestors: The Deane-Freeman Collections from the Bloods', in *American Indian Art Magazine* (Summer 2002: 38–77).
Burant, J. (1998), 'Using Photography to Assert Canadian Sovereignty in the Arctic: The A. P. Low Expedition of 1903–04 aboard the CGS Neptune', in, King, J. C. H. and Lidchi, H., *Imaging the Arctic*, London: British Museum Press, pp.77–87.
Burnet, J. R. and Palmer, H. (1988), *Coming Canadians: an introduction to a history of Canada's peoples*, Toronto: McClelland & Stewart.
Butlin, R. (2009), *Geographies of Empire: European Empires and Colonies, c.1880–1960*, Cambridge: Cambridge University Press.
Carrington, B. (2010), *Race, Sport and Politics: The Sporting Black Diaspora*, London: Sage.
Charland, M. (1986), 'Technological Nationalism', in *Canadian Journal of Political and Social Theory* (10: 196–221).
Charland, M. (2009), 'Technological Nationalism', in Robinson, D. (ed.). *Communication History in Canada*, Don Mills, Ontario: Oxford University Press, pp.50–72.
Clarke, G. E. (2005), 'This is no hearsay: Reading the Canadian Slave Narratives', in *Papers of the Bibliographical Society of Canada* (43: 1, 7–32).
Clayton, D. (2000), *Islands of Truth: the Imperial Fashioning of Vancouver Island*, London: University of British Columbia Press.
Cobb, M. and Duffy, D. (1981), '"A Picture of Prosperity": The British Columbia Interior in Promotional Photography, 1890–1914, in *B. C. Studies* (52: 142–56).
Coe, B. and Gates, P. (1977), *The Snapshot Photograph: The Rise of Popular Photography, 1888–1939*, London: Ash and Grant Ltd.
Cook, T. (2003), 'Immortalising the Canadian Soldier: Lord Beaverbrook and the Canadian War Records Office in the First World War', in Busch, B. C. (ed.), *Canada and the Great War: Western Front Association Papers*, Montreal: McGill-Queen's University Press (pp.46–65).
Cook, T. (2005), 'Canada's Great War on Film: *Lest We Forget* (1935)', in *Canadian Military History* (14: 3, article 2).
Cook, T. (2006), *Clio's Warriors: Canadian Historians and the writing of the world wars*, Vancouver: UBC Press.
Cooper, F. and Stoler, A. L. (1989), 'Tensions of Empire: Colonial Control and Visions of Rule', in *American Ethnologist* (16: 609–21).
Cosgrove, D. (2000), 'The Measures of America', in Corner, J. and MacLean, A. S. (2000), *Taking Measures Across the American Landscape*, New Haven: Yale University Press, pp.3–13.
Cosgrove, D. and Fox, W. L. (2010), *Photography and Flight*, London: Reaktion Books.
Cowan, P. (1982), *The Kid Who Couldn't Miss*, Ontario: National Film Board of Canada.
Cowtan, R. (1872), *Memories of the British Museum*, London: Richard Bentley and Son Publishers.
Craggs, R. (2008), 'Situating the Imperial Archive: The Royal Empire Society Library, 1868–1945', in *Journal of Historical Geography* (34: 48–67).
Craig, D. (1997), *Royal Geographical Society Illustrated: A Unique Record of Exploration and Photography*, London: Scriptum Editions.
Crang, M. (1993), 'On Display', in Blunt, A. et al. (eds), *Cultural Geography in Practice*, London: Hodder Arnold, pp.255–68.
Cronin, M. (2007), 'Northern Visions: Aerial Surveying and the Canadian Mining Industry, 1919–1928', in *Technology and Culture* (48: 303–30).
Dali, S. (1927), 'Photography, pure creation of the mind', in *L'Amic de les Arts* (no.18, 30 September 1927), reprinted in *Oui* 12.
Dali, S. (1929), 'Photographic Data', in *La Gaceta Literaria* (no.6, February 1929), reprinted in *Oui* 70–1.

Daniels, S. (1993), *Fields of Vision: Landscape Imagery and National Identity in England and the United States*, Cambridge: Polity Press.
Daniels, S. and Nash, C. (2004), 'Lifepaths: Geography and Biography', in *Journal of Historical Geography* (30: 449–58).
Daniels, S. (2010), 'Putting Maps in Place', in *Journal of Historical Geography* (36: 473–80).
Dempsey, H. A. (1983), 'A. Rafton-Canning, Lethbridge Photographer: a Pictorial Feature', in Dempsey, H. A. (ed.), *Alberta History* (31: 16–23).
Dempsey, L. J. (2007), *Blackfoot War Art: Pictographs of the Reservation Period, 1880–2000*, Norman: University of Oklahoma Press.
Dennis, R. (2008), *Cities in Modernity: Representations and Productions of Metropolitan Space, 1840–1930*, Cambridge: Cambridge University Press.
Dippie, B. W. (1994), 'Representing the Other: The North American Indian', in Edwards, E. (ed.), *Anthropology and Photography: 1860–1920*, London: Yale University Press, pp.13–26.
Dodds, G., Hall, R. and Triggs, S. (1994), *The World of William Notman: The Nineteenth Century Through a Master Lens*, Toronto: McClelland & Stewart.
Domosh, M. (1996), *Invented Cities: The Creation of Landscape in Nineteenth-Century New York and Boston*, London: Yale University Press.
Dorin, P. C. (1975), *The Canadian National Railways' Story*, Seattle: Superior Publishing Co.
Driver, F. and Gilbert, D. (1998), 'Heart of Empire? Landscape, Space and Performance in Imperial London', in *Environment and Planning D* (16: 11–28).
Driver, F. and Gilbert, D. (eds) (1999), *Imperial Cities: Landscape, Display and Identity*, Manchester: Manchester University Press.
Driver, F. and Gilbert, D. (1999), 'Imperial Cities: Overlapping Territories, Intertwined Histories', in Driver and Gilbert (eds), *Imperial Cities: Landscape, Display and Identity*, Manchester: Manchester University Press, pp.1–20.
Driver, F. and Jones, L. (2009), *Hidden Histories of Exploration*, London: Royal Holloway, University of London and the Royal Geographical Society (with IBG).
Druick, Z. (2007), *Projecting Canada: Government Policy and Documentary Film at the National Film Board*, London: McGill-Queen's University Press.
Eagle, J. A. (1989), *The Canadian Pacific Railway and the Development of Western Canada, 1896–1914*, Kingston: McGill-Queen's University Press, pp.173–212.
Eber, D. (1989), *When the Whalers were up North: Inuit Memories from the Eastern Arctic*, Montreal: McGill-Queen's University Press.
Eber, D. (1994), 'A Feminine Focus on the Last Frontier', in *Arctic Circle* (Spring: 16–21).
Edwards, E. (ed.) (1994), *Anthropology and Photography: 1860–1920*, London: Yale University Press.
Edwards, E. (1994), 'Introduction', in Edwards, E. (ed.), *Anthropology and Photography 1860–1920*, London: Yale University Press, pp.3–17.
Edwards, E. (1996), 'Postcards: Greetings From Another World', in Selwyn, T. (ed.), *The Tourist Image: Myths and Myth Making in Tourism*, Chichester: John Wiley and Sons Ltd, pp.197–222.
Edwards, E. (2001), *Raw Histories: Photographs, Anthropology and Museums*, Oxford: Berg.
Edwards, E. and Hart, J. (2004), 'Introduction: Photographs as Objects', in Edwards and Hart (eds), *Photographs, Objects Histories: On the Materiality of Images*, London: Routledge, pp.1–15.
Edwards, E. and Hart, J. (2004), 'Mixed Box: the Cultural Biography of a Box of "Ethnographic" Photographs', in Edwards and Hart (eds), *Photographs, Objects, Histories: On the Materiality of Images*, London: Routledge, pp.47–61.
Esdaile, A. (1946), *The British Museum Library: a Short History and Survey*, London: George Allen and Unwin Ltd.
Evans-Lewin, P. (1913), *Royal Colonial Institute Yearbook, 1913*, London: Royal Colonial Institute.
Falconer, J. and Hide, L. (2009), *Points of View: Capturing the Nineteenth Century in Photographs*, London: British Library.
Faris, J. (2003), 'Navajo and Photography', in Pinney and Peterson (eds), *Photography's Other Histories*, London: Duke University Press (pp. 85–99).
Featherstone, M. et al. (2004), *Automobilities*, London: Sage.
Featherstone, M. (2004), 'An Introduction', in Featherstone et al. (eds), *Automobilities*, London: Sage, pp.1–24.
Foster, J. (2003), 'Capturing and Losing the "Lie of the Land": Railway Photography and Colonial Nationalism in Early Twentieth-Century South Africa', in Schwartz and Ryan (eds), *Picturing Place: Photography and the Geographical Imagination*, London: I. B. Tauris, pp.141–61.

Francis, D. (1992), *The Imaginary Indian: The Image of the Indian in Culture*, Vancouver, B. C.: Arsenal Pulp Press.

Freeman, M. (1999), *Railways and the Victorian Imagination*, London: Yale University Press.

Fujiwara, A. (ed.) (2012), *Ethnic Elites and Canadian Identity: Japanese, Ukrainian and Scots, 1919–1971*, Winnipeg: University of Manitoba Press.

Geary, C. M. and Webb, V. L. (1998), 'Introduction: Views on Postcards', in Geary, C. M. and Webb, V. L. (eds), *Delivering Views: Distant Cultures in Early Postcards*, London: Smithsonian Institution Press.

Gemmell, J. (2004), *The Politics of South African Cricket*, London: Routledge.

Gems, G. R. (2005), 'Negotiating a First Peoples Identity Through Sport: Assimilation, Adaptation and the Role of the Trickster', in King, C. R. (ed.), *Native Athletes in Sport and Society: A Reader*, London: University of Nebraska Press, pp.1–21.

Gendreau, Y., Nordemann, A. and Oesch, R. (eds) (1999), *Copyright and Photographs: An International Survey*, London: Kluwer Law International.

Geoghegan, H. (2010), 'Museum Geography: Exploring Museums, Collections and Museum Practice in the U. K.', in *Geography Compass* (4: 1462–76).

Girard, P. (2008), 'British Justice, English Law and Canadian Legal Culture', in Buckner, P. (ed.), *Canada and the British Empire*, Oxford: Oxford University Press, pp.259–77.

Glazebrook, G. P. de T. (1964), *A History of Transportation in Canada: Volume II, National Economy (1864–1936)*, Toronto: Carleton Library and McClelland & Stewart Ltd.

Greenhalgh, P. (1988), *Ephemeral Vistas: The Expositions Universelles, Great Exhibitions and World's Fairs, 1851–1939*, Manchester: Manchester University Press.

Gregson, H. (1970), *A History of Victoria, 1842–1970*, Victoria: Victoria Observer Publishing Co. Ltd.

Guerra, F. and Pilot, L. (2000), 'Historic Photoplanes', in *International Archives of Photogrammetry and Remote Sensing* (33: 611–18).

Hamlett, J. (2006), '"Nicely Feminine Yet Learned": Student Rooms at Royal Holloway and the Oxford and Cambridge Colleges in Late Nineteenth Century Britain', in *Women's History Review* (15: 137–61).

Hannavy, J. (2008), 'Markets, Photographic', in Hannavay, J. (ed.), *Encyclopaedia of Nineteenth-Century Photography*, London: Routledge, pp.896–8.

Hannavay, J. (2008), 'Printing-Out Paper', in Hannavay, J. (ed.), *Encyclopaedia of Nineteenth-Century Photography*, London: Routledge, pp.1174–5.

Hannouda, N. (1994), 'Two Portraits of Auresian Women', in Edwards (ed.), *Anthropology and Photography: 1860–1920*, London: Yale University Press, pp.206–10.

Harding, C. (2008), 'Camera Design: General', in Hannavay, J. (ed.), *Encyclopaedia of Nineteenth-Century Photography*, London: Routledge, pp.254–5.

Hales, P. B. (2005), *Silver Cities: Photographic American Urbanization, 1839–1939*, Albuquerque: University of New Mexico Press.

Harris, R. C. (1987), *Historical Atlas of Canada: Vol.1 From the Beginning to 1800*, London: University of Toronto Press.

Harris, R. C. (1991), *Canada Before Confederation: a Study in Historical Geography*, Ottawa: Carleton University Press.

Harris, R. C. (2008), *The Reluctant Land: Society, Space and Environment in Canada before Confederation*, Vancouver: University of British Columbia Press.

Harris, P. R. (1998), *A History of the British Museum Library, 1753–1973*, London: The British Library.

Hatfield, P. J. (2006), 'Drawing Back the Curtain: Geraldine Moodie and the Canadian Arctic, 1904–1905', University of London, MA thesis.

Hauser, K. (2007), *Shadow Sites: Photography, Archaeology and the British Landscape, 1927–1955*, Oxford: Oxford University Press.

Hawton-Booth, M. (1997), *Photography: An Independent Art – Photographs from the V & A Museum, 1839–1996*, London: V & A Publications.

Headrick, D. R. (1981), *The Tools of Empire: Technology and European Imperialism in the Nineteenth Century*, Oxford: Oxford University Press.

Heinsch, H. K. and Heinsch, B. A. (1994), *The Photographic Experience, 1839–1914*, University Park: Pennsylvania State University Press.

Helibrun, F. (2009), 'Portraiture', in Helibrun, F. (ed.), *A History of Photography: The Musée d'Orsay Collection, 1839 – 1925*, Paris: Flammarion, pp.103–24.

Helibrun, F. and Bocard, H. (2009), *A History of Photography: the Musée d'Orsay Collection 1839–1925*, London: Flammarion.
Hill, J. (2004), 'Cultures and Networks of Collecting: Henry Wellcome's Collection, London': Royal Holloway, University of London, PhD thesis.
Hill, J. (2006), 'Travelling Objects: the Wellcome Collection in Los Angeles, London and Beyond', *Cultural Geographies* (13: 340–66).
Hobsbawm, E. and Ranger, T. (eds) (1983), *The Invention of Tradition*, Cambridge: Cambridge University Press.
Hutchinson, R. (1996), *Empire Games: The British Invention of Twentieth-Century Sport*, London: Mainstream Publishing.
Huyda, R. J. (1996), 'Photography and the Choice of Canada's Capital', in *History of Photography: Special Issue on Canadian Photography* (20: 104–7).
Innis, H. (1923), *A History of the Canadian Pacific Railway*, Toronto: McClelland & Stewart Ltd.
Innis, H. (1950), *Empire and Communications*, Oxford: The Clarendon Press.
Jackson, P. (1992), 'Constructions of culture, representations of race: Edward Curtis's "way of seeing"' in Anderson, K., and Gale, F., *Inventing Places*, Longman, pp.89–106.
Jacobs, J. (1996), *Edge of Empire: Postcolonialism and the City*, London: Routledge.
James, C. L. R. (2005, Orig. 1963), *Beyond a Boundary*, London: Yellow Jersey Press.
James, P. (2012), *Canada and Conflict*, Don Mills, Ont.: Oxford University Press.
Jasanoff, M. (2011), *Liberty's Exiles: the loss of America and the Remaking of the British Empire*, London: Harper Press.
Kaye, V. J. (1964), *Early Ukrainian Settlements in Canada 1895–1900*, Toronto: University of Toronto Press.
Keene, D. (2005), 'Cities and Empire', in *Journal of Urban History* (32: 8–21).
Kelley, N. and Trebilcock, M., *The Making of the Mosaic: a History of Canadian Immigration Policy*, London: University of Toronto Press.
Kennedy, D. (1996), *The Magic Mountains: Hill Stations and the British Raj*, Berkeley: University of California Press.
Keshen, J. (2003), 'The Great War Soldier as Nation Builder in Canada and Australia', in Busch, B. C. (ed.), *Canada and the Great War: Western Front Association Papers*, Montreal: McGill-Queen's University Press (pp.3–26).
Kidd, B. (1980), *Tom Longboat*, Don Mills, Ont.: Fitzhenry and Whiteside.
King, C. R. (2005), 'Identities, Opportunities, Inequities: An Introduction', in King, C. R. (ed.), *Native Athletes in Sport and Society: A Reader*, London: University of Nebraska Press, pp.xi–xxxiii.
Knowles, V. (2007, rev. ed.), *Strangers at Our Gates: Canadian Immigration and Immigration Policy, 1540–2006*, Toronto: Dundurn.
Kõdar, T. (1996), 'The Canadian Photographic Periodical Press', in *History of Photography: Special Issue on Canadian Photography* (20: 138–45).
Kordan, B. S. (2002), *Enemy Aliens, Prisoners of War: Internment in Canada during the Great War*, Montreal: McGill-Queen's University Press.
Koltun, L. (1984) (ed.), *Private Realms of Light*, Markham, Ont.: Fitzhenry and Whiteside.
Kroker, A. (1984), *Technology and the Canadian Mind: Innis/McLuhan/Grant*, New York: St. Martin's Press.
Lambert, D. and Lester, A. (2006), 'Introduction: Imperial Spaces, Imperial Subjects', in Lambert and Lester (eds), *Colonial Lives Across the British Empire: Imperial Careering in the Long Nineteenth Century*, Cambridge: Cambridge University Press, pp.1–31.
Langford, M. (2008), *Suspended Conversations: The Afterlife of Memory in Photographs*, London: McGill-Queen's University Press.
Larson, F. (2009), *An Infinity of Things: How Sir Henry Wellcome Collected the World*, Oxford: Oxford University Press.
Le Corbusier (1988, first published 1935), *Aircraft*, New York: Universe.
Lester, A. (2001), *Imperial Networks: Creating Identities in Nineteenth-Century South Africa and Britain*, London: Routledge.
Lister, M. (2009, 4th ed.), 'Photography in the Age of Electronic Imaging', in Wells, L. (ed.), *Photography: A Critical Introduction*, London: Routledge, p.311–44.
Littau, K. (2003), 'Eye Hunger: Physical Pleasure and Non-Narrative Camera', in Arthurs, J. and Grant, I. (eds), *Crash Cultures*, Bristol: Intellect, pp.35–51.
Lowe, J. L. (1982), *Walden's Postcard Enthusiast Revisited*, Ridley Park, Penn.: Deltiologists of America.

Luciuk, L. and Hryniuk, S. (1991), *Canada's Ukrainians: Negotiating an Identity*, Toronto: University of Toronto Press.

Lutz, C. A. and Collins, J. L. (1993), *Reading National Geographic*, London: The University of Chicago Press.

MacQuire, S. (1998), *Visions of Modernity: Representations, Memory, Time and Space in the Age of the Camera*, London: Sage.

Mandelbrote, G. and Taylor, B. (eds) (2009), *Libraries Within the Library: the Origins of the British Library's Printed Collections*, London: British Library.

Mangan, J. A. (1992), 'Prologue: Britain's Chief Cultural Export: Imperial Sport as Moral Metaphor, Political Symbol and Cultural Bond', in Mangan, J. A. (ed.), *The Cultural Bond: Sport, Empire and Society*, London: Frank Cass, pp.1–10.

Marien, M. W. (2006, 2nd ed.), *Photography: A Cultural History*, London: Laurence King Publishing.

Mattison, D. (1985), *Camera Workers: The British Columbia Photographers Directory, 1858–1900*, Victoria, BC: Camera Workers Press.

McCannon, J. (2012), *A History of the Arctic: nature, exploration and exploitation*, London: Reaktion.

McCauley, E. A. (1985), *A. E. A. Disdéri and the Carte de Visite Portrait Photograph*, New Haven, CT: Yale University Press.

McDougall, M. H. (1981), 'R. H. Trueman, Artist and Documentarian', in *B. C. Studies* (52: 129–41).

McEwan, C. (1994), 'Encounters with West African Women: Textual representations of difference by white women abroad', in, Blunt, A. and Rose, G., *Writing Women and Space: Colonial and Postcolonial Geographies*, London: The Guildford Press, pp.73–100.

McKinley, A. C. (1929), *Applied Aerial Photography*, London: Chapman & Hall, Ltd.

McMaster, G. (1996), 'Creating spaces', in Greenberg, R. et al. (eds), *Thinking About Exhibitions*, London: Routledge, pp.191–200.

McQueen, R. (1998), *The Eatons: The Rise and Fall of Canada's Royal Family*, Toronto: Stoddart.

Miller, C. (1993), *Painting the Map Red: Canada and the South African War, 1899–1902*, London: McGill-Queen's University Press and the Canadian War Museum.

Mills, S. (1991), *Discourses of Difference: an Analysis of Women's Travel Writing and Colonialism*, London: Routledge.

Mitchell, T. (1989), 'The World as Exhibition', in *Comparative Studies in Society and History* (30: 217–36).

Mitchell, T. (1992), 'Orientalism and the Exhibitionary Order', in, Dirks, N. B. (ed.), *Colonialism and Culture*, Michigan: University of Michigan Press, pp.289–316.

Moholy-Nagy, L. (1967), *Painting, Photography, Film*, London: Lund Humphries.

Morrison, E. W. B. (1901), *With the Guns in South Africa*, Hamilton: Spectator Printing Co.

Nabokov, P. (1981), *Indian Running*, Santa Barbara: Capra Press.

Nasmith, G. G. (1923), *Timothy Eaton*, Toronto: McClelland & Stewart.

Neiberg, M. S. (2008), 'Toward a Transnational History of World War I', in *Canadian Military History* (17: 1, article 4).

Nelson, C. A. (2010), 'Introduction', in Nelson, C. A. (ed.), *Ebony Roots, Northern Soil: Perspectives on Blackness in Canada*, Newcastle: Cambridge Scholars Publishing (pp.1–35).

Nye, D. E. (1994), *The American Technological Sublime*, London: The MIT Press.

Ogborn, M. (2007), *Indian Ink: Script and Print in the Making of the English East India Company*, Chicago: University of Chicago Press.

O'Neill, P. B. (1984), 'Canadiana Deposited in the British Museum Library between 1895 and 1924', in *British Library Occasional Papers: Canadian Studies* (1: 83–90).

O'Neill, P. B. (ed.) (1989), *A Checklist of Canadian Copyright Deposits in the British Museum, 1895–1923: Volume I, Maps*, Halifax, N. S.: Dalhousie University School of Library and Information Studies.

O'Neill, P. B. (ed.) (1989), *A Checklist of Canadian Copyright Deposits in the British Museum, 1895–1923: Volume II, Insurance Plans*, Halifax, N. S.: Dalhousie University School of Library and Information Studies.

O'Neill, P. B. (ed.) (1989), *A Checklist of Canadian Copyright Deposits in the British Museum, 1895–1923: Volume III, City and Area Directories*, Halifax, N. S.: Dalhousie University School of Library and Information Studies.

O'Neill, P. B. (ed.) (1989), *A Checklist of Canadian Copyright Deposits in the British Museum, 1895–1923: Volume IV, Sheet Music*, Halifax, N. S.: Dalhousie University School of Library and Information Studies.

O'Neill, P. B. (ed.) (1989), *A Checklist of Canadian Copyright Deposits in the British Museum, 1895–1923: Vol. V Photographs*, Halifax, N. S.: Dalhousie University School of Library and Information Studies.
Ondaatje, M. (1988), *In the Skin of a Lion*, London: Picador.
Osborne, B. S. (1988), 'The Iconography of Nationhood in Canadian Art', in Cosgrove, D. and Daniels, S. (eds), *The Iconography of Landscape*, Cambridge: Cambridge University Press, pp.162–78.
Osborne, B. S. (2003), 'Constructing the State, Managing the Corporation, Transforming the Individual: Photography, immigration and the Canadian national railways, 1925–30', in Schwartz, J. M. and Ryan, J. R. (eds), *Picturing Place: Photography and the Geographical Imagination*, London: I. B. Tauris, pp.162–92.
Pakenham, T. (1993, orig. 1979), *The Boer War*, London: Weidenfeld & Nicolson.
Padfield, T. (2008), 'Copyright', in Hannavay, J. (ed.), *Encyclopaedia of Nineteenth-Century Photography*, London: Routledge, pp.337–8.
Patterson, S. (2006), 'Postcards from the Raj', in *Patterns of Prejudice* (40: 142–58).
Payne, C. and Junard, A. (eds) (2011), *The Cultural Work of Photography in Canada*, Montreal, Que.: McGill-Queen's University Press.
Payne, C. (2013), *The Official Picture: The National Film Board of Canada's Still Photography Division and the Image of Canada, 1941–1971*, Montreal, Que.: McGill-Queen's University Press.
Pearson, D. (2009), 'Introduction: from Texts to Collections', in Mandelbrote, G. and Taylor, D. (eds), *Libraries Within the Library: the Origins of the British Library's Printed Collections*, London: British Library, pp.1–7.
Pettipas, K. (1994), *Severing the Ties That Bind: Government Repression of Indigenous Religious Ceremonies on the Prairies*, Winnipeg: University of Manitoba Press.
Phillips, G. C. (1997), *The Western Canada Photographers List (1860–1925)*, London, Ont.: Iron Gate Publishing Co.
Pierce, P. (1985), *Canada: The Missing Years*, London: Hamlyn.
Pinney, C. (1994), 'The Parallel Histories of Anthropology and Photography', in Edwards, E. (ed.), *Anthropology and Photography: 1860–1920*, London: Yale University Press, pp.74–93.
Poole, D. (1997), *Vision, Race and Modernity: a Visual Economy of the Andean Image World*, Chichester: Princeton University Press.
Pratt, M. L. (1992), *Imperial Eyes: Travel Writing and Transculturation*, London: Routledge.
Price, D. (2000), 'Surveyors and the Surveyed: Photography Out and About', in Wells, L. (2000, 2nd ed.), *Photography: A Critical Introduction*, London: Routledge, pp.65–116.
Price, D. and Wells, L. (2009, 4th ed.), 'Thinking About Photography: Debates, Historically and now', in Wells, L. (ed.), *Photography: A Critical Introduction*, London: Routledge, pp.9–64.
Qulaut, G. Q. (1998), 'Keynote Address', in King, J. C. H. and Lidchi, H., *Imaging the Arctic*, London: British Museum Press, pp.19–23.
Racette, S. F. (2009), 'Haunted: First Peoples Children in Residential School Photography', in Lerner, L. (ed.), *Depicting Canada's Children*, Waterloo: Wilfrid Laurier University Press, pp.49–84.
Ralph, W. (2007, 2nd ed.), *William Barker, V. C.: The Life, Death and Legend of Canada's Most Decorated War Hero*, Mississauga, Ont.: John Wiley and Sons Ltd.
Rattray, A. (1862), *Vancouver Island and British Columbia: Where They Are; What They Are; and What They May Become*, London: Smith, Elder & Co.
Regehr, T. H. (1976), *The Canadian Northern Railway: Pioneer Road of the Northern Prairies, 1895–1918*, Toronto: Macmillan of Canada.
Richards, T. (1993), *The Imperial Archive: Knowledge and the Fantasy of Empire*, London: Verso.
Robinson, D. (ed.) (2009), *Communication History in Canada*, Don Mills, Ontario: Oxford University Press.
Rodger, A. (1984), 'So Few Earnest Workers: 1914–1930', in Koltun, L. (ed.), *Private Realms of Light*, Markham, Ont.: Fitzhenry and Whiteside, pp.72–87.
Rose, G. (2000), 'Practising Photography: an Archive, a Study, some Photographs and a Researcher', in *Journal of Historical Geography* (26: 555–71).
Rose, G. (2007, 2nd ed.), *Visual Methodologies: An Introduction to the Interpretation of Visual Images*, London: Routledge.
Ross, W. G. (1984), *An Arctic Whaling Diary: The Journal of Captain George Comer in Hudson Bay 1903–05*, London: University of Toronto Press.

Roy, P. (1976), 'The Illumination of Victoria: Late Nineteenth Century Technology and Municipal Enterprise', in *B. C. Studies* (32: 79–92).
Rudisill, R. (1991), 'Directories of Photographers: An Annotated World Bibliography', in Palmquist, P. E. (ed.) *Photographers: A Sourcebook for Historical Research*, Brownsville, CA: Carl Mautz Publishing, pp.52–101.
Ryan, J. R. (1997), *Picturing Empire: Photography and the Visualisation of the British Empire*, London: Reaktion Books.
Ryan, J. (2000), 'Photos and Frames: Towards an Historical Geography of Photography', in *Journal of Historical Geography* (26: 119–24).
Rydell, R. W. (1998), 'Souvenirs of Imperialism: World's Fair Postcards', in Geary, C. M. and Webb, V. L. (eds), *Delivering Views: Distant Cultures in Early Postcards*, London: Smithsonian Institution Press, pp.47–63.
Rydell, R. W. (2006), 'World Fairs and Museums', in Macdonald, S. (ed.), *A Companion to Museum Studies*, London: Blackwell, pp.135–51.
Santink, J. L. (1990), *Timothy Eaton and the Rise of his Department Store*, Toronto: University of Toronto Press.
Sassoon, J. (2004), 'Photographic Materiality in the Age of Digital Reproduction', in Edwards and Hart (eds), *Photographs, Objects, Histories: On the Materiality of Images*, London: Routledge, pp.186–202.
Saumarez-Smith, C. (1989), 'Museums, artefacts and meanings', in Vergo, P. (ed.) (1989), *The New Museology*, London: Reaktion Books, pp.6–21.
Schama, S. (2009), *Rough Crossings: Britain, the slaves and the American Revolution*, London: Vintage Books.
Schein, R. H. (1993), 'Representing Urban America: 19th Century Views of Landscape, Space and Power', in *Environment and Planning D* (11: 7–21).
Schnapp, J. T. (1999), 'Crash (Speed as Engine of Individuation)', in *Modernism/Modernity* (6: 1–49).
Schwartz, J. M. (1981), 'The Past in Focus: Photography and British Columbia, 1858–1914', in *B. C. Studies* (52: 5–15).
Schwartz, J. M. (1996), 'Guest Editorial', in *History of Photography: Special Issue on Canadian Photography* (20: ii).
Schwartz, J. M. and Ryan, J. R. (2003), 'Introduction: Photography and the Geographical Imagination', in Schwartz, J. M. and Ryan, J. R. (eds), *Picturing Place: Photography and the Geographical Imagination*, London: I. B. Tauris, pp.1–18.
Schwartz, J. M. (2004), 'Un Beau Souvenir du Canada: Object, Image, Symbolic Space', in Edwards and Hart (eds), *Photographs, Objects, Histories: On the Materiality of Images*, London: Routledge, pp.16–31.
Schwartz, J. M. (2007), 'Photographic Reflections: Nature, Landscape, and Environment', in *Environmental History* (12: 966–93).
Schwartz, J. M. (2010), 'Oh! What a Parade: Context and Materiality in the British Library Exhibition "Points of View: Capturing the Nineteenth Century in Photographs"', in *Photography and Culture* (3: 195–206).
Shaw, S. B. (2001), *Photographing Canada from Flying Canoes*, Brunstown, Ont.: General Store Publishing House.
Simpson, K. (2005), 'Sporting Dreams Die on the "Rez"', in Eitzen, D. S. (ed.), *Sport in Contemporary Society: An Anthology*, London: Paradigm, pp.259–65.
Skidmore, C (2002), 'Photography in the Convent: Grey Nuns, Québec, 1861', in *Histoire Sociale/Social History* (70: 279–310).
Skidmore, C. (ed.) (2006), *This Wild Spirit: Women in the Rocky Mountains of Canada*, Edmonton: University of Alberta Press.
Skidmore, C. (2008), 'Notman, William and Sons (1856–1935)', in Hannavay, J. (ed.), *Encyclopaedia of Nineteenth-Century Photography*, London: Routledge, pp.1011–12.
Sloane, H. (1707–25), *A Voyage to the Islands of Madera, Barbados, Nieves, St. Christopher's and Jamaica*, London.
Sontag, S. (1973), *On Photography*, London: Farrar, Straus and Giroux.
Springwood, C. F. (2005), 'Playing Football, Playing Indian: A History of the First Peoples Who Were the NFL's Oorang Indians', in King, C. R. (ed.), *Native Athletes in Sport and Society: A Reader*, London: University of Nebraska Press, pp.123–42.
Staff, F. (1979, 2nd ed.), *The Picture Postcard and its Origins*, London: Lutterworth Press.

Steinheimer, R. and Brouws, J. (2004), *A Passion for Trains: The Railway Photography of Richard Steinheimer*, London: W. W. Norton and Co.
Sternberg, I. (1991), 'The British Museum Library and Colonial Copyright Deposit', in *The British Library Journal* (17: 61–82).
Sternberg, I. (1991), 'Acquisitions of Printed Books at the British Library, 1837–1960', London: University of London PhD thesis.
Stevens, G. R. (1960), *Canadian National Railways: Volume 1, Sixty Years of Trial and Error (1836–1896)*, Toronto: Clarke, Irwin and Co. Ltd.
Stevens, G. R. (1960), *Canadian National Railways: Volume 2, Towards the Inevitable (1896–1922)*, Toronto: Clarke, Irwin and Co. Ltd.
Story, R. (1980), *The Forging of an Aristocracy: Harvard & the Boston Upper Class, 1800–1870*, Middletown, Con.: Wesleyan University Press.
Street, B. (1994), 'British Popular Anthropology: Exhibiting and Photographing the Other', in, Edwards, E. (ed.), *Anthropology and Photography: 1860–1920*, London: Yale University Press, pp.122–31.
Strong, D. C. (1996), 'Sidney Carter and Alfred Stieglitz: The Canadian Pictorialist Exhibition (1907)', in *History of Photography: Special Issue on Canadian Photography* (20: 160–2).
Subtelny, O. (1991), *Ukrainians in North America: An Illustrated History*, Toronto: University of Toronto Press.
T. Eaton Co. (1901), *Toronto, Album of Views*, Toronto: Dominion Publishing Co.
Tagg, J. (1988), *The Burden of Representation*, London: Macmillan.
Thomas, N. (1994), *Colonialism's Culture: Anthropology, Travel and Government*, London: Polity Press.
Thomas, N. (2004), 'Exploring the Boundaries of Biography: the Family and Friendship Networks of Lady Curzon, Vicereine of India 1898–1905', in *Journal of Historical Geography* (30: 496–519).
Tippett, M. (1984), *Art at the Service of War: Canada, Art and the Great War*, Toronto: University of Toronto Press.
Tobias, J. L. (1983), 'Canada's Subjugation of the Plains Cree, 1879–1885', in *The Canadian Historical Review* (64: 519–48).
Toman, C. (2007), *An Officer and a Lady: Canadian nursing and the Second World War*, Vancouver: UBC Press.
Trachtenberg, A. (1989), *Reading American Photographs: Images as History Mathew Brady to Walker Evans*, New York: Hill and Wang.
Triggs, S. (1994), *The World of William Notman: The Nineteenth Century Through a Master Lens*, Toronto: McClelland & Stewart.
Troper, H. M. (1972), *Only Farmers Need Apply: Official Canadian Government Encouragement of Immigration from the United States, 1896–1911*, Toronto: Griffin House.
Virilio, P. (2007, trans. Rose, J.), *The Original Accident*, London: Polity Press.
Walden, K. (1997), *Becoming Modern in Toronto: The Industrial Exhibition and the Shaping of a Late Victorian Culture*, London: University of Toronto Press.
Ward, J. (2008), 'Dry Plate Negatives: Gelatine', in Hannavay, J. (ed.), *Encyclopaedia of Nineteenth-Century Photography*, London: Routledge, pp.438–9.
West, S. (2004), *Portraiture*, Oxford: Oxford University Press.
White, D. (1998), *In Search of Geraldine Moodie*, Saskatchewan: Canadian Plains Research Center.
Widdis, R. W. (1998), *With Scarcely a Ripple: Anglo-Canadian migration into the United States and Western Canada, 1880–1920*, London: McGill-Queen's University Press.
Williams, D. (2009), *Media, Memory, and the First World War*, Montreal: McGill-Queen's University Press.
Willoughby, M. (1992), *A History of Postcards: A Pictorial Record from the Turn of the Century to the Present Day*, London: Studio Editions.
Winegard, T. C. (2012), *For King and Kanata: Canadian Indians and the First World War*, Winnipeg: University of Manitoba Press.
Woody, H. (1998), 'International Postcards: Their History, Production and Distribution (circa 1895–1915)', in Geary, C. M. and Webb, V. L. (eds), *Delivering Views: Distant Cultures in Early Postcards*, London: Smithsonian Institution Press, pp.13–45.
Zeller, S. (2009, 2nd ed.), *Inventing Canada: Early Victorian Science and the Idea of a Transcontinental Nation*, London: McGill-Queen's University Press, Carleton Library Series.
Zeman, B. (1988), *To Run With Longboat: Twelve Stories of Indian Athletes in Canada*, Edmonton, Alberta: GMS Ventures Inc.

Index

Page numbers in italics are figures

CPSIA information can be obtained
at www.ICGtesting.com
Printed in the USA
BVHW060711101118
532599BV00020B/160/P

9 781787 353008